A Decade of Nigeria

A Decade of Nigeria

Politics, Economy and Society
2004–2016

By

Heinrich Bergstresser

BRILL

LEIDEN | BOSTON

The chapters on Nigeria 2004–2015 were previously published in Brill's *Africa Yearbook. Politics, Economy and Society South of the Sahara* 2004–2015. The chapter on Nigeria 2016 will be published in the forthcoming *Africa Yearbook. Politics, Economy and Society South of the Sahara* 2016.

Library of Congress Cataloging-in-Publication Data

Names: Bergstresser, Heinrich, author.
Title: A decade of Nigeria : politics, economy and society, 2004–2016 / by
    Heinrich Bergstresser.
Description: Leiden ; Boston : Brill, 2017. | Series: A decade of … series
    | "Based on chapters previously published in the Africa Yearbook.
    Politics, Economy and Society South of the Sahara"—Acknowledgment page. |
    Includes bibliographical references and index.
Identifiers: LCCN 2017012385 (print) | LCCN 2017013797 (ebook) | ISBN
    9789004347410 (E-book) | ISBN 9789004346970 (pbk. : alk. paper)
Subjects: LCSH: Nigeria—Politics and government—1993–2007. |
    Nigeria—Politics and government—2007– | Nigeria—Economic
    conditions—21st century. | Nigeria—Social conditions—21st century.
Classification: LCC DT515.22 (ebook) | LCC DT515.22 .B45 2017 (print) | DDC
    966.905/4—dc23
LC record available at https://lccn.loc.gov/2017012385

Typeface for the Latin, Greek, and Cyrillic scripts: "Brill". See and download: brill.com/brill-typeface.

ISBN 978-90-04-34697-0 (paperback)
ISBN 978-90-04-34741-0 (e-book)

Contents

Acknowledgement

This publication in the series "*A Decade of...*" is like the earlier three (featuring Mozambique, Ghana and Namibia, respectively), based on chapters previously published in the *Africa Yearbook. Politics, Economy and Society South of the Sahara.*

The author wishes to thank the former and current editors of the West African chapters, Klaas van Walraven and Sebastian Elischer, respectively, for their continued support in this project during all the years and Peter Colenbrander and Carol Rowe for their meticulous language editing. Last but not least, the author is grateful to Ayodele Aderinwale, Ubale Musa, Joe McIntyre, alias Malam Gambo, and his beloved wife Sibylle Pohly-Bergstresser, who, over a period of more than two decades, were always accessible as the need arose in resolving crucial questions concerning Nigerian affairs.

Nigeria in 2004

In 2004, Nigeria experienced a wave of hitherto unknown political violence, ethnic and religious conflict and organised crime, affecting almost all the 36 states and Abuja. The conflicts sometimes reached a level that threatened the political system and endangered the still infant democratisation process. While the shariah issue lost political momentum in the world's biggest Christian-Islamic country, infighting for resource and financial control, especially at state and council level, reached new heights. Several local militias were able to increase their political influence and some even successfully turned themselves into local and regional powerbrokers. The federal government responded by pursuing a strategy of political dialogue and force, depending on the perceived relevance of the issue for the central government. In conjunction with the intensity and variety of conflicts, this policy revealed the weakness of the modern institutions and caused widespread frustration with the political and very limited economic progress. Against this background, President Olusegun Obasanjo and his government started a new economic and social reform programme and scheduled a national conference for early 2005 to create at least some legacy of 'democracy dividend' and economic progress.

Domestic Politics

The long-overdue *elections for the 774 local councils* took place in most of the 36 federal states and the Federal Capital Territory (FCT) on 27 March, and were aimed at completing the election marathon begun in 2003. In Sokoto and Niger states the electorate went to the polls in January, while voting for various councils in some states had to be postponed due to civil strife and violence. In one state, voting had to be cancelled. The ruling People's Democratic Party (PDP) of

© KONINKLIJKE BRILL NV, LEIDEN, 2017 | DOI 10.1163/9789004347410_002

President Obasanjo, which already controlled most state governments and both chambers (senate and house of representatives) of the National Assembly confirmed its dominant position. The northern-based main opposition All Nigeria People's Party (ANPP) and the southwest based Alliance for Democracy (AD) only just retained their strongholds in states such as Zamfara and Lagos respectively. Voter turnout was extremely low, and the elections were largely marred by widespread fraud, violence and rather flagrant ballot rigging. According to the local transition monitoring group, the ballot could not be considered to reflect the will of the people.

A *constitutional crisis* developed over statutory allocations to local councils from the Federation Account. The 1999 constitution listed 768 local governments and 6 area councils within the FCT. But some state assemblies created additional councils. Lagos state, for example, the only state the Yoruba AD party ruled, established 37 new councils in addition to the listed 20. Consequently, the federal government denied those local governments funding allocations until the states reverted to the number enshrined in the constitution.

In April, the Lagos state government took the case to the *supreme court*, which declared in December that the president had no constitutional powers to withhold statutory funds to any tier of government. Nevertheless, the federal government continued withholding the funds and asked the supreme court for clarification of the verdict against the background of the first schedule, part I, section 3 of the constitution that lists the states of the federation, the local government areas and the area councils of the FCT, Abuja.

The legal battle over the outcome of the presidential elections of 2003 went on throughout the year. The defeated ANPP presidential candidate, former junta chairman Maj. Gen. Muhammadu Buhari (retd), challenged the re-election of President Obasanjo, himself a former junta chairman and retired four star general, in the court of appeal that had been mandated to act as the *presidential election tribunal*. He asked the court to annul the 2003 elections because of substantial rigging in at least 16 states and maintained that Obasanjo was not qualified to stand. On 20 December, the court in a three-to-one verdict generally rejected Buhari's petition. It confirmed vote rigging in some areas, including Obasanjo's home state, Ogun, where Buhari got just 680 votes as against 1,360,170 in favour of the incumbent. However, it found no evidence that this had tipped the overall result. The tribunal thus annulled the election in Ogun state on the basis of serious infractions there, ranging from violence and official intimidation to falsification of results.

At the beginning of the year, a power struggle within PDP between Anambra state Governor Chris Ngige and his closest former ally and sponsor Chris Uba caused a serious political and constitutional crisis in the state that even *endangered national security and stability*. On 2 January the Enugu high court ordered the inspector general of police, Tafa Balogun, to remove Ngige from office. The order was based on a lawsuit instituted by the suspended member of the Anambra state house of assembly, Nelson Achukwu, on the grounds that the governor had resigned in July the previous year. Another order from the Awka high court restrained the inspector general of police from executing the order. On 12 January, the court of appeal upheld this order, and on 27 January the Awka high court voided Ngige's purported resignation in 2003, after which he was temporarily arrested by special police forces on 10 July 2004 when he denied having resigned and refused to leave government house. On 30 November, however, the court of appeal finally set aside the decision by the Enugu high court, pointing out that it had no jurisdiction over the Anambra state government.

Between 10 and 12 November, supporters of the governor and Chris Uba clashed several times and the postponed council elections were put on hold indefinitely. The state-owned television and radio stations in the capital Awka, in Onitsha, in Enugu-Ukwu and a building of the Independent National Electoral Commission (INEC) in the capital were torched and some vehicles burnt. The federal government sent police reinforcements to Anambra state to quell the riots and there were conflicting reports about several people being killed. In an open letter on 6 December, Innocent Audu Ogbeh, the national chairman of the PDP, sharply criticised President Obasanjo and his government for the way the crisis had been handled. In a quick response Obasanjo blamed Ogbeh for shirking his responsibility as party chairman to attempt to resolve it. Then, Obasanjo urged the PDP leadership to force Governor Ngige to resign, and an emergency meeting of the executive committee was set for early January 2005.

Plateau state and its border area with Taraba state in the Middle Belt region became another serious conflict area. Here *deep ethnic and religious divisions* as well as competition between farmers and nomads over control of land, grazing rights and the allocation of funds fuelled political tensions. On 13 February, at least 11 people died in the Muslim-dominated village of Mavo (Wase local government) after being attacked by ethnic Tarok militias. The majority of Tarok are Christian. Around Tunga village on 19 February, four patrolling policemen were killed by assailants suspected of being ethnic Fulani. A week later, military and police forces were deployed to Yelwa town (Shendam local government) after Fulani herdsman killed some 100 people, allegedly including 48 seeking shelter in a church. In another attack around the same time by Christian militias in Garkawa, at least 40 Hausa-Fulani and Fulani of the Muslim faith were killed. And on the eve of the local government elections in Wase, at least 20 Muslims died after a raid by Christian militiamen.

Despite the peace initiative committee on Plateau state, inaugurated by President Obasanjo and comprising eminent people and stakeholders from the greater Plateau area under the chairmanship of the Emir of Zaria, Shehu Idris, the killings continued. In mid-April, Tarok militia attacked three villages near the town of Ibi on the Taraba state side, killing seven people and razing many houses. In Barkin Chiyawa (Qua'an Pan local government) more than 30 Muslims died when Christian militia raided the village. At the end of April, half a dozen villages along the Plateau-Taraba border reported at least 120 victims. After another attack on Muslims in the central market in Yelwa on 2 May, leaving 200–300 people dead, the government of Plateau state imposed a *dusk-to dawn-curfew* on 5 May and ordered policemen to shoot troublemakers on sight.

The Yelwa incident even spilled over into the ancient city of Kano where Muslim youths went on the rampage, killing dozens of Christians and driving several thousand people from their homes. The Christian Association of Nigeria (CAN), Kano branch, put the number of victims at almost 600, much higher than police estimates. A week-long dusk-to-dawn curfew was imposed on 11 May.

However, on 18 May, President Obasanjo declared a *state of emergency over Plateau state* because, according to him, national security was at stake. He suspended Governor Joshua Dariye and the State Assembly and appointed a former military governor of Plateau state and army chief of staff, Maj. Gen. Chris Alli (retd) as sole administrator. Within 48 hours, as stipulated by the constitution, both houses of the National Assembly confirmed the state of emergency in Plateau with the required two-thirds majority. The state of emergency was renewable after six months. On 1 June, parliament passed the new law, with eight regulations, sought by the president to enforce the emergency rule he had invoked in Plateau with the appointment of the administrator.

Apart from the ongoing killing that lasted until late June, more than 50,000 people, mostly Muslim, took refuge in neighbouring Nasarawa and Bauchi states. According to the Plateau state committee on the census of displaced persons, some 250,000 were displaced in Plateau state alone and had to live in camps. The national commission for refugees put the number living in relief camps nationwide at some *800,000 internally displaced persons*. On 16 November, the state of emergency was lifted, Joshua Dariye was reinstated as governor and the State Assembly reinstituted as parliament. This move was followed by an anti-corruption campaign against Dariye aimed at ensuring he was deposed. The federal government cited Dariye's involvement in a money-laundering enterprise under investigation in Britain. In late November, the state parliament declined to probe the governor, and in December courts in Abuja and Kaduna ruled in favour of the governor's constitutional immunity from civil or criminal prosecution while in office.

The oil and gas producing Niger Delta and its major cities Port Harcourt and Warri continued to be extremely volatile, despite the presence of some 5,000 troops. Violence caused by armed robbers, kidnappers, pirates, oil thieves, militias, militant youths and state security operations directly affected oil production by the major companies Shell, ExxonMobil, ChevronTexaco and Nigerian National Petroleum Corporation (NNPC). In addition, an internal power struggle between two ethnic Ijaw warlords in Rivers state, Mujahid Dokubo-Asari and Ateke Tom, to a large extent mirrored the proxy war between rival factions in PDP. Moreover, a struggle over the control of stolen crude oil aggravated the volatile situation still further. It was estimated that between at least 50,000 and 100,000 barrels of oil were stolen per day. However, both warlords were offspring of the rigged 2003 elections in favour of Governor Odili and President Obasanjo because both played a vital role in intimidating opponents of the PDP. On the other hand, civil strife between ethnic Ijaw and Itsekiri in greater Warri area in Delta state had its roots in the longstanding struggle for political and financial control of resources at local level.

The Niger Delta People's Volunteer Force (NDPVF) led by Mujahid Dokubo-Asari and the Niger Delta Vigilante Group (NDVG), led by Ateke Tom, clashed on 1 February in Bugama near Port Harcourt over the right to collect compensation from Shell over an oil spill in the community. Bugama in Kalabari kingdom was the stronghold of Dokubo-Asari, where at least two-dozen people were reported killed. In early June, troops descended on Bugama, killing 20. Soon after, Dokubo-Asari, supported by 2,000 armed men, claimed to control three local governments in Rivers state. In mid-July, military forces, supported by the NDVG of Ateke Tom, killed 11 members of the NDPVF in the Amadi-Ama district of Port Harcourt. At the end of the month, gunmen opened fire in a bar in the oil city and shot several people. On 15 August, a longstanding dispute over a chief-tancy title in the village of Ataba (Rivers state) culminated in the shooting of 13 people. By mid-September, an estimated *500 people had been reported killed in Port Harcourt* and its surrounding creeks.

On 27 September, Dokubo-Asari issued a communiqué, 'Opera-tion Locust Feast', to wage war against foreign oil companies on Independence Day, 1 October, to highlight the will of the Ijaw peo-ple for self-determination. However, after the federal government agreed to peace talks with both *warlords* in Abuja, the attack was suspended. Having met the president, Dokubo-Asari and Ateke Tom agreed to a ceasefire and signed a disarmament and amnesty deal on 1 October. They promised to disband and totally disarm all militias and militant groups before the end of the year when the presiden-tial amnesty expired. By the end of October, Dokubo-Asari's faction started handing over weapons to the government allegedly in return for cash. By mid-November, Dokubo-Asari stopped further disarma-ment, claiming that his rival was not abiding by the disarmament agreement. But the ceasefire held, and on 7 December Dokubo-Asari resumed the peace process.

On 17–18 January, Itsekiri militias invaded four Okpe communi-ties in Sapele local government (Delta state) and killed 17 indigenes. Some seven people died after clashes between *Ijaw and Itsekiri mi-litia* groups in Ogbeh Ijoh and Ode Itsekiri on the outskirts of Warri one week later. In April, a new peace initiative by the Delta state government set up a 14-member committee of leading local politi-cians representing both ethnic groups. On 23 June, a peace accord was signed, but later, three Ijaw signatories retracted their agree-ment, among them the well-known Chief Edwin Clark.

On 23 April, *pirates killed two US oil workers*, two local boatmen and three navy troopers on the Benin River in Warri North. The US citizens were working for ChevronTexaco, which indefinite-ly suspended oil production in the area, a loss of 140,000 b/d. On 2 February, militant Itsekiri kidnapped local oil workers of Shell in Sapele (Delta) and killed a naval officer. The hostages were released a few days later. On 20 November, about 80 youths from the Ijaw village of Ojobo (Delta state) occupied a Shell oilrig for almost four days. Soldiers of the 'Operation Restore Hope' joint task force came to disperse them and used their guns, wounding more than a dozen protesters. Ojobo community leaders, however, claimed that seven demonstrators had been killed. The military and Shell's new managing director, Basil Omiyi, denied the accusation. Towards the end of the year, the situation escalated when on 5 December unarmed protesters from the Ijaw village of Kula (Rivers state) near the Bonny oil terminal seized two oil platforms operated by Shell and one operated by ChevronTexaco, cutting off oil flows and demanding talks on jobs and development. The occupation ended two days later but Shell agreed not to restart production until the dispute had been resolved. This forced both companies to suspend oil exports of 134,000 b/d.

In the northeastern states of Borno and Yobe, a *radical Islamic sect* called Muhajirun or Hijrah and inspired by the Afghan Taliban movement attacked police stations in Damaturu, Kanamma and Geidam area (Yobe state) in early January, killing two policemen. The core of the sect was made up of students and young graduates. In September, they attacked Bama and Gwoza (Borno state), where three policemen and some civilians lost their lives. And in October, in another attack in the same state at Kala-Balge near the Cameroon border, they killed three people and took half a dozen hostages. The military and police forces launched several counterattacks, killing some 50 members, and five sect members were arrested in Cameroon by local security forces.

In Numan in neighbouring Adamawa state, Christian Bachama clashed with Hausa and Fulani Muslims in early June over the reconstruction of a mosque overlooking the palace walls of the local traditional Bachama chief. Some 130 people died, almost 4,000 were displaced and many houses were destroyed. On 11 June, a dusk-to-dawn curfew was imposed and extended to the capital Yola, where displaced Muslims from Numan were seeking refuge. Moreover, the state government deposed the chief because of his complicity in the violence.

The institutions of higher learning continued to be volatile places where for years *cult and gang violence*, especially in the southern parts of the country, had claimed hundreds of lives. At the Lagos State University and the Ambrose Ali University in Edo state, widespread cult violence resulted in the death of at least three students. After two students were killed at the Olabisi Onabanjo University (Ogun state) in early June, more than 80 were expelled on 21 June for alleged murder and secret cult activities. At about the same time, three students were killed at the country's oldest university in Ibadan (Oyo state). In March, a magistrate's court in Ahoada (Rivers state) sentenced seven suspected cult members to various terms of imprisonment. And in November, a high court in Owerri (Imo state) sentenced to death a man who had killed his wife to sell her organs to ritualists. In early August, the Nigerian public was shocked when the police uncovered *fetish shrines* in Okija in Ihiala local government (Anambra state) filled with dozens of mutilated corpses, skeletons and skulls. Forensic tests proved that some of these victims were killed and their organs used to worship traditional gods. The police arrested some 20 people, most of them priests at the shrines, and charged them with murder.

Some well-known people were assassinated and several policemen and ordinary persons were victims of armed robbers, mainly operating along highways. A chieftain of the PDP in Delta state, Aminosoari Kalu Dikibo, was assassinated on 6 February. In early March, a local politician and an INEC commissioner in Kogi state, Luke Shigaba and Phillip Olorunnipa, and the former managing director of Nigerian Airways, Andrew Agom, were gunned down. Eshu Egbola, a close aide of the governor of Cross River, was murdered in his home state in August. In Kwara state, state civil servant Michael Agboola was murdered on 15 October, and Jerry Agbeyegbe, a captain and leading member of the Nigerian aviation safety initiative was killed in Lagos on 12 October.

Some 50 policemen lost their lives while on duty, most of them in Edo state. In Kwara, four were killed in July during a failed attack on an armoured van carrying money. In neighbouring Kogi state, armed robbers gunned down another four officers and a soldier in December. In October, two policemen attached to the governor of Delta state died after being attacked on the Asaba-Benin road. Prior to this, in April, the police claimed to have shot more than 400 armed robbers within three months.

A shake-up in the police force took place in early May, and several state police commissioners were redeployed, while 13 deputies were promoted to the rank of commissioner. Despite the loss of many lives and the poor salaries, the 300,000-strong police force retained its reputation for extortion, corruption and abetting crime, even though hundreds of policemen were dismissed and dozens arrested. To curb abuses against citizens, the Nigerian police set up a human rights service in July and launched a sophisticated nationwide PR media campaign.

In October, Transparency International listed Nigeria as the world's third most corrupt country. This was a clear indication that Obasanjo's anti-corruption campaign had so far largely failed. Although 500 suspects were in custody, neither the Independent Corrupt Practice Commission (ICPC) nor the Economic and Financial Crimes Commission (EFCC) were able to produce convincing evidence to bring a single prominent figure to book. Even the new *Money Laundering Bill*, introduced in March, has not yet yielded results. For example, the federal government withdrew the $ 214 m national identity card fraud case in June, after one suspect, former minister Sunday Afolabi, passed away. However, ICPC filed new charges against the suspects, among them two other former ministers, Hussaini Akwanga and Mohammed Shata. The biggest fraud trial so far, concerning the defrauding a Brazilian bank of $ 242 m, was pending in the Ikeja high court (Lagos state). In November, a trial of three rear admirals (Babatunde Samuel Kolawole, Francis Agbiti, Anthonio Ibinabo Bob-Manuel), charged with conspiracy and serious fraud, began in a *military court*. Allegedly, they were implicated in the disappearance of an impounded Russian oil tanker, whose crude oil was siphoned off to a Nigerian oil tanker and replaced with water. The Russian crew was tried in a criminal court in Lagos for oil theft. Even the efforts to recover funds allegedly looted by the late dictator Sani Abacha were put on hold by the Kaduna federal high court on 24 September. In its judgment, the court voided the government's move to retrieve the funds from Abacha's cronies. The federal government accordingly took the case to the court of appeal.

The five-year trial of five imprisoned high-ranking officers and close allies of Abacha (Hamza al-Mustapha, Ishaya Bamaiyi, James Danbaba, Bala Jibrin Yakubu and Rabo Lawal) dragged on without a verdict. They were charged with the attempted murder of the 'Guardian' (Lagos) publisher Alex Ibru in 1995. In another trial in Ibadan (Oyo state), the main suspect, Iyiola Omisore, accused of murdering Minister of Justice Bola Ige in 2001, was acquitted in June. The other 11 suspects were later discharged because of lack of evidence. The case made headlines for more than a year because Omisore became a senator on the PDP platform while in detention. Another trial in Lagos in October caused serious concerns about the loyalty of the security forces. In April, local print media speculated about a *possible coup d'état*. However, the chief of defence staff, General Alexander Ogomudia, struck a panel to investigate the issue. Prominent among the suspects in the alleged coup attempt was Hamza al-Mustapha, already on trial for attempted murder. He was accused of holding secret meetings in Lagos's Kirikiri maximum security prison with military officers. Finally, he, along with two military officers, one of them on the run, and one civilian were charged with treasonable felony because they had planned to overthrow the president.

The *shariah* issue lost momentum despite the fact that shariah courts in northern Nigeria kept on handing down death sentences by *stoning* and other penalties such as amputation and flogging.

However, nobody has been 'lawfully' stoned to death since 12 states introduced the shariah law in 2000 and 2001. The death sentences were either overturned on appeal or appeals were still pending. Nevertheless, on 5 January, a shariah court in Alkaleri (Bauchi state) sentenced Umar Tori to death by stoning for incest. In two other areas (Tafawa Balewa and Ningi) in the same state, two women, Hajara Ibrahim and Daso Adamu, were given the same sentences in September and October for having sex out of wedlock, but the verdicts were overruled in shariah courts of appeal. The same was true in March of a death sentence passed in 2003 against Jibrin Babaji for sodomy. In Niger state, the death sentence against Fatima Usman and her former lover Ahmadu Ibrahim, passed in 2001, was still pending. However, at the end of the year a shariah court in Gwarzo (Kano state) sentenced Danliti Rabiu to death by stoning for sodomy.

A minor *cabinet reshuffle* took place in June when two ministers of state (foreign and internal affairs) swapped portfolios. After a long battle in the senate, the president swore in the former minister of education, Professor Babaloba Borishade, as minister of state for power and steel. However, more importantly, on 30 April President Obasanjo appointed his special economic adviser, Chukwuema C. Soludo, as the new governor of the Central Bank of Nigeria, thereby replacing Joseph Sanusi. For the first time, a woman, Wahir Mshelia, assumed a leading position by becoming deputy governor. Jacob Buba Jang became the new comptroller general of the Nigerian customs service.

Against the background of the poor security situation the record on *human and civil rights deteriorated.* Irritated about critical reports in the United States, Europe and at home, the federal government put pressure on local and foreign media. On 1 April, the national broadcasting commission banned local broadcasters from taking over live transmission of news broadcasts from foreign stations. The scripts of foreign news and related programmes were to be rewritten and voiced locally before being broadcast. This decision directly affected stations like the BBC, CNN, VOA and Deutsche Welle. On 4 September, the State Security Service (SSS) confiscated 15,000 copies of the magazine 'Insider Weekly', known for its strong criticism of President Obasanjo. Three staff members were briefly detained and computers confiscated. However, the magazine was back on the newsstands on 20 September, although security agents besieged the office. In February, the freelance reporter of the 'Economist', Silvia Sansoni, was deported. The federal government justified its decision on the basis of her disregard of immigration laws and abuse of accreditation terms. In November, Stephan Faris of the US magazine 'Time' was refused entry at Lagos airport by the SSS, even though he had a valid visa.

For years, poor prison conditions remained unaddressed. Some 26,000 of the 40,000 prison inmates nationwide were still on remand without being convicted. More than 400 were waiting in death row, some for years. In Kaduna, civil rights activists accused police of *extra-judicial killings*, a practice that was on the rise. In October, 12 people were shot, and police claimed they had killed suspected armed robbers trying to break out of jail. In June, a vigilante mob, indirectly protected by the police, lynched at least a dozen suspected armed robbers in the city of Ughelli (Delta state). In June and September, a dozen members of the banned militant Movement for the Actualisation of the Sovereign State of Biafra (MASSOB) were arrested for holding illegal assemblies. In May, the federal government had already foreclosed the release of the official report of the human rights violations investigation commission, better known as the Oputa Panel Report on human rights abuses by past governments. The decision was based on the supreme court judgment that annulled the probe of the panel because of its unconstitutionality. The report had been submitted to the federal government as far back as May 2002.

The judiciary, embedded in a highly complicated legal system, technically called *legal pluralism*, still suffered from many years of military dictatorship. Moreover, the already overburdened courts were confronted with widespread corruption at every level that made it difficult to pass sentence and almost impossible to maintain independence. However, the highest courts are highly politicised and the vast majority of their verdicts were aimed at stabilising the political system, explicitly demonstrated in suits concerning the results of the elections in 2003.

Foreign Affairs

Nigeria's foreign policy focused on maintaining good relations with the US, enforcing its interests in the Bakassi conflict with neighbouring Cameroon and mediating in the Darfur conflict. Nigeria also tried to intensify its relations with Asian countries, especially China.

In February the US appointed career diplomat John Campbell as ambassador to Nigeria and removed Nigeria from a list of countries (in October) whose ports did not comply with US security standards. These decisions underlined the interests of both parties to keep close relations. The US increased its efforts to assist the Nigerian government in the Niger Delta by donating navy patrol ships and training Nigerian crews. Moreover, in July General Charles Wald, deputy commander of European Command (EUCOM), which also covers Africa, visited Nigeria. In August, General Robert Foglesong, commander of the US Air Force in Europe and Senator Chuck Hagel followed suit. Soon afterwards, it was agreed to hold *joint military training* in the Niger Delta. The first exercises took place in September as part of Joint-Combined Exchange Training (JCET). In addition, the US pledged to the military a modern medical laboratory, and in October US military transport planes flew Nigerian soldiers to Darfur. President Obasanjo met President Bush in Washington on 2 December, and the latter voiced strong support for Nigeria's efforts to help settle the conflicts in Darfur and Côte d'Ivoire. Serious legal problems arose towards the end of the year when the US refused Nigeria's new national carrier, Virgin Nigeria

Airlines, to operate direct flights, due to begin in early 2005, into the US. In February, 115 Nigerians were deported for a variety of reasons ranging from overstaying to drug trafficking.

Through President Obasanjo's chairmanship of the AU, Nigeria was directly involved in the *Darfur crisis in Sudan*. In July, he sent the former junta leader Gen. Abdulsalami Abubakar (retd) to Sudan and Chad for talks on Darfur, which he viewed as a problem to be resolved by the AU. On 1 August, Obasanjo met his counterpart al-Bashir in Khartoum and shortly afterwards Nigeria sent a battalion of peacekeeping troops as part of an AU force to the war-torn area. Towards the end of August, peace talks between the two warring factions and the Sudan government began in Abuja under AU auspices. Despite Nigerian mediation, peace talks broke down several times and at year's end no real solution was in sight. In November, the AU named the former career diplomat and well-known politician Baba Gana Kingibe as its special envoy in Sudan.

The handover of the potentially oil-rich *Bakassi* peninsula by Nigeria to Cameroon, originally scheduled for May, did not take place during the year. The International Court of Justice (ICJ) in The Hague had ruled in 2002 that Bakassi belonged to Cameroon and re-drew parts of the 1,600-kilometre land border stretching from Lake Chad to the Gulf of Guinea. Despite a meeting between Obasanjo and President Biya of Cameroon in Geneva at the end of January, initiated by UN Secretary-General Annan, and several further rounds of talks within the joint commission between February and November, Nigeria deliberately delayed the talks. On the domestic front the government was under political pressure to ignore the ICJ ruling, but within diplomatic circles it confirmed its alleged commitment to abide by it. At the same time, together with its counterpart, Nigeria used diplomatic channels to get the international community to financially support the demanding logistical exercise. An estimated $ 12 m was required, and the UN set up a trust fund. Both countries had already paid in $ 2.5 m, the EU contributed $ 500,000 and Britain $ 1.8 m. However, both heads of state met again in Yaounde on 29 July and agreed that all Nigerian troops would be out of Bakassi by 15 September at the latest. Despite the delay, two villages were exchanged on 13 July. Cameroon handed over Ndabuka to Nigeria and assumed sovereignty over Narki. Two days before the deadline, *Nigeria postponed the withdrawal of its forces* and a statement by Nigerian Foreign Minister Oluyemi Adeniji that a referendum would be the best way of deciding Bakassi's future put the whole issue on hold. Thus, the 13th meeting of the joint commission, scheduled for 7 December, was postponed to February 2005.

Nigeria continued to play a modest role in tackling the *Côte d'Ivoire conflict*, although President Obasanjo, AU chairman and head of the newly established Peace and Security Council, called several meetings to resolve the crisis. On 20 June, Obasanjo invited the Ivorian President Laurent Gbagbo, Ghanaian Head of State John Kufuor, Togo's President Gnassingbé Eyadéma and the executive secretary of ECOWAS, Mohammed Ibn Chambas for talks. In an emergency meeting on 14 November in Abuja, Obasanjo, Kufuor and Eyadéma were joined by Senegal's President Abdoulaye Wade, Blaise Campaoré of Burkina Faso, Gabon's President Omar Bongo and Alpha Konaré, chairman of the AU commission. They called for an immediate arms embargo on the government and rebel groups. Shortly thereafter, the UN Security Council voted unanimously for an arms embargo. On the eve of the meeting of francophone nations in Ouagadougou, Obasanjo discussed the Ivorian crisis with French President Chirac, whom he had already met at the 'Autorité du Basin du Niger' summit in Paris in April.

Nigeria continued its *peacekeeping activities* with military and police forces as part of the UN Mission in Liberia (UNMIL). Nevertheless, the exiled former Liberian President Charles Taylor, granted residence in Nigeria in 2003, began to haunt the government. The special court for Sierra Leone, mandated by the UN, had indicted Taylor for war crimes and in June a court in Abuja allowed a request by the Nigerian Coalition on the International Criminal Court (NCICC) for Taylor's repatriation to Sierra Leone to face war crimes charges. In September, the Nigerian government urged the court to strike the suit on the grounds that Nigeria granted residence to Taylor on humanitarian grounds and partly to resolve the Liberian crisis. The court upheld the objection and dismissed the suit. In October, UNHCR began repatriating some 1,000 Liberian refugees who had volunteered to return home.

The *joint offshore fields in the Gulf of Guinea* determined Nigeria's relationship with São Tomé and Príncipe. President Obasanjo and his counterpart Menezes met on 26 June and signed a joint declaration on transparency and governance in the Joint Development Zone (JDZ). Nigeria owned 60% and São Tomé and Príncipe 40% of the JDZ, which was divided into nine potentially lucrative oil exploration blocks. Under the agreement, all payments for exploration licences in the JDZ would be made public, the income audited and the accounts of a joint supervisory authority published. All nine oil blocks were first tendered in 2003, but only one was taken up. In November, five blocks were again put up for tender in Abuja, and 26 oil companies, including indigenous ones, submitted bids. In July, Nigeria granted São Tomé and Príncipe a loan of $ 5 m after an emergency request. In a similar move, Nigeria gave Ghana a loan of $ 40 m that was supposed to finance Ghana's share in the West African gas pipeline project.

Nigeria's *orientation towards Asia* first yielded results when NNPC entered into a service contract agreement with the state China Petroleum and Chemical (Petrochemical) Corporation (SINOPEC) for the development of two shallow water oil blocks in April. In May, NNPC's top manager Funsho Kupolokun signed an agreement with the China International United Petroleum and Chemical Company (UNIPEC) for the supply of 50,000 b/d crude oil. In September, a delegation from the Chinese National Petroleum Development Corporation (CNPC) held talks in Nigeria and signed a memorandum of understanding on cooperation in the oil and gas sectors. Around the same time, the Nigeria-China business investment forum took place in Shanghai. This was followed by the inauguration of a technical committee one month later to work out details of how to effectively execute a joint venture investment agreement. On 6 November, the chairman of the standing committee of the National People's Congress, Wu Bangguo, visited Nigeria, and both sides signed a cooperation accord on oil, technology and telecommunication. The accord included a grant of $ 2.2 m to Nigeria. As a political gesture, President Obasanjo ordered the closure of the Taiwanese commercial office in the capital, but it was permitted to relocate to Lagos state. Last but not least, the Nigerian Defence Minister Rabiu Kwankwaso officially visited China in June.

President Obasanjo and his ministers Oluyemi Adeniji (foreign affairs), Mrs. Ngozi Okonjo-Iweala (finance) and Adamu Idris Waziri (commerce) took part in an international development conference in Tokyo in early November. This Asian-African conference was part of a Japanese initiative to boost Africa's development. According to Prime Minister Junichiro Koizumi, Japan wanted Nigerian development to be a model for surrounding African countries. After the conference, the Nigerian president and his delegation proceeded to India. On 2 November, they held talks with the newly elected Prime Minister Manmohan Singh and had a session with the Indian Chambers of Commerce and Industry. In October, the Indian Oil Corporation signed a term contract for 40,000 b/d crude oil from Nigeria. Nevertheless, Nigeria tried to intensify the longstanding *military relationship with India's neighbour Pakistan.* The five-day visit to Nigeria (1–5 March) of the chairman of Pakistan's joint chiefs of staff committee, General Mohammed Aziz Khan, was aimed at increasing military cooperation in the fields of equipment and training.

Since the Iraq war, the relationship with the former colonial power Britain has cooled. Nevertheless, Hilary Benn, secretary of state for international development announced during his three-day visit in September that the British government through the department for international development would double its development assistance to Nigeria from £ 35 m in 2003–04 to £ 70 m in 2005–06.

This was in line with the Country Assistance Plan (CAP) for 2004–07. In November, the president went on an official visit to Britain. Both governments agreed to step up the *fight against trafficking in people.* The bilateral accord targeted improved cross-border cooperation and tougher prosecution of traffickers. The agreement was signed by Britain's Solicitor-General Harriet Harman and Nigeria's Attorney-General Akinlolu Olujinmi. Against this background, Obasanjo undertook some important trips to London in his capacity as chairman of the *Commonwealth.*

Since it was revealed that *Swiss banks* harboured $ 700 m looted by the late military dictator Sani Abacha, the elected Nigerian government used legal and diplomatic means fairly successfully to get the money back. Some $ 500 m was still frozen when in August the Swiss government ordered its return to Nigeria. The Abacha family appealed this decision in the highest court of Switzerland, and the case was still pending at year's end. On 9 December, Abba Abacha, son of the late dictator, was arrested in Germany, after Swiss authorities issued an arrest warrant, but extradition to Switzerland was still pending.

Against the background of possible reform of the UN, President Obasanjo declared in his address to the General Assembly on 23 September that "Nigeria was qualified to be a permanent member of the *UN Security Council.*" The 48th annual conference of the International Atomic Energy Agency elected Nigeria on to the board of governors, just before it put its first nuclear research reactor, at Ahmadu Bello University in Zaria, into operation on 30 September. Earlier, the UN honoured Nigeria's active role in Africa, particularly West Africa, when the Security Council visited Abuja on 26 June as part of its West Africa tour. Shortly before, President Obasanjo attended the G8 summit in the US, and in March he took part in a special meeting of ECOWAS and the World Bank in Accra and received the bank's president, James Wolfensohn, during his three-day visit to Nigeria.

In early August, the new managing director of the IMF, Rodrigo de Rato, started his first trip to Africa with a two-day visit to Nigeria.

He underlined the IMF's rather positive attitude towards the critical role Nigeria had assumed as political and economic leader and its commitment to the new home-grown economic and social reform programme, the National Economic Empowerment and Development Strategy (NEEDS). Moreover, de Rato offered every assistance to repatriate Nigerian funds stashed in foreign countries by corrupt leaders and government officials. The visit followed the Article IV consultations between Nigeria and the IMF executive board on 16 July.

Socioeconomic Developments

Socioeconomic development was dominated by soaring oil prices, the boom in the mobile phone sector, the slowed privatisation programme and a political and legal battle between the federal government and the Nigerian Labour Congress (NLC) over new fuel prices. Living conditions for most Nigerians, however, did not really improve, as indicated by an HDI of 0.466 (HDR 2004) that put Nigeria 151st of 177 countries.

Rising oil prices on the international market also inflated the annual budget. In addition, much bargaining between the presidency, the senate and the house of representatives to harmonise the bill, seriously delayed the naira 1.3 trillion ($ 9.6 bn) budget for 2004, which came into force on 21 April. The budget was related to the benchmark of $ 25 per barrel of crude oil and an exchange rate of naira 136 to the dollar. Nigeria produced some 2.3 m b/d, despite turmoil in the Niger Delta. The price of benchmark Brent North Sea crude went up from some $ 30 in January to $ 45 in August, to more than $ 50 in October and fell just below $ 40 in December. Thus, Nigeria's foreign reserves doubled from $ 8.2 bn at the beginning of the year to $ 16.1 bn at the end of it. Nevertheless, *external debts* increased and stood at $ 34 bn, because Nigeria pinned its debt service at $ 1 bn for the Paris Club, which it owed almost $ 28 bn, far below its obligation of almost $ 3 bn, thereby significantly increasing arrears. However, GDP increased by 5.5% and average inflation rate fell to 15%.

Throughout the year, NLC and the federal government confronted each other, using political and legal means over the sensitive fuel price issue. Fuel subsidies had been partly removed after an elected government took power in 1999, but fuel was still highly subsidised at the rate of $ 1.8 bn per annum, as most Nigerians considered cheap fuel a birthright. The introduction of a fuel tax of naira 1.50 per litre on petrol, diesel and kerosene, which came into force on 1 January, had to be suspended. NLC called off a *nationwide strike* on 21 January only a few hours after a court had ordered that both the strike and the intended tax collection be suspended pending a ruling on that issue. In early May, fuel marketers slightly increased the price to almost naira 43 and by the end of the month to naira 50 to 55. This was in line with a modest deregulation policy that allowed private marketers to import fuel and fix prices. NLC responded by calling a nationwide strike on 9 June, but it suspended the action on 11 June after filling stations slashed the petrol price.

After failed negotiations with the federal government in early October, NLC launched a four-day strike on 11 October to get the 20% price hike reversed. Only two days before, NLC leader Adams Oshiomhole was briefly detained by the SSS. NLC threatened to call another nationwide strike on 16 November, but on the eve of the strike suspended it after the federal government backed down and reduced the price of fuel and, more importantly, kerosene, which most Nigerians use for cooking. However, the court of appeal ruled on 16 December that NLC could not call a nationwide strike because of the fuel tax.

Shell was also hit by strike action by its staff. The two oil workers' unions, National Union of Petrol and National Gas and Petroleum and Natural Gas Senior Staff Association of Nigeria called a two-day warning strike in June and another in October to protest a planned cut of 1,000 jobs. Just before Christmas in a silent move, NNPC sacked 2,355 staff. The National Association of Resident Doctors (NARD) called a two-day warning strike in November to press for the payment of salary arrears, and in mid-December NARD began an open-ended strike.

The *privatisation programme* slowed down again despite the ambitious five-year reform programme (NEEDS), launched in March. In November, Obasanjo ruled out privatising the nation's four refineries for the foreseeable future, after 13 companies were given federal government approval in October to commence construction of private refineries. In addition, the Aluminium Smelter Company of Nigeria (ALSCON), Ajaokuta Steel Company and Nigerian Telecommunication Limited (NITEL) were all causing serious problems. In August, Nigeria terminated the contract with the US company Solgas Energy. Instead, it signed a ten-year accord with an Indian company to complete and manage Ajaokuta. At the end of the year, Solgas Energy took the federal government before an arbitration panel of the International Chamber of Commerce for breach of contract. In July, a core investor from the US, the BFI Group Corporation, failed to acquire a majority stake in ALSCON. The federal government disqualified the company's bid because it had allegedly missed the deadline to pay the required 10% deposit.

Nigeria belongs to Africa's fastest growing *mobile phone market*. In recent years, $ 4 bn have been invested, mainly by private companies like MTN, M-Tel, Globacom and V-Mobile. According to the Nigerian Communication Commission some 5 m mobile and 1 m landlines were available in July and it expected to hit the 10 m benchmark within a year. But the heavily loss-making, state-run NITEL failed again (as in 2002) to find a strategic investor to acquire a 51% share. The Dutch consultancy company Pentascope International, contracted in 2003 to manage NITEL, admitted in November that it was overwhelmed by the company's problems and could not even meet 20% of the projected number of lines for the first year.

After overcoming all the legal issues concerning the liquida-
tion of the national carrier Nigeria Airways, in February the federal
government appointed South African Airways as strategic investor
and technical partner to launch the new national carrier Nigerian
Eagle Airline by the end of the year. However, subsequent negotiations broke down and the federal government chose the British airline Virgin Atlantic as its new partner in the creation of the new
Virgin Nigeria Airlines.

The *power situation* went from bad to worse, since the National
Electric Power Authority was able to generate just 3,000 megawatts
per day, while estimated national demand was 6,000 megawatts.
The launch of a second, small independent power supply project
in Lagos state in August to some extent eased the industry's dire circumstances in the state and served as a potential model for further
private investment in the power sector.

The *World Bank* approved a $ 120 m credit to improve urban water
supplies, a $ 140 m credit to support the economic reform and gover-
nance programme, another $ 120 m credit for sustainable manage-
ment of mineral resources, and it finally administered a $ 900,000
Japanese grant for the preparation of the Nigerian Urban Youth and
Empowerment Project.

Africa's biggest industrial project, *Nigeria Liquefied Natural Gas*,
was expanded again after the joint venture partners decided in July
to invest a further $ 1.25 bn to build the sixth production train. Soon
afterwards, NNPC and a subsidiary of ExxonMobil signed the financing documents for the more than $ 1 bn liquid natural gas expansion
project.

Nigeria became the epicentre and source of the latest and *fastest-
growing polio outbreak* and accounted for 80% of the world's polio
cases. The international vaccine programme, targeted at 35 million
children, met stiff opposition in some Muslim-dominated states,
especially Kano and Zamfara. Radical Islamic clerics claimed that
the US-made vaccine was manipulated to cause infertility. After a
long political battle with the federal government, the international

community and some influential Muslim moderates, the radicals capitulated, and in October WHO and UNICEF carried the campaign to the north.

The *spread of HIV/AIDS continued*, and in terms of absolute numbers Nigeria was second only to South Africa. About 3.8 m people were infected, most of them living in Lagos, and at least 13 states had prevalence rates of more than the critical benchmark of 5%.

Nigeria in 2005

In 2005, the Nigerian government demonstrated convincing leadership for the first time since it came to power as an elected body in 1999. Under the undisputed leadership of President Olusegun Obasanjo, it revealed a hitherto unknown capacity for managing and, to a fairly large extent, preventing a threatening internal crisis by withdrawing the most powerful local militias from the field of operations, largely by legal means. In fact, in what was a remarkable achievement, the government even reached a debt relief deal with the Paris Club, unprecedented in the history of the creditors' club. This, in conjunction with a personal triumph in the supreme court over the outcome of the 2003 presidential elections and wide-ranging banking reform, paved the way for the commencement of a public debate on amending the constitution in favour of the incumbent. Notwithstanding these achievements, in comparative terms the level of violence in the country was still fairly high. Interestingly, while the federal government was able to mobilise sustainable support from Western countries and institutions in stabilising Nigeria, there was not too much progress registered in crisis management on the African home front, in particular the serious crisis in Sudan's Darfur region.

Domestic Politics

The legal battle over the outcome of the presidential elections of 2003 went into its last round. In early January, the petitioner and main challenger, the defeated candidate of the All Nigeria People's Party (ANPP), former junta chairman Maj. Gen. Muhammadu Buhari (retd), went to the *supreme court*. He asked the court to allow his appeal against the conduct of the 2003 presidential elections and to quash the majority judgement of the court of appeal that acted as the presidential tribunal. At the same time, President Olusegun Obasanjo of the ruling People's Democratic Party (PDP) challenged the verdict of that tribunal, which had cancelled the results in his home state, Ogun. On 1 July, the supreme court unanimously dismissed the challenge by Buhari, ending the legal battle by Obasanjo's main opponent to have the presidential elections annulled. Furthermore, the court reversed the decision on Ogun state in favour of the president, stating that there was insufficient evidence to annul the poll. The outcome of this long legal battle was not only a personal triumph for the incumbent but also strengthened his position as president and almost undisputed leader of Nigeria.

Anambra state Governor Chris Ngige had survived a protracted power struggle within the PDP in 2004 that had even endangered national security and stability. However, the national chairman of the PDP, Innocent Audu Ogbeh, was forced to resign on 10 January following a very public row with Obasanjo over the handling of the political crisis in Anambra state. In March, the PDP national executive elected a former senior military officer, Colonel Amadu Adah Ali (retd), as the new party chairman. He had served in the military government when Obasanjo was the head of the military junta from 1976–79. Against this background, it came as a shock to the incumbent when on 12 August the Anambra state election petition tribunal in Awka nullified Ngige's election. In Ngige's stead the tribunal declared the petitioner Peter Obi of the All Progressive Grand Alliance (APGA) the validly elected candidate who ought to have been declared winner by the *Independent National Election Commission* (INEC). Notwithstanding the tribunal's verdict, the incumbent remained in office, and in November he filed a petition in the court of appeal, Enugu division, challenging the nullification. The court, however, adjourned the matter to mid-January 2006 for a definite and accelerated hearing. Thus by year's end, apart from the Ngige case, only the validity of the governorship of James Ibori in Delta state was still pending.

After the national council of state had approved the guidelines, the federal government constituted the national conference to be known as *National Political Reform Conference* in the capital, Abuja, in February. It was supposed to recommend amendments to the 1999 constitution to make up for the credibility it lacked as a result of its having been promulgated by decree by the outgoing military government under General Abdulsalami Abubakar in May 1999. The well-known retired Justice Nike Tobi became chairman, and Alhaji Sule Katagum, a former commissioner of the federal civil service, deputy chairman. Reverend Father Mathew Hassan Kukah, who had been the secretary-general of the Catholic Church for ten years and a member of the Oputa Panel on Human Rights Violations, served as secretary.

The most controversial issues related to the *presidential and gubernatorial terms* and the sharing of oil and gas revenues. While the committee in charge proposed a six-year single term for the president and a five-year term for governors, the committee on revenue-sharing proposed the adoption of a 17% derivation principle for revenue allocation from the federation account – as against the current 13% – in favour of the oil producing states. The supreme court confirmed this figure and dismissed a suit by northern governors on 15 December. The delegates from the oil and gas producing areas in the south demanded a minimum of 25%. In early July, they walked out of the conference and refused to endorse the final report. On 26 July, the president passed the report to the National Assembly for consideration and action. According to the 1999 Constitution, part II, section 9, however, any provisions that alter the constitution require a two-thirds majority of all members of both chambers of the National Assembly and approval by resolution of the houses of assembly of not less than two-thirds of the 36 federal states.

The public debate on a possible third term for the president and the governors gained momentum by the end of the year, when a sub-committee of the National Assembly, influential businessmen and the vast majority of governors supported the notion that they be allowed to serve three terms of four years each. This was not at all surprising, and highlighted their fear that they would be charged by the *Economic and Financial Crime Commission* (EFCC) after leaving office. Outspoken critics such as the former head of the military junta during the civil war, retired General Yakubu Gowon, whose opinion represented large parts of the Middle Belt region, openly warned Obasanjo against standing for a third term. However, the president was well aware of his strong position, which might serve him well if he stood in the presidential elections in early 2007. Thus, Vice-President Atiku Abubakar, Obasanjo's potential successor, was one of his first prominent victims when on 28 August the president publicly accused him of disloyalty. He was even accused of having had prior knowledge of a planned coup d'état in 2004. Yet Obasanjo did not dare to remove his vice-president from office, because the latter could still mobilise support from within the ruling party PDP.

Opposition groups and famous activists like Nobel literature prize laureate Wole Soyinka, elder statesman Anthony Enahoro and civil rights activist Beko Ransome-Kuti were supposed to take part in the national conference. However, they considered it to be a mere government talking shop and continued to advocate for a *National Sovereign Conference*, an idea that had long been circulating. In this spirit, they began organising an alternative Pro-National Conference (PRONACO) that started in Lagos on independence day, 1 October, under the chairmanship of Enahoro. However, from the very beginning the leading figures could not agree on a common platform. By the end of October, Enahoro as well as Soyinka were absent from the general assembly meeting and shunned the much-touted mobilisation rally, fuelling the impression that things had fallen apart in the organisation.

In recent years, local militias had seriously threatened state security and endangered the democratisation process. Now, for the first time, the elected federal government put the expansion of militias on hold by arresting certain leading figures and charging them in court. On 20 September, Mujahid Dokubo-Asari, the leader of the illegal ethnic *Ijaw militia* Niger Delta People's Volunteer Force (NDPVF), was detained and charged in court in Abuja on allegations that he was planning a fresh uprising in the Niger Delta and was bent on overthrowing the state. Dokubo-Asari, whom many Ijaw regarded as a freedom fighter, was refused bail and the trial was postponed for procedural reasons until 10 January 2006.

On 22 October, security forces detained Ganiyu Adams and Frederick Fasehun, the two factional leaders of the banned ethnic *Yoruba militia* O'odua People's Congress (OPC), which mainly concentrated its action in the greater Lagos area. The group had originally been created to defend the rights of the Yoruba people. However, the two men were charged with conspiracy and murder, but released on 14 November after the director of public prosecutions for Lagos state admitted that they had no case to answer. Shortly thereafter, Fasehun and Adams were re-arrested and confronted with fresh charges, including illegal possession of arms and subverting the government or promoting its overthrow. The court adjourned the case to 1 February 2006 and remanded the accused in custody.

The leader of the banned ethnic *Igbo militia*, Movement for the Actualisation of the Sovereign State of Biafra (MASSOB), Ralph Uwazuruike, suffered a similar fate on 26 October and was charged with treason. The court in Abuja, however, adjourned the case to 17 January 2006. MASSOB advocated the secession of parts of southeastern Nigeria referred to as Biafra, and largely inhabited by ethnic Igbo.

These actions indicated that the federal government and the security services had been planning the arrests well in advance, only awaiting the right moment to put the plan into action. Additionally, the courts in many cases applied new and harsh bail conditions to make it more difficult for the accused to escape criminal charges. A factional power struggle within the NDPVF led in May to the dismissal of Columbus Richman, who claimed to be the founder of the organisation and its commanding officer. In July, the *State Security*

Service (sss) interrogated Dokubo-Asari in connection with allegations that he was planning to destroy facilities belonging to foreign oil companies. He denied the allegations and was released without charge. However, after his arrest on 20 September, some NDPVF commanders rather surprisingly backed away from threats of violence, thereby confirming the structural weakness of the organisation. Its leaders feared a severe military reaction, because all federal army units in the area had been put on high alert.

The prelude to the arrests of the two OPC faction leaders began in mid-February when members of the two factions clashed and left at least three people dead and several policemen seriously injured. Some weeks later, the faction leaders were supposed to have settled their longstanding differences over ways and means to fight for the rights of the Yoruba people. However, a violent incident in Ilorin, the capital of Kwara state, in late September caused the death of five civilians and a policeman. OPC supporters were opposed to the turbanning of a traditional ruler by the Emir of Ilorin, and in the aftermath they clashed with opposing sides and the police. OPC members were also involved in another bloody incident in Lagos in October, when 12 people, including a policeman, were brutally murdered and cars and properties destroyed.

Fifty-three suspected members of MASSOB were detained in September 2004 after launching the Biafra freedom football tournament and were charged with treason. In July 2005, almost one year on, a court in Lagos quashed the charge of treason and conspiracy and discharged 25 of those being held. The court, however, found that 28 persons still had a case to answer, having admitted that they belonged to MASSOB, an unlawful society. Notwithstanding these verdicts, the security forces arrested another batch of 42 suspected members in Imo state in August, followed by the arrest of Uwazuruike in October. On 7 November, demonstrators marched through the commercial centre of Onitsha to press for his release. The march degenerated into a violent protest and the residence of Nigeria's first president, the late Nnamdi Azikiwe, was set ablaze.

On 5–6 December, in Anambra, Enugu, Imo and Ebonyi states public life was disrupted by a *two-day stay-at-home strike* that was called
to protest the arrest and trial of Uwazuruike. Onitsha and Owerri
saw the most violent clashes between MASSOB militants and heavily armed police forces, which resulted in several casualties and
much damage. MASSOB put the death toll at 20 people, while the
Nigerian press put it at between three and 20.

The governor of Bayelsa state, Diepreye Alamieyeseigha, was arrested at London's Heathrow airport on 15 September in connection
with allegations of *money laundering*. It soon became apparent that
the arrest was the product of close collaboration between the British
police and Nigeria's EFCC. Initially, Alamieyeseigha was granted bail
but was later re-arrested and charged with laundering £ 1.8 m found
in cash and bank accounts. The funds and his passport were confiscated and his assets frozen. The trial was fixed for 8 December and
Alamieyeseigha was released on 13 October, after a British court formally granted bail upon six conditions, among them a £ 500,000 bail
bond, daily reporting to a police station known to the court, and an
order not to leave the country. The court applied these harsh conditions after taking into consideration the fact that another Nigerian
governor, Joshua Dariye of Plateau state, was briefly arrested in
London on September 2004 on suspicion of fraud. He was released
on bail on signed condition that he would return to London to face
further questioning. However, he failed to return and the court issued an international arrest warrant and ordered the freezing of all
his assets and bank accounts.

To the surprise of British and Nigerian officials, Alamieyeseigha
broke his bail conditions and fled from Britain. On the 21 November,
he showed up in his home state, believing he would be protected by
his immunity as governor. However, in the meantime, public opinion in Nigeria and the political climate in his home state had turned
against him. In addition, some sources pointed to his dubious relations with the arrested warlord Dokubo-Asari. Within days, the
state assembly began a legal *impeachment* procedure. It mandated

the chief judge of Bayelsa state to constitute a seven-man investigation to look into allegations of gross misconduct. The panel began sitting on 6 December and found the governor guilty on all these allegations. Two days later, on 8 December, the state assembly impeached Governor Alamieyeseigha with the necessary two-thirds majority, and his deputy and the acting governor Goodluck Jonathan was sworn in as the new governor. Having now lost his immunity, Alamieyeseigha was arrested and detained by the EFCC and charged in a Lagos court with money laundering, illegal acquisition of property and false declaration of assets.

During the year, Obasanjo's *anti-corruption campaign* gathered momentum. Some senior officials were convicted in a drive to stamp out corruption. Nevertheless, in October Transparency International, in its corruption perception index, ranked Nigeria as the sixth most corrupt country in the world. In January, the inspector-general of police, Tafa Adebayo Balogun, had to retire before being detained and charged with money laundering and stealing huge amounts of money belonging to the Nigeria police force. In November, a court in Abuja sentenced him to six months imprisonment and fined him $ 30,000. In addition, the government seized property and cash from Balogun worth some $ 150 m.

In January, a *military court* passed verdict on three rear-admirals who were allegedly implicated in the disappearance of a ship carrying large quantities of stolen crude oil. One of the accused, Anthonio Ibinabo Bob-Manuel, was discharged, while Babatunde Samuel Kolawole and Francis Agbiti were convicted and then demoted to the rank of commodore and dismissed from the navy. In December, the detained crew members who had been involved in the oil theft, almost all of them Russian nationals, were sentenced to six months imprisonment. However, they were allowed to leave Nigeria immediately, thereby avoiding a possible diplomatic row over this case between Moscow and Abuja.

The biggest *international fraud trial* to date, that concerning the defrauding of a Brazilian bank of $ 242 m, ended in November.

Mrs. Amaka Anajemba got off lightly with two-and-a-half years in prison, while the other two suspects, Frank Nwude and Nzweribe Okoli, were sentenced to 25 and 12 years imprisonment respectively. In addition, they had to surrender most of their assets to compensate the victims.

The *anti-corruption campaign* did not stop there, and the EFCC and the Independent Corrupt Practices and Related Offences Commission (ICPC) even aimed at several top politicians. In April, the president sacked Education Minister Fabian Osuji for allegedly offering a bribe of naira 55 m to some legislators to have an inflated education budget passed. This amount was the equivalent of approximately $ 400,000. The *president of the senate*, Adolphus Wabara, was allegedly involved as well. He was forced to resign and was eventually succeeded by Senator Ken Nnamani, again representing the southeast, one of six geopolitical zones. Since the beginning of the democratisation process in 1999, all presidents of the senate have represented that zone. The two top politicians and five legislators were charged with corruption in a court in Abuja. In a further move, the president dismissed the minister for housing and urban development, Alice Mobolaji Osomo, for attempting to secretly sell state-owned luxury houses in Lagos to a cross-section of the political and military elite, instead of having them advertised. All sales were cancelled and paid deposits refunded. Many more cases against high-level officials were still pending, underscoring efforts by the federal government to tackle endemic corruption. Yet, despite the obvious breakthroughs by the anti-corruption commissions, the Paris-based Financial Action Task Force (FATF) did not remove Nigeria from the list of uncooperative countries.

A *major cabinet reshuffle* took place in July. The most important changes affected the ministries of justice and petroleum. Incumbent president of the Nigerian Bar Association (NBA) Bayo Oyo replaced Justice Minister Akinlolu Olujinmi, while the special advisor on petroleum resources, Edmund Daukoru, was promoted minister of state, the meaning of this being that Obasanjo kept the petroleum

portfolio. In addition to the cabinet reshuffle, the president changed
the leadership of several institutions and approved new boards of
parastatals and government agencies. Sunday Gabriel Ehindero
was appointed the new inspector-general of police, Rear-Admiral
Ganiyu Adeleye chief of naval staff and Maurice Iwu chairman of
the election commission, INEC. Joseph Chukwurah took over the
Nigerian immigration service and Irene Nkechi Chigbue the privatisation agency, Bureau of Public Enterprises (BPE). Bashir Gwandu
became the executive secretary of the national communications
commission and Justice Emmanuel Olayinka Ayoola was appointed
the new chairman of the anti-corruption commission, ICPC.

As in previous years, the Middle Belt and the southern parts of
the country were particularly crime-ridden, but the number of assassinations declined significantly. *Armed robbers* mainly targeted
banks and long-distance buses. Near Benin City, 15 passengers
and two policemen were killed in March in two incidents. On the
Gwagwala-Abuja expressway, armed robbers killed six people, including a police escort, on 25 April. In Ethiope East local government in Delta state, a gang attempted to raid a community bank on
23 June but was resisted by policemen. Two officers lost their lives.
In three other bank robberies in Umuahia and Aba, Abia state, and
Abakaliki, Ebonyi state, in November and December, nine people,
including seven policemen, were killed. By the end of 2005 some
26 policemen had lost their lives while on duty, according to the
inspector-general of police, and some 2,600 armed robbery suspects
had been arrested and more than 1,000 firearms recovered.

Despite the loss of so many lives, the police retained their reputation for abetting crime, especially after killing six persons in Apo
area in Abuja on 7 June. The police patrol claimed to have killed suspected armed robbers. The special rapporteur of the United Nations
Commission on Human Rights, Philip Alston, however, warned that
extra-judicial killings might not abate unless the government looked
into the Apo affair and similar occurrences in the recent past.
A panel of inquiry proved that although the policemen were acting

on a distress call in connection with a robbery attack, the shooting of the six was reprehensible and unjustifiable and the officers
therefore had to face trial. Significantly, the federal government
paid compensation to the families of the victims. In August, the inspector-general of police paraded nine policemen for the illegal sale
and movement of arms and ammunition to demonstrate that the
police force was looking inward in its onslaught on violent crimes.
In December, he unfolded a reform programme that was aimed at
purging the force of criminals. Eventually, security forces arrested a
number of suspects believed to have killed two US oil workers, three
navy sailors and two civilians in April 2004.

Nigeria's overall human and civil rights record improved slightly
but was nevertheless mixed. The publication of the Oputa Panel
report on *human rights abuses* by past governments was appreciated in many circles. As a result of a court ruling in 2004, the report
had never been officially published. But, remarkably, in January the
civil society forum put the report on the internet. As was widely
expected, the report's main finding was that three former military
rulers, Muhammadu Buhari, Ibrahim Babangida and Abdulsalami
Abubakar were personally liable for extra-judicial killings perpetrated while they were in power. The report recommended that in
future all three men be banned from holding high office. Babangida
was, nevertheless, tipped as one of the main contenders for the presidency in 2007.

The European parliament's Sakharov prize for outstanding bravery and determination in the battle for universal human rights was
awarded on 26 October to barrister Hauwa Ibrahim. She belongs to a
tiny *female Muslim elite* in northern Nigeria and made headlines by
successfully defending Amina Lawal, who was sentenced to death
by stoning for adultery in a shariah court in 2002. However, an appeal court voided the verdict.

In fact, state security services mainly *harassed journalists*, in
particular at state level in the Niger Delta during the last quarter
of the year when tension in the delta was rising. On 11 October, the

publisher of the 'Weekly Star' in Port Harcourt, River state, Owei Kobina Sikpi, was detained and charged with publishing a false report about the governor's alleged involvement in money laundering. Close to the day of remembrance of the extra-legal killing of writer and civil rights activist Ken Saro-Wiwa on 10 November 1995, editors of the 'The Hard Truth' and the 'Port Harcourt Argus' were briefly arrested. In December, two broadcasters from the Rhythm 93.7 FM radio station in Port Harcourt, Klem Ofuokwu and Cleopatra Taiwo, were detained and charged with airing a news item that was later found to be false. In Lagos state, the Bellview air crash in October caused the temporary shutdown of the biggest private radio and TV station, 'Ray Power' and 'African Independent Television', by the Nigerian authorities. Their reporters were the first to locate the crash site, transmit shots of body parts and even provided information that there were no survivors before the proper authorities were able to assess the situation.

While cult and gang violence in institutions of higher learning in the southern parts of the country went on unabated, the *shariah* issue lost further momentum. This was in stark contrast to the fact that shariah law appeared to have retained popular support in the northern states. Most verdicts of shariah courts on amputation, however, were overturned on appeal or were pending. Furthermore, two men in Katsina accused of homosexuality and therefore facing the death penalty by stoning, were finally discharged on 6 December. In the pending case of Umar Tori, who was convicted of incest in 2004, a shariah court of appeal in Bauchi state upheld his appeal and ordered that his case be tried before another upper shariah court. In November, a shariah judge in Kano ordered two young men, Aminu Iliyasu and Shu'aibu Yusuf, to be hanged for killing a three-year-old girl. While the convicts appealed, they were the first to be sentenced to death by a shariah court since Kano state began implementing the shariah code.

In July, the government of Kano state imposed a ban on men and women of Muslim faith travelling together on public transport.

However, women could still travel with their male relations. Some 9,000 *religious marshals* were supposed to enforce the new law in the city of Kano alone, which includes many people of Christian faith from the Middle Belt and the south. Since there were not enough vehicles available, the ban was contentious from the start. As a result, marshals clashed with motorbike taxi riders in December who, together with women, were defying the ban by pretending to be related. In another incident, Islamic militants in the city burnt down four houses within the police barracks from which beer was being sold.

Between February and June, several *sectarian clashes* exacerbated tensions in Sokoto, home of the sultan. Members of so-called 'Shiite' groups clashed with mainstream Sunni Muslims over doctrinal differences and access to the central mosque. While there are no Shiite Muslims in Nigeria, Muslims and Islamic groups sympathising with the Iranian revolution are wrongly called Shiites. More than a dozen people were killed in these incidents, several wounded and houses burnt, including a local government office.

The oil- and gas-producing *Niger Delta* continued to be volatile. Shell and Chevron Texaco were the main targets of protest, which caused serious damage, the death of some dozens of people and temporary closures of flow stations. Internal power tussles over the control of the largesse from oil companies cost lives as well and left many badly injured. A deadly chain of events was triggered off when 12 people in the mainly ethnic Ijaw Bayelsa state, including four councillors of Nembe local government, were killed on 3 February. The councillors were on their way to settle the rift between Odioma and Obiaku communities over the ownership of land that Shell had started developing. On 4 February, *security forces* shot dead six protesters from the Ugborodo community in Delta state at the ChevronTexaco oil export terminal in Escravos. At the end of the year, 12 suspected pipeline vandals were killed at Oghara in Delta State during a gun battle with security operatives. Despite all these incidents, the general level of organised violence in this region declined slightly, given the failure of the Ijaw militias in particular to mount an uprising after the arrest of Dokubo-Asari.

As in previous years, *deep ethnic divisions* and competition for control of land continued to fuel political tensions at the local level. However, inter-religious clashes in this Christian-Islamic country that had cost so many lives in the northern regions in the past almost disappeared during 2005. Nevertheless, ethnic Fulani nomads killed some 14 farmers from the Tiv tribe near Katsina Ala in Benue state in April. Furthermore, the border area between Cross River and Ebonyi state in the far southeast saw a communal war over disputed farm leases, lasting from April till June and leaving more than 100 people dead.

Foreign Affairs

On the one hand, Nigeria maintained good relations with the US, strengthened its relations with China, increased its cooperation with Britain, made significant progress in settling the huge debts with the Paris Club and tried to mediate in the Darfur conflict and the crisis in Togo. On the other hand, it further delayed the demarcation of the land border with Cameroon and the handover of the Bakassi peninsula.

In early March, Nigeria received four gunboats from the United States to be deployed in checking the activities of oil thieves. At the same time, a high-ranking international conference on energy and security in Africa took place in Abuja, organised by the defence ministries of both countries. Against this background, both sides agreed in December to establish a joint committee with the task of coordinating comprehensive action against insecurity in the Niger Delta and establishing close partnerships with the EFCC, ICPC and the office of the accountant-general. At a meeting with President George W. Bush in Washington in May, Obasanjo expressed his willingness to explore how to address concerns in the US that the Liberian

Charles Taylor be brought to justice. However, in his address to the plenary debate of the UN General Assembly on 17 September, Obasanjo maintained his position that Taylor's return from exile in Nigeria to face trial could in the short-term do more harm than good. Nevertheless, the US honoured Nigeria's fight against corruption by revoking the entry visas of several politicians and officials believed to be involved in corrupt practices. Towards the end of the year, the US committed some $ 30 m for the next four years to assist Nigeria in its reform programme and finally entitled Nigeria to draw under the *African Growth and Opportunity Act* (AGOA).

Obasanjo's visits to China in April and May were supposed to strengthen and consolidate bilateral relations. The outcome was a $ 200 m partnership agreement for the telecom sector in Nigeria and an oil supply pact of over 30,000 b/d for China. In September, the government approved the purchase of 12 combat aircraft, worth some $ 250 m. The contract was awarded to the China National Aero Technical Import and Export Corporation. The *influx of Chinese* increased significantly and they were very visible in daily life. Estimates put the figure at 50,000, although local analysts suggested the number was even higher. Local small- and medium-scale traders as well as the Manufacture Association of Nigeria (MAN) were already complaining that many Chinese had taken over parts of their business and were flooding the market with prohibited and sub-standard products from abroad. In addition, they accused Chinese traders of running illegal shopping centres. In April, the president used his trip to China to visit Vietnam and Indonesia, where he attended the summit of the non-aligned movement. In January, he had already received the then Iranian President Mohammad Khatami.

In his capacity as chairman of the AU, President Obasanjo continued to be directly involved in the *Darfur crisis* in Sudan. This topic was also high on the agenda of the fourth AU summit in Abuja (28–31 January), which was addressed by UN Secretary-General Kofi Annan. Nigeria significantly increased its contingent in the AU force and sent three battalions and 45 police officers to the war-torn area.

At the same time, the capital Abuja continued to serve as the venue for peace talks under AU auspices between the warring factions. Several rounds of talks between June and December failed to produce any positive results, and in early October the *Nigerian peace-keeping force* suffered its first losses of life when three soldiers were killed in an ambush.

Nigerian crisis management also failed to a large extent in Togo. After the death of Africa's longest serving dictator Gnassingbé Eyadéma on 5 February, his son Faure Gnassingbé was named president in violation of the constitution. The federal government took a hard line by imposing *sanctions on* Togo, and Obasanjo even called the situation a threat to peace in Africa. The Nigerian government had to back down in March when Faure resigned his position and agreed to submit to presidential elections, which he won in disputed circumstances.

Nigeria continued its activities as part of the UN Mission in Liberia (UNMIL). In January, Lt. Gen. Joseph Olorungbon Owonibi was appointed the peacekeeping force commander. Three hundred *Liberian policemen* underwent special training in Nigeria as part of the transition to an elected government in October. In addition, both governments signed an accord in June to repatriate some 2,000 Liberian refugees under the auspices of UNHCR.

For the second year running, the handover of the potentially oil-rich *Bakassi* peninsula failed to take place. Nigeria deliberately delayed the re-marking of the land border. The International Court of Justice (ICJ) had ruled in 2002 that Bakassi belonged to Cameroon and, in addition, issued rulings on parts of the 1,600-kilometre long border that were unfavourable to Nigeria. On 11 May, Obasanjo and Cameroon's President Paul Biya met Kofi Annan at a tripartite summit in Geneva and an agreement was reached to work out a new programme of Nigerian troop withdrawal from Bakassi. However, it took the joint border commission, chaired by the UN Special Representative Ahmedou Ould-Abdallah, more than two months to gather in Yaounde for their first meeting of 2005. The killing of a

Cameroonian soldier in the Bakassi border region by Nigerian forces in June raised serious doubts about whether the exercise would proceed. However, Nigeria maintained that the incident was an accident. In early July, Nigeria began a gradual pull-out of some of its troops, and in September it handed over a Cameroonian soldier who had been arrested in the occupied territory. Despite these concessions, the joint commission failed to set a new deadline for final troop withdrawal. Eventually, some progress was achieved in favour of Cameroon by readjusting the common border in Adamawa state. At the Commonwealth summit in Malta on 27 November, Obasanjo and Cameroon Prime Minister Ephrahim Inoni resolved that both countries would collaborate with the UN Secretary-General. On 27 December, the United Nations office in West Africa announced that 260 kilometres had finally been demarcated south of Lake Chad. Last but not least, in October the European Commission approved $ 4.8 m to help pay for the border demarcation.

The relationship with *Britain* improved further, taking into account the significant increase in the British development programme in Nigeria. This was in line with the Nigerian reform efforts as well as with Britain's wish to win back lost ground in its former colony. Consequently, the Country Assistance Plan (CAP) executed by the Department for International Development (DFID) was increased for a second time to the tune of £ 100 m for the period 2006–07. The allocation for 2005–06 was £ 70 m. Hilary Benn, secretary of state for international development, visited Nigeria in May to coordinate the pressing African debt issue for the forthcoming G8 summit in Britain. In this context, Obasanjo briefly met Prime Minister Tony Blair in London ahead of the summit, which he attended in July.

Nigeria also tried to strengthen its relationship with *France*. During his four-day visit to France in May, Nigeria's president met his French counterpart Jacques Chirac and several business leaders, thereby underlining the fact that France had become the second biggest investor in Nigeria after the US. Unsurprisingly, Chirac assured his guest of his willingness to be generous in considering the debt issue within the Paris Club. Ahead of this visit, French Trade Minister François Loos made a trip to Nigeria aimed at further strengthening existing commercial ties.

In a protracted legal battle with *Swiss authorities* and the family of late military dictator Sani Abacha, the federal government finally succeeded in getting back some $ 500 m stolen by Abacha during his time in office (1993–98). The Swiss government delayed the repatriation of funds for several months with the intention of having the World Bank oversee the spending of the repatriated loot. However, the Bank was only ready to assist in working out the modalities of the repatriation. Its new president, Paul Wolfowitz, intervened personally to press the Swiss to release the money. Finally, both sides signed an agreement on the repatriation of the funds on 27 September.

This Nigerian success story was topped by the deal with the *Paris Club* that settled $ 30 bn of external debts. For years, President Obasanjo had tirelessly confronted Western leaders with the demand for debt relief and debt cancellation for Africa, but, of course, with Nigeria foremost on his mind. His efforts finally paid off, and his finance minister, a former vice president of the World Bank, Mrs. Ngozi Okonjo-Iweala, handled the issue professionally. Despite the fact that the international political climate was not really in favour of Nigeria during the first months of the year, the Paris Club creditor countries met in Paris on 20 June ready to enter into negotiations on a comprehensive debt treatment. In recognition of Nigeria's reform drive, in October the IMF approved a two-year Policy Support Instrument (PSI) for Nigeria under the newly created PSI framework. This served as a decisive condition for the *debt relief deal* with Nigeria on 20 October, worth some $ 18 bn. In addition, Nigeria had to agree that it would clear arrears of some $ 6.4 bn immediately and the remaining $ 6 bn debts through a debt buy-back operation to be completed in 2006. Thanks to the unprecedented windfall profits from oil and external reserves at an all-time high ($ 29.5 bn at the end of October), this was supposed to be a fairly easy undertaking. Indeed, this exceptional treatment, unprecedented in the Club's history, actually proved that the creditor countries had deliberately extended their support in stabilising Africa's most populous nation. This approach had already been demonstrated by the visits of the managing director of the IMF, Rodrigo de Rato, in May, and the new president of the World Bank, Paul Wolfowitz, in June. During the latter's African trip, Nigeria was the first port of call.

In January, Mohammed El-Baradei, director-general of the international atomic energy agency, went to Nigeria to inspect the country's first *nuclear research reactor* at Ahmadu Bello University in Zaria. After the two-day visit, the reactor was given a clean bill of health. The federal government pointed out its intention to build two 1,000 megawatt nuclear power plants within the foreseeable future.

The relationship with Latin American countries was rather poorly developed. In improving these relations, the president went on a four-day visit (30 July–2 August) to Trinidad and Tobago and stopped over in Jamaica on 2 August. On 4–6 September, Obasanjo paid an official visit to Mexico. However, Brazil continued to be more important for Nigeria. Because of significant crude oil exports, Nigeria was Brazil's most important trading partner in Africa. Both countries were still vying for a permanent seat on the UN Security Council, highlighting their common interests. This was underlined by the visit of President Luiz Inácio 'Lula' da Silva on 11–12 April and the return visit by Obasanjo on 6–8 September. During talks with Foreign Minister Celso Amorion on 17 January in Abuja, both governments committed themselves to the restoration of a direct air link in the near future.

To the disappointment of the Nigerian leadership, Nigeria failed for the second time running to install its candidate as president of the African Development Bank (AfDB). Instead of Olabisi Ogunjobi, the board elected Rwandan Finance Minister Donald Kaberuka on 21 July.

Socioeconomic Developments

Socioeconomic developments were dominated by continually soaring oil prices, far-reaching reform of the banking sector and a new labour law. However, to some extent these developments were overshadowed by a couple of devastating *air disasters*, which demonstrated that Nigeria's air safety was far below reasonable standards.

On 22 October, a Bellview aircraft crashed on an internal flight soon after take-off from Lagos airport, killing the crew and all 117 passengers. Almost the same number of people, including 60 students of Loyosa Jesuit college in Abuja, lost their lives when a Sosoliso aircraft crashed in Port Harcourt on 9 December. A small private plane crashed in Kaduna on 28 November, leaving all three people on board dead. While the black boxes of the ill-fated plane crash in Port Harcourt were recovered, the black boxes of the Bellview flight could not be found, indicating that the plane had not been properly equipped. Since one of the victims was the chief of defence cooperation at the US-embassy, US air safety experts joined the probe into the crash. The temporary closure of Lagos airport in November, caused by urgent repairs to a faulty runway, was another symptom of the situation and compounded the already poor reputation of the aviation sector. The federal government reacted to the fatal incidents by grounding planes and sacking several high-ranking officials from the ministry of aviation, the Nigerian civil aviation authority and the Nigerian airspace management agency.

Oil and gas prices on the international market rose sharply. The price for light sweet crude and brent, comparable to Nigeria's high quality crude oil, rose from the high $ 40 mark at the start of 2005 and passed through the psychological barrier of $ 60 a barrel in June. By the end of December, oil production stood at some 2.4 m b/d. Thus, Nigeria was able to settle the external debt issue with the Paris Club and finally passed the naira 1.8 trillion ($ 13.5 bn) budget for 2005 in April, which was related to a benchmark of $ 30 per barrel. The president, however, in agreement with the National Assembly, later cut it down to naira 1.7 trillion ($ 12.7 bn) to demonstrate to the international financial institutions that the government was serious about improving its monetary policy. However, the budget was 13% higher than the one for 2004. Yet remarkably, the naira held its exchange rate of 132 to the dollar throughout the year, which meant that it had appreciated since the previous year. Notwithstanding external debt relief, the domestic debt still stood at naira 1.5 trillion ($ 11.2 bn). Most of the debts were arrears for pensioners.

Soaring energy prices and the extremely positive long-term prospects for marketing *liquefied gas* encouraged international oil companies, including the Nigerian National Petroleum Corporation (NNPC), to further invest in the Niger Delta and offshore. ChevronTexaco and its joint venture partner NNPC awarded a contract for the execution of the Escravos gas-to-liquids project to an international consortium in April, to be completed in 2008. Both partners sealed a deal to collaborate in the construction of a 30,000 b/d capacity refinery nearby. Moreover, the US-based company began to build a floating oil platform off the coast, which, after completion, will produce 250,000 b/d.

The number one oil company in Nigeria, Shell, announced major changes to its leadership structure in August. The managing director Basil Omiyi was appointed the chairman of all Shell companies in Nigeria. Ann Pickard became the executive vice-president for Africa, and Lagos remained the headquarters for all activities on the continent. In November, a new international player emerged in the form of the *Russian state oil firm* Zarubezhneft, after it struck an oil deal to explore two offshore blocks.

In line with economic reforms commended by the IMF and World Bank, the price of fuel was increased twice, to naira 45–55 per litre in April and eventually to naira 60–69 per litre in August. This move was aimed at significantly reducing the huge subsidy of some $ 1.4 bn a year. In fact, most of the refined fuels had to be imported because the four state-owned refineries operated, if at all, at a very low level for most of the time. Nigeria's main workers' union, the Nigerian

Labour Congress (NLC), under its leader Adams Oshiomhole organised peaceful *nationwide street protests* during the second half of September, which recalled its successful actions against price hikes in 2004. However, following a stampede during student protests over the price hike in the city of Benin on 30 August, three people were killed and several injured.

The situation on the ground changed significantly as a result of a *new labour law* that came into force on 31 March and broke NLC's monopoly. The new law made union membership voluntary and demanded that a strike call be sanctioned by a majority of members in a vote. In fact, it gave the federal government sole power to decide whether unions could form a confederation. On 8 August, the government granted formal approval to a second central labour movement, the Trade Union Congress under the leadership of Mrs. Peace Obiajulu with 16 affiliated, mainly senior staff, unions.

Temporary strike actions by resident doctors, nurses, tanker drivers, oil workers, judiciary staff and staff of Nigeria's state radio, television network, news agency and theatres were overshadowed by massive *retrenchments of personnel* in various parastatals and other institutions. Between July 2004 and March 2005, the monetisation of in-kind benefits and the restructuring of pilot ministries along with NNPC and the central bank led to the retrenchment of 17,000 employees and 5,000 ghost workers. In October, the central bank of Nigeria sacked another 1,040 staff under a restructuring exercise, and the minister of the federal capital territory was given the task of supervising the sacking of about 30,000 federal workers as part of a public sector reform.

The *privatisation programme* slowed down again, thanks to another failure in getting the heavily loss-making Nigerian Telecommunication Limited (NITEL) privatised. As had already been indicated at the end of 2004, the government finally terminated the three-year management contract with the Dutch consultancy company Pentascope International in February. In July, six prospective investors were short-listed by the BPE to take over the 51%

equity stake in NITEL and its mobile section M-TEL. However, during the bidding procedure at the end of December, four withdrew when the government insisted that the transaction would not include the highly lucrative fibre cable SAT-3. The fifth contender backed out soon after. Thus, the Egyptian Orascom Telecom Holding emerged as the sole bidder, offering a paltry $ 256 m for the controlling shares, and was eventually declared winner. Immediately, however, there were growing indications that the government would cancel the poor deal.

While the privatisation of the nation's biggest refinery in Port Harcourt failed as well, Capital Leisure and Hospitality Limited, a subsidiary of the Nigerian Transnational Corporation Limited (Transcorp), acquired 51% equity in NICON Hilton Hotel in Abuja and finally took over ownership of Nigeria's most prestigious hotel in December, which by then was renamed Transcorp Hilton Hotel. Modest progress was achieved in reforming the *ailing power sector* when the reform bill for the sector came into force in March, paving the way for further private investment. One month later, the Nigerian Electric Power Authority (NEPA) was incorporated into a new company called Power Holding Company of Nigeria Plc (PHCN), which inherited NEPA's assets. BPE said it had sold 24 companies in 2005, realising naira 43 m. The government also eventually approved six new private universities, bringing the total number of licensed universities to 23.

Against all the odds, the long overdue *banking reform* became a reality. The central bank of Nigeria stuck to its deadline of year's end for restructuring and consolidating the banking sector. The decisive condition for a bank to operate was set at a minimum capital base of naira 25 bn. Eventually, through mergers and acquisitions involving 76 banks, the number of banks was reduced to 25. The remaining 14 banks were supposed to be liquidated by early 2006.

After a long political battle with radical Islamic clerics in 2004, federal and state governments continued with several rounds of vaccination campaigns to *eradicate polio,* particularly in the northern

Muslim-dominated regions, which had become the epicentre of the disease. Thus, the health authorities were able to halt the spread of the disease, and were supported politically by the Nigerian Forum of Religious and Traditional Leaders and the Media on Immunisation and Child Survival. On top of this, some 1,000 people, crippled by polio, staged a rally in Kano in November to encourage parents to allow their children to be vaccinated. The World Bank and the African Development Bank granted $ 51.7 m and $ 500,000 respectively to fight highly infectious polio. The spread of HIV/AIDS, however, continued unabated, and another disease, tuberculosis, seemed to be on the increase, with some 260,000 new cases annually. In June, the government launched the national health insurance scheme as part of the Millennium Development Goals, and President Obasanjo was the first person to be registered, with registration number P1.

Despite all these socioeconomic achievements, football crazy Nigeria was shocked when the Nigerian football team tripped up in the qualifiers, and for the first time since 1994 missed a place in the final round of the World Cup.

Nigeria in 2006

In 2006, the failed third-term campaign by supporters of incumbent President Olusegun Obasanjo coincided with a deep constitutional and political crisis in four states that threatened the political system and endangered the run-up to the forthcoming election marathon in April 2007. These events may have far-reaching repercussions for the democratic transition to a new leadership. The contentious and even dubious impeachments of four state governors caused nationwide uncertainty and raised serious constitutional and legal questions about Nigeria's federal system. It even highlighted the arbitrariness with which elected and appointed bodies tried to break legal rules whenever they saw fit. In relation to the domestic security situation, there was a frustrating paradox between an increasing number of police, expanded organised crime and the re-emergence of a deep social and ethnic-religious divide, demonstrated by the Danish cartoon controversy. Notwithstanding the general security decay, thanks to soaring oil prices the government accumulated huge foreign reserves, which paved the way for a possible exit strategy with the London Club of creditors and remarkably stabilised macroeconomic performance.

Domestic Politics

An anti-third term campaign inside and outside the National Assembly and the ruling People's Democratic Party (PDP) successfully placed in question President Obasanjo's almost undisputed leadership position. Despite months of public discussion, the senate put an end to the extremely contentious constitutional issue at the commencement of the legal process on 16 May by halting any amendment of the *constitution*, which stipulates that presidents and governors should serve a maximum of two terms. Although the president had never publicly said he wanted to stand for re-election, maintaining he would make his decision if the constitution were amended, he was nevertheless aiming for a third term. Moreover, incumbent and former governors would have benefited from such an amendment as well.

The failed third-term bid also highlighted the intense factional struggles within the political class (particularly within the PDP) in the run-up to the 2007 election to secure access to the immense financial resources generated by oil and gas revenues. These struggles increased because the governors receive and administer huge statutory allocations to states and local governments, thereby enjoying considerable powers. On 7 July, the *supreme court* actually strengthened these powers by declaring legislation unconstitutional that empowered the federal government to monitor the statutory disbursement of local government allocations by state governments.

The federal government's *anti-corruption campaign*, mainly executed by the Economic and Financial Crimes Commission (EFCC), had recovered some $ 5 bn in illegally acquired monies within just three years. In addition, the commission also took aim at several incumbent and former governors. In the case of Diepreye Alamieyeseigha, former governor of Bayelsa state, for example, British police handed back about £ 1 m to the Nigerian government, while his South African mansion was auctioned. However, gubernatorial immunity prevented the commission from taking legal action against governors while in office. This contrasted starkly with the position of legislators at all levels, who enjoyed such protection only with regard to proceedings on the floor of the house. Several governors were, nonetheless, under investigation, and the EFCC regularly fed legislators with information on corruption charges and sometimes put pressure on those who were under scrutiny to cooperate with the commission. Once again, dubious impeachment proceedings, which were in fact power struggles within the ruling PDP, brought to light the widespread culture of political deviousness among the political class.

The *impeachment saga* began in Oyo state in the northern Yoruba heartland on 12 January, when the state legislators impeached Governor Rashidi Adewole Ladoja (PDP). His deputy, Christopher Alao-Akala, took over. After ten months of vigorous legal battles, a unanimous judgment by the court of appeal nullified the impeachment of Ladoja as unconstitutional. On 7 December, the supreme court upheld the ruling and Ladoja returned to the governor's house in the state capital, Ibadan.

The political crisis in Anambra state in the Igbo heartland continued unabated, despite the fact that Peter Obi of the All Progressive Grand Alliance (APGA) was sworn in as governor on 17 March, thereby ending the long-lasting legal contest with the then PDP governor, Chris Ngige. Against the background of a deeper crisis that cost many lives, involving militias such as the banned Movement for the Actualisation of a Sovereign State of Biafra (MASSOB) and the Bakassi Boys, Peter Obi could not maintain his leadership position. From the day he took office, he was locked in a power struggle with Andy Uba, a close advisor of the president and a PDP aspirant for the next governorship of the state. Under dubious circumstances, the PDP-dominated state assembly finally impeached the incumbent, and his deputy Virginia Etiaba reluctantly took over on 3 November, just 24 hours after declining to be sworn in. Thus she became the first *female governor* in the history of the country. Nevertheless, on 28 December, the high court in the state capital of Awka declared the impeachment of Peter Obi null and void, but this had no immediate political impact.

Governor Joshua Dariye (PDP) of the crisis-ridden Plateau state in the volatile minority area in the Middle Belt was the next impeachment victim. In the wake of increasing turmoil and violence in the state, testimony by a detective from the Metropolitan Police in London detailing the circumstances leading to the arrest and questioning of the governor in Britain in 2004, caused the state house to impeach Dariye on 13 November with just eight of the 24 legislators present. Notwithstanding this *illegal act*, his deputy, Chief Michael Botmang, took over the same day.

With the impeachment of another PDP governor, Ayodele Fayose of Ekiti state in the eastern part of Yorubaland, on 16 October and the declaration of a *state of emergency* three days later by President Obasanjo, the impeachment saga reached its climax. The political and constitutional crisis in the state escalated after the former speaker of the state house, Friday Aderemi, became governor after he had supervised the impeachment of Fayose and his deputy, Mrs. Biodun Olujimi. While the impeached governor did not accept the verdict and went into hiding, his deputy claimed to be the acting governor. The upshot was that there were three potential governors in the state.

The federal government took the view that the whole impeachment process was *unconstitutional* and used the ridiculous situation of having three governors as the main argument to declare a state of emergency. The president suspended the office of governor and the legislature for six months and appointed a former head of the West African peacekeeping force in Liberia, retired Maj. Gen. Adetunji Olurin, as administrator. After a long and controversial debate, the National Assembly eventually endorsed Obasanjo's decision with the required two-thirds majority of both chambers on 26 October.

By the end of December, the National Judicial Council (NJC) had suspended the chief judge of Anambra state, a high court judge in Plateau state and the chief judge and a high court judge in Ekiti state. In the view of the NJC, they had not followed due process during recent impeachments of state governors. However, on 14 July, the court of appeal finally resolved the last case arising from the 2003 gubernatorial elections and confirmed the validity of James Ibori's governorship (PDP) in Delta state, which had been challenged by Chief Great Ogboru.

The failed third-term bid paved the way for several rounds of fierce contest within the ruling PDP. Despite his own defeat, Obasanjo was still able to steer the selection process in a particular direction. Vice-President Atiku Abubakar and former military dictator Ibrahim Babangida, both considered as strong potential successors, were the most prominent victims on the PDP platform. The vice-president was suspended from the party over *corruption allegations*, which were orchestrated by the presidency. Obasanjo finally sacked his vice-president on 23 December while the latter was on a private visit in the US, thereby executing a long-awaited but constitutionally contentious decision. Babangida, however, reluctantly withdrew from the race in the run-up to the convention in December, realising that he would face public humiliation at the convention.

In the aftermath of this political manoeuvre, the election of Umaru Musa Yar'Adua, governor of Katsina state, as *PDP presidential candidate* came as a surprise to many analysts. With no real military background but backed by Obasanjo, he thus succeeded as the consensus candidate on 17 December. Most delegates saw him, even as a Muslim, as someone who would probably be acceptable to large parts of the Middle Belt and of the establishment in the south and southwest. The son of one of the richest and most famous Hausa-Fulani families in northern Nigeria's Muslim establishment, Umaru Yar'Adua grew up under the shadow of his older brother, retired Maj. Gen. Shehu Musa Yar'Adua, number two under General Obasanjo when the latter was junta chairman from 1976–79. The Yar'Adua family was one of the very few Hausa-Fulani families who spent much time in the then capital of Lagos and were familiar with Yoruba politics and culture. Because of that, the general was able to establish and sponsor a powerful nationwide political network with the ultimate aim of being elected president. Imprisoned in 1995 and assassinated by military dictator Abacha in 1997, Shehu Musa Yar'Adua's network eventually served as the main platform for the PDP. Hardly had Umaru Yar'Adua been elected PDP presidential candidate than he named Goodluck Jonathan, governor of the southern oil state of Bayelsa, as his running mate. Obasanjo, however, convinced the delegates to amend the party rules in his favour, thereby becoming PDP chairman of the board of trustees after leaving office.

During the year, Vice-President Abubakar, who also belonged to the pre-PDP network, strategically established a new political platform made up of factions of other parties. Supported by an alliance of prominent politicians, such as former PDP chairman Innocent Audu Ogbeh and Bisi Akande of the Alliance for Democracy (AD), Abubakar was chosen by the Action Congress (AC) as presidential candidate at a convention in Lagos on 20 December. The former junta chairman, retired Maj. Gen. Muhammadu Buhari, runner-up in the 2003 presidential election, became the consensus candidate of the All Nigeria People's Party (ANPP).

As in previous elections, the *electoral commission* was not able to live by its own rules and regulations. The Electoral Act stipulated that the electoral register was to be completed 120 days before the start of elections for governors and state assemblies and for president and National Assembly (14 and 21 April 2007 respectively). The exercise began on 25 October, but because of poor logistics as well as serious technical, administrative and managerial problems, only some 20 m of an estimated 60 m eligible voters were registered by the 14 December deadline. INEC, the Independent National Electoral Commission, had no choice but to extend the exercise and set a new deadline of 30 January 2007. This legally contentious decision was made possible after the National Assembly began the procedure to amend the Electoral Act before 30 January 2007.

During the second half of the year, several ministers and special advisors resigned or were relieved of their posts. The first major *cabinet reshuffle* took place on 1 June. The most prominent figure among those removed from the cabinet was the national security advisor, retired Lt. Gen. Aliyu Gusau, who was replaced by retired Maj. Gen. Sarki Mukhtar. Finance minister, Mrs. Ngozi Okonjo-Iweala, who had taken credit for the debt agreement with the Paris Club in 2005, reluctantly replaced Oluyemi Adeniji as foreign minister. The latter was moved to the ministry of internal affairs. Okonjo-Iweala's deputy, Mrs. Nenadi Usman, became minister of finance and after a short and bitter power struggle with her former superior took over the powerful presidential economic team as well. After Ngozi Okonjo-Iweala claimed to have uncovered alleged fraud at the ministry, the presidency dismissed her claims, clearing her predecessor of any wrongdoing. On 3 August, she resigned and Joy Ogwu, director-general of the Nigerian Institute of International Affairs (NIIA), took over her portfolio.

In November, the second major cabinet reshuffle included the resignation of the defence minister, Rabiu Musa Kwankwaso, a former governor of Kano state, who again had political ambitions in his home state. Minister of State Thomas Aguiyi-Ironsi, son of Nigeria's first military ruler, took over. In addition, Babalola Borishade (aviation) swapped his portfolio with Femi Fani-Kayode (culture and tourism) after a *devastating air disaster* on 29 October, which left some 100 people dead, among them Muhammadu Maccido, Sultan of Sokoto, his son and other dignitaries. On 12 June, Justice Salihu Modibo Alfa Belgore replaced Chief Justice Muhammad Uwais, who had reached the mandatory retirement age of 70.

By the end of December, the government announced the pruning of federal ministries from 27 to 19. Accordingly, it merged aviation, transport and works into the ministry of transport, while the ministry of police affairs was taken over by the ministry of internal affairs. The most important decisions affected the oil and power portfolios, which were merged into the energy ministry, and the ministry for information, which assumed the functions of the communications ministry.

The decision regarding personnel affected the *military* as well. On 30 May, the president retired General Alexander Ogomudia (chief of defence staff) and Air Marshal Jonah Wuyep (chief or air staff) and replaced them with chief of army staff Lt. Gen. Martin Agwai and Air Vice Marshal Paul Dike respectively. Lt. Gen. Owoye Andrew Azazi was appointed chief of army staff, while Vice Admiral Ganiyu Adekeye retained his position as chief of naval staff. Agwai was promoted to the rank of general and Dike to that of air marshal. Dike became the first ethnic Igbo to rise to that position, while Azazi was the first ethnic Ijaw to head the army.

However, an air disaster hit the top military brass of the army when a Dornier *military aircraft crashed* on 17 September, leaving only five survivors. The officers had been en route to the Obudu cattle ranch in Cross River state for a meeting ordered by the chief of army staff to discuss the future of the military in the next decade. Four days later, 23 senior officers, including eight major generals and two brigadier generals, were buried with national honours in the capital Abuja.

The *Danish cartoons* of the Prophet Mohammad led to the re-emergence in their worst form of deep ethnic and religious divisions in the world's largest Christian-Islamic country. The cartoons even triggered several bloody clashes, namely in Shendam and Namu in Qua'an Pan local government area, Plateau state and in Ihima, Kogi state in April, and in Offa and Enrinle, Kwara state in June. Although the cartoons had been published in Denmark in September 2005, the worldwide protests against the publication reached the predominantly Muslim north only in early February 2006. The Kano state house of assembly immediately banned all Danish goods and cancelled negotiations with a Danish company over the building of a power station. The issue escalated when members of the state house set ablaze Danish and Norwegian flags within the assembly's premises on 7 February. On 18 February, the issue got out of hand and exploded in Maiduguri, the Borno state capital, in the northeast. A mob of Muslims turned on local Christians, mostly ethnic Igbo, after police had broken up a rally against the cartoons. Several people were killed and a number of churches and shops looted and set on fire. Thousands of Christians sought sanctuary in army barracks and police stations while bloody clashes spread to other cities in the north. The arrival of the first corpses in the southern commercial city of Onitsha, Anambra state, sparked two days of riots (22–23 February) against the tiny northern Muslim community, mostly Hausa-Fulani. At least 80 died during the massacre before the governor imposed a curfew. Notwithstanding this action, reprisal attacks spread to neighbouring Enugu state, causing more deaths. In total, the riots over the cartoon cost some 130 Nigerian lives, by far the highest number worldwide.

At the same time, the inspector-general of police banned the activities of *religious marshals*, known as 'Hisbah', in Kano state: they were entitled by the state government to enforce shariah law. However, the state government refused to abide by the ban, maintaining that the 'Hisbah' volunteer group had been properly established by state law. In January, the southern Abia state had passed a similar law, which brought back the outlawed Bakassi vigilante group. In a swift reaction, however, the federal government accused the Kano state government of turning the 'Hisbah' vigilante group into a parallel police force and of seeking foreign sponsorship to train religious militants, thereby posing a threat to national security. On 9 February, the police arrested two of its leading figures, Yahaya Faruk Chedi and Abubakar Rabo Abdulkareem, and charged them in court in Abuja. After a three-month legal battle, the court of appeal overturned the verdict of the federal court and granted the detainees bail. Notwithstanding this, the Kano state government had already filed an application in the supreme court in February demanding that the court stop the federal government from disbanding 'Hisbah'. The federal government filed a counterclaim in April, asking the court to dismiss the constitutional case, and the court adjourned the case till 2 March 2007. In view of the cartoon and 'Hisbah' incidents, the public increasingly lost interest in archaic shariah court verdicts, which were becoming less frequent anyway, while several had been overturned or deemed to be pending.

On 2 November, because of the fatal air disaster that cost the life of Sultan Maccido, his younger brother Muhammad Sa'ad Abubakar, then a serving colonel, emerged as the 20th sultan of Sokoto. He immediately retired from the army and was subsequently promoted to the rank of brigadier general.

Anambra state and the Niger Delta were the most volatile parts of the country. The predominantly ethnic Igbo state in the southeast, centre of the banned militia MASSOB, the outlawed Bakassi Boys and the Anambra vigilante service, experienced another wave of violence between May and August. The multidimensional struggle for power and local revenues, in which militias, vigilantes, the state government, political parties and organised transport owners and transport workers were involved, escalated almost day by day. The prelude to this crisis began in late May when policemen from Abuja arrested more than 200 people, claiming them to be members of MASSOB. On 18 June, Governor Peter Obi imposed a one-week *dusk-to-dawn curfew* in the commercial capital, Onitsha, after a crowd had gone on the rampage the previous day and burned down two police stations. MASSOB claimed that police had killed eight of its members in a raid, a charge the police denied. However, the acts of violence increased when militants stormed Onitsha prison and set some 240 inmates free. That action forced the governor to extend the curfew to six neighbouring communities. Notwithstanding the curfews, clashes between police, militias and the feuding groups continued, leaving about 20 dead, including policemen. With good reason, the state government extended the curfew in Onitsha until mid-August.

MASSOB leader Ralph Uwazuruike, who had been arrested and detained the previous year, faced new *treason charges* and was denied bail. Mujahid Dokubo-Asari, the leader of the Ijaw militia, the Niger Delta People's Volunteer Force (NDPVF), suffered a similar fate. By contrast, Frederick Fasehun, leader of the banned Yoruba militia, the O'odua People's Congress (OPC), was granted bail because of serious health problems, with the federal government eventually dropping the treason charges against him, while Ganiyu Adams, factional leader of OPC, was released on bail on 19 December.

The continuing crisis in the oil- and gas-producing Niger Delta at times turned into *local warfare*, cutting annual oil production by more than 20%. Shoot-outs between soldiers and militias, military bombardments, car bomb explosions, kidnappings for ransom, armed robbery and the killing of innocent people were the order of the day. In the course of the year, some 160 foreign oil workers from Europe, Asia and the US were taken hostage. In several statements, militant groups gave the continued detention of militant leader Mujahid Dokubo-Asari and former Bayelsa state Governor Diepreye Alamieyeseigha as factors driving their actions. In most cases, hostages were released unharmed within hours or days, usually after a financial deal was struck, in several cases mediated by the rather moderate Federated Niger Delta Ijaw Communities (FNDIC) under the leadership of Chief Bello Oboko or the state government. In short, *hostage-taking* had become a flourishing business. Consequently, these payments, which were kept secret, fuelled the violence and the proliferation of armed groups almost by the day. One US citizen was assassinated on 10 May in Port Harcourt, while a Briton lost his life during a rescue attempt on 22 November.

The military lost about 40 soldiers during several *gun battles* with militia forces, including the Movement for the Emancipation of the Niger Delta (MEND), the Joint Revolutionary Council (JRC), Coalition for Militant Action in the Niger Delta (COMA), Movement of the Niger Delta People (MONDP), Niger Delta Vigilante (NDV), Iduwini Volunteer Force (IVF) and, last but not least, the NDPVF. Security services, however, had a reputation for overkill in executing crackdowns, with the result that local communities, which the government needed on its side, were further alienated and made allegations of army brutality. The replacement of Brigadier Elias Zamani by Brigadier Alfred Ilogho in March as head of the military task force, which had been demanded by militia groups for some time, did not really change matters. The number of militia and civilian casualties was several hundred at least. Estimates by local observers put the figure even higher. Whatever the accurate figure, the bloodiest battles took place at Shell's Benisede flow station on 15 January and its Cawthorn Channel gas-gathering plant on 7 June and 2 October. On 15 February in Warri, the *military task force* bombarded the Ijaw community, who were suspected of harbouring militant youths. According to community leaders, 20 people died. At year's end, four foreigners who were taken hostage on 7 December by members of MEND were still being held and only a small number of militants had been arrested and charged.

In November, despite widespread hostilities, the chief of army staff opened a rare *dialogue with militants*. In addition, more stakeholders, such as the Nobel laureates' commission comprising Wole Soyinka and 64 other laureates, UNDP and USAID got involved to reverse the longstanding neglect of development of the Niger Delta. The commission was established to address injustice, mitigate suffering and prevent conflict from escalating and spilling across Nigeria's borders, and presented its comprehensive report on 1 December.

While cult and gang violence went on almost unabated, Nigeria experienced a wave of hitherto unknown organised crime and *politically motivated killings*. In the run-up to the elections in 2007, several well-known politicians at state and local level were assassinated. Governorship aspirants Jesse Aruku in Plateau state (end of June), Funso Williams in Lagos state (27 July), Ayo Daramola in Ekiti state (14 August) were killed by unknown assailants, and Sa'adatu Abubakar Rimi, wife of a former Kano state governor, was hacked to death in Kano city on 14 January. On 14 February, Shuaibu Sabon Birnin, director in the ministry of internal affairs, fell victim to gunmen wearing military uniforms. On 7 March, a former attorney-general of Kaduna state, Muhammadu Sani Aminu, was gunned down, and on 18 December, Ibrahim Bakare, a PDP campaigner in Lagos state, suffered the same fate. Segun Enrile, a former top civil servant in Ekiti state, was murdered on 22 October; Godwin Agbroko, chairman of the editorial board of the national daily 'This Day', was shot dead on 22 December; and Vincent Makanju, lecturer involved in peace education at Obafemi Awolowo University in Oyo state, was killed on 11 October. Local observers estimated that contract killings could be arranged cheaply and could cost as little as naira 100,000, equivalent to $ 775, depending on the victim's reputation.

As in previous years, *armed robbers* targeted long-distance buses, but the number of bank raids, raids on bureaux de change and armoured personnel carriers also increased significantly. An unknown number of retired and active security service staff were involved in these activities. Although most robberies took place in the southern part of the country, especially in Lagos and Port Harcourt, the crime wave also penetrated Abuja and bigger cities in the far north, such as Sokoto, Kaduna and Kano.

On 4 December, about 30 robbers targeted the international airport of Lagos just after midnight. In a four-hour operation, the gang took naira 150 m from the bureau de change and got away unscathed. On this particular occasion, no one was killed. On 17 November and 14 December, the famous Alaba international market along the Lagos-Badagry expressway was raided, leaving at least 26 persons dead, including some policemen. In fact, armed robbers raided no fewer than 12 banks during December alone. In the face of this *crime wave*, Nigeria's 25 banks decided to spend $ 15 m in upgrading security. However, for the first time security staff discovered explosives in the luggage of a passenger, one Samuel Dickson Adima, who was about to check in for an Abuja-bound flight in Lagos on 18 November. He was arrested and later four other suspects were taken into custody by security personnel.

Some 100 policemen lost their lives on duty – 67 alone within the fourth quarter of the year. Despite this unprecedented loss, the police retained their reputation for corruption and ongoing *extra-judicial killings*. The ugliest incident happened in crime-ridden Abia state on 10 August, when the police paraded 12 robbery suspects who had survived a deadly shoot-out with security forces. The following day, the 12 suspects were found dumped in a mortuary. The police did not comment on the incident and started an internal investigation. The federal government's reaction to the incessant crime, however, was just a major shake-up of the police in August, with the appointment of ten new deputy and assistant inspectors-general and the promotion of several officers within the top echelons of the police force in September. Nevertheless, in a remarkable verdict, the supreme court confirmed the death sentences against three policemen sentenced in 2001 for culpable homicide and armed robbery. In a highly symbolic gesture, 1,520 ethnic Igbo officers who were dismissed from the police force shortly after the civil war of 1967–70 were issued retirement letters by the police service commission with effect from 29 May 2000. This was in compliance with the approval of a presidential amnesty for police officers affected by the civil war.

Because of the worsening security situation, Nigeria's overall *human and civil rights* record was rather mixed. Harassment of journalists decreased slightly. In early February, charges were dropped against two broadcasters from Rhythm FM in Port Harcourt who were standing trial. Klem Ofuokwu and Cleopatra Taiwo were detained and charged in December the previous year with airing a news item that was later found to be false. TV presenter Mike Gbenga Aruleba of the private Africa International Television (AIT) and Rotimi Durojaiye, correspondent of the 'Daily Independent', were arrested in June and charged with sedition over a report questioning the airworthiness and cost of the new presidential jet, but the charges were eventually dropped. On 14 May, two days before the third-term bid was put to rest in the senate, the State Security Service (SSS) ordered AIT to immediately stop broadcasting a documentary on the extension of the tenure of officeholders and removed the master tape. In March, the Nigeria Broadcasting Commission (NBC) imposed a partial ban on Radio Freedom in Kano, the first privately owned radio station in the far north, for an alleged violation of the broadcasting code. On 16 June, the Nigerian navy detained an American photographer of the 'National Geographic', Ed Kashi, in Bayelsa state for photographing gas flares at a flow station. After three days in detention, however, he was released by the SSS. On 10 February, Bekololari Ransome-Kuti, member of the famous Kuti family and one of Nigeria's staunchest human rights and pro-democracy leaders, passed away at the age of 65.

A new law, the Advance Fee Fraud and Other Related Offences Act 2006, which came into effect on 5 June, forced all internet service providers to register with the EFCC. In July alone, the EFCC raided more than 20 cyber cafes. In August, as part of *prison reforms*, the federal government announced the release of 10,000 of some

40,000 inmates, those released having spent up to a decade in jail awaiting trial. Another 15,000 similar cases were to be considered in 2007. Large numbers of non-convicted inmates remained in jail because of delays in the justice system, missing police files, absent witnesses and poor prison management. On top of that, more than 400 convicted inmates had been waiting on death row for years.

Throughout Nigeria's colonial and postcolonial history the *national census* has always been a highly political and consequently contentious issue. The 2006 census was no different. Violence (which cost several lives), poor logistics, lack of material, widespread confusion and rows over payments to officials characterised the ambitious exercise (24–25 March). In fact, counting had to be extended by two days. At year's end, the national population commission released the provisional results, a figure of 140 m. In other words, Nigeria's population would have grown by 51 m since the last official census in 1991, meaning that the annual growth rate stood at 3.2%, with the ratio of males to females at 105 to 100.

Foreign Affairs

Nigeria's foreign policy focused on maintaining good relations with the US, which received more than 50% of all Nigerian exports; expanding existing relations with China; further increasing cooperation with Britain; leading African states in establishing closer ties with Latin America; and putting the Bakassi conflict with neighbouring Cameroon to rest.

Top-ranking politicians, military personnel and personalities from the US visited Nigeria during the year. George W. Bush's wife Laura arrived on 16 January on her three-nation West African tour and announced that the US was providing $ 163 m in 2006 to combat HIV/AIDS in the country. Former US President Bill Clinton joined the 7th biennial Leon Sullivan summit in Abuja (17–20 July), together with World Bank President Paul Wolfowitz and several African heads of state. On 16 July, North American Airlines opened a new chapter in direct US-Nigeria flights and flew in several summit delegates. *Cooperation with the US* was again confirmed by the visit in March of the commander of the allied joint force command in Naples, Admiral Henry Ulrich, and the arrival of a missile destroyer at the end of May to join the Nigerian navy's golden jubilee celebrations. In addition, security personnel from both countries took part in two high-level rounds of talks on security and safety issues in the Gulf of Guinea in May and July, while the US significantly increased its naval presence in the region. In December, Military Professional Resources Incorporated (MPRI), which works for the US government and comprises former top-ranking US military personnel, submitted a blueprint for a new defence policy to Nigeria's military top brass, both serving and retired. Ever since the end of military dictatorship in 1999, MPRI has acted as consultant to the Nigerian military leadership and provided special courses.

Bilateral relations got a boost after the federal government approved the extradition of war crimes suspect and former Liberian President Charles Taylor to his home country on 16 March. The decision paid off and Obasanjo was invited to the White House on 29 March. The close cooperation in combating financial crimes, money laundering and fraud was strengthened, and the US department of justice trained more than 130 Nigerian anti-corruption officials in February. In a joint action by the Nigerian and US *drug enforcement agencies*, some 14 metric tonnes of a mélange of cocaine and white cement were intercepted at the port of Lagos in June. While the US Exim Bank approved $ 300 m for 14 of the 25 Nigerian banks to support US exports to Nigeria, it committed $ 15 m to promote the conduct of proper elections.

Nigeria extended and consolidated its *relations with China* on the economic front. In January, the China National Offshore Oil Company (CNOOP) bought a $ 2.3 bn stake in a Nigerian oil and gas field. Interestingly, India's largest oil and gas company had won the bidding in December 2005, only to have the purchase blocked by its government, which considered the bid commercially unviable and too risky. However, China's massive investment drive went on unabated, supported politically by the visit of its foreign minister in January, President Hu Jintao's two-day state visit on 26–27 April and the visit of the vice-president of China's Exim Bank in November. The Chinese president even addressed a joint session of the National Assembly, pointing out that China would forge a new type of Sino-African strategic partnership. In April, work spanning over 10 years commenced in Lagos on the Lekki free zone project. In addition, China agreed to finance the rehabilitation of the dilapidated railway system, build the Mambilla hydro power plant, which would cost some $ 2.5 bn, and to continue with the national rural telephone project. In August, Huawei Technologies, a leading private Chinese high-tech network equipment vendor, won a contract worth $ 100 m to provide the local Multi-Links company with sophisticated and state-of-the-art technology for multiple communication services in six core cities, namely Lagos, Ibadan, Port Harcourt, Abuja, Kaduna and Kano. After Obasanjo attended the three-day forum on Sino-African cooperation in Bejing (3–5 November), China Southern Airlines began direct air services to Nigeria on New Year's Eve. The temporary closure of the Chinese village in Lagos by the Nigerian customs service and the trial of some Chinese who had allegedly imported prohibited items caused some friction, but eventually proved to be a rather minor matter.

The strong orientation towards Asia did not stop there. With the three-day state visit by President Roh Moo-hyun (9–11 March), *South Korea* increased its engagement and investment by signing two wide-ranging agreements on energy cooperation and oil exploration. Obasanjo paid a return visit on 6 November. In October, the Malaysian-Nigerian Global Formwork joint venture started to build the $ 600 m 'Malaysian Gardens' residential housing scheme in Abuja, partly financed by Malaysia's external trade development corporation. His trips to Asia took President Obasanjo to the D8 summit in Indonesia (12–13 May) and to the annual meeting of the IMF and World Bank in Singapore in September, where he met consultants from JP Morgan and Fitch Ratings on 17 September and discussed his plan to pay back all debts of the *London Club* of private creditors. The president also met members of the global business community and assured them that elections would be peaceful, free and transparent. Then he stopped over in Japan to hold talks with Japanese Prime Minister Junichiro Koizumi and the president of Chubu Electric Power Company, one of the world's largest users of liquefied gas.

Top British politicians visited Nigeria as well, underlining growing *British interest* in its former colony. On 14 February, the secretary of state for foreign and Commonwealth affairs, Jack Straw, delivered a lecture on the role of the late junta leader, Gen. Murtala Ramat Muhammed, in nation building. Britain donated £ 250,000 for the retraining of policemen and fighting corruption, while £ 230,000 was given to the EFCC to strengthen its war on money laundering and other related crimes. Chancellor of the Exchequer Gordon Brown took part in an international conference on financing development in Africa in Abuja in May. In addition, Prince Charles went to northern Nigeria on a three-day visit (28–30 November) where he was treated to a traditional durbar similar to the one held 50 years ago for his mother, Queen Elizabeth II. The main purpose of the visit was, however, the inauguration of a peacekeeping training centre at the military college in Jaji, Kaduna state, which was built with £ 500,000 of British government funding. The government's aid agency, the Department of International Development (DFID), had already opened an office in Kano to manage the increased support to the Islamic north and to indicate a long-term commitment to Britain's former colony. President Obasanjo, along with several top ministers and Nigerian business tycoons, attended the Nigerian investment forum organised under the auspices of Baroness Linda Chalker in London (15–16 June).

The long lasting *Bakassi peninsula* and land border conflict with neighbouring Cameroon was finally put to rest in Archibong town on 14 August. In compliance with a ruling by the ICJ in 2002 and a UN-brokered deadline, authority over Bakassi was transferred, the Nigerian flag lowered and the Cameroonian flag hoisted in its place. The 12 June Greentree agreement paved the way for the final withdrawal of Nigerian troops. On 14 June, Obasanjo informed the public and defended the decision in a nationwide broadcast. Interestingly, the outcome of this costly and unnecessary legal and political battle exactly matched the findings by the late attorney-general of the federation, Taslim Olawale Elias, in 1970.

Nigeria's efforts to mediate and conclude the peace talks on the *Darfur crisis* in Sudan produced only mixed results. With the US deputy secretary of state, Robert Zoellick, and Britain's secretary of state for international development, Hilary Benn, in attendance as international mediators, an agreement with the main faction of the Sudan Liberation Movement (SLM) was signed on 5 May in Abuja. However, a splinter group of the SLM walked out of the signing ceremony and the other rebel group, the Justice and Equality Movement (JEM), also refused to join the accord. On 4 January, Maj. Gen. Collins Remy Umunakwe Iherike took over command of the AU intervention force in Darfur from his colleague Festus Okonkwo. However, on 19 August, three Nigerian peacekeeping soldiers were shot dead in an ambush.

Apart from Bakassi, Sudan, an African cocoa producers' summit in Abuja in May, an AU conference on security in the capital in September, and the extraordinary ECOWAS summit on Côte d'Ivoire on 6 October at the same location, the Nigerian leadership did not pay too much attention to continental or sub-regional politics. Obasanjo focused rather on getting the necessary support from the AU for the inaugural *Africa-South America Summit* in Abuja (26–30 November). A number of African and Latin American heads of state and government attended, among them Luiz Inácio 'Lula' da Silva from Brazil, Bolivian President Evo Ayma Morales, Blaise Compaoré of Burkina Faso and Muammar Kadhafi from Libya. The summit adopted a declaration that contained a plan of action intended to implement a wide-ranging cooperation programme. In addition, it was agreed that future summits would be held every two years and would alternate between Africa and Latin America, with the next summit scheduled for 2008 in Venezuela.

Nigeria's relationship with the EU was more or less defined by the financing of traditional development projects and projects that would strengthen democratic institutions. Accordingly, the EU provided funds to combat corruption and promote democracy. During a three-day visit (19–22 November) to Nigeria, the president of the European parliament, Josep Borell Fontelles, donated $ 50 m to the electoral commission, INEC, and the anti-corruption agency, EFCC. On 26 June, a delegation of the EU commission, in collaboration with the national planning commission, launched two major programmes worth some $ 20 m aimed at institutional and economic reform of state and local governments as well as water and sanitation projects in six states, Anambra, Cross River, Osun, Kano, Jigawa and Yobe. In July, the Nigerian ministry of defence signed an $ 84 m contract with the Italian aircraft manufacture Alenia Aermacchi for the maintenance of 12 jet trainers.

After the meeting of OPEC in Abuja on 14 December, it was announced that Nigeria's minister of state for petroleum resources, Edmund Daukoru, would assume the OPEC presidency on 1 January 2007. In addition, on 17 November, Minister of Justice and Attorney-General Bayo Ojo was elected to the UN's prestigious International Law Commission.

Socioeconomic Developments

As in the previous year, socioeconomic developments were dominated by continually *soaring oil prices*, thereby stabilising the economy at the macroeconomic level. These developments were, however, overshadowed by the insurgency in the Niger Delta, which at times was akin to civil war, and devastating air and oil pipeline disasters.

Oil and gas prices on the international market rose sharply to historic heights. The price of light sweet crude and Brent, comparable to Nigeria's high quality crude, rose from the high $ 50 mark per barrel at the start of 2006 to $ 78 in August, before it fell to the $ 60 mark towards the end of the year. The permanent upheaval in the Delta region forced all oil companies to cut production, which cost Nigeria $ 4 bn in fiscal 2006. Nevertheless, the losses were to some extent offset by the extraordinarily high oil prices, which actually enabled the federal government to accumulate foreign reserves of an unprecedented $ 41 bn. Thus, the government appointed *external asset managers* to manage its foreign reserves and assets, including JP Morgan Chase and Credit Suisse from abroad and the local First Bank of Nigeria and Zenith Bank. At the end of May, President Obasanjo informed the senate that his government would negotiate repayment of some $ 2.3 bn owed to the London Club of creditors. By year's end, $ 1.4 bn had been paid back. Notwithstanding Obasanjo's ambitious aim to get rid of the debts owed to the Paris and London Clubs before leaving office, *domestic indebtedness* still amounted to $ 12 bn at the end of June. In a remarkable political move, the federal government commenced the payment of naira 75 bn in retirement arrears to an estimated 200,000 pensioners across the country in August. In July, it had already disbursed naira 4.5 bn of some naira 150 bn debts owed to local contractors.

Although it is a major oil producer, Nigeria showed that its gas production was becoming more important, indicated by the fact that liquefied natural gas production stood at some 22 m tonnes, which was delivered to the huge US market and the Mediterranean countries in the EU and Turkey. Thus, with *gas reserves* of some five trillion cubic metres, it had one of the largest reserves in the world at its disposal, more than double its oil reserves. Notwithstanding the prosperous outlook, fuel scarcity prevailed most of the time, even disrupting international flights and leading to power failures. As in previous years, most petroleum products had to be imported and were still subsidised to the tune of almost $ 1.4 bn. The black market rate for fuel rose to naira 130–250 a litre in urban centres, although the official pump price was only naira 65.

A side effect of the huge reserves of foreign currency was the merger of the official and parallel market exchange rates for the local currency in May, which resulted in an exchange rate of naira 129 to the dollar. In recognition of Nigeria's general financial reforms, the country received its first credit rating by Fitch as well as by Standard & Poor's, two international rating agencies, in January and February. On 23 June, the Paris-based international finance task force even removed Nigeria from a list of countries that do not cooperate in the fight against money laundering. On 22 February, Obasanjo signed the naira 1.9 trillion ($ 14.5 bn) *budget* for 2006, which was related to a benchmark of $ 35 per barrel. Of the $ 4.2 bn capital budget, 40% was appropriated for key infrastructural areas such as power, roads, water supply and railways.

As in the previous year, Nigeria experienced devastating air disasters, which demonstrated again that the country's *air safety* was far below reasonable standards, although some $ 150 m was made available in April to improve safety at airports. On 14 November, President Obasanjo signed the new Civil Aviation Authority Act 2006 into law, which established flight safeguards, improved security checks and laid down tougher eligibility rules for air transport licences.

In the greater Lagos area, two petrol pipelines exploded on 12 May and 26 December, killing about 200 and 500 persons respectively. In early November, no fewer than 20 *pipeline vandals* were burnt to death in northern Adamawa state while tapping fuel. The blasts were probably ignited by sparks or candlelight shortly after the thieves had punctured the high pressure pipelines and tapped the fuel in order to sell it on the lucrative black market. This crime often attracts ordinary and poor people living next to the pipelines, who try to get fuel free of charge, ignoring the extreme dangers.

At the end of 2005, the federal government had within days cancelled the poor deal with the Egyptian Orascom Telecom Holding, which had offered a paltry $ 256 m for controlling shares in Nigerian Telecommunication Limited (NITEL). To put an end to the NITEL saga, the bureau of public enterprises *privatisation agency* dropped further competitive bidding in favour of a negotiated sale. On 3 July, the Nigerian Transnational Corporation Limited (Transcorp) took over 75% of NITEL and its mobile subsidiary M-TEL for the sum of $ 750 m. British Telecom, the operator and non-equity-holding technical partner, seconded Steve Brookman and John Weir to become chief executive officer of NITEL and head of M-TEL respectively. The booming Nigerian mobile phone market, with some 32 m subscribers towards year's end, saw another major takeover in May/June when Celtel, a subsidiary of Kuwait's MTC, acquired a controlling 65% share in V-mobile for $ 1.5 bn.

The second half of the year saw the retrenchment of thousands of civil servants under the public service reform programme. According to the president, the downsizing of the bloated service of some 1.5 m civil servants would enable government to spend more on the hitherto poor provision of services and infrastructure. Given the generally volatile political and socioeconomic situation, the National Industrial Court Act 2006 was passed in July, stripping federal and state high courts of jurisdiction to adjudicate suits relating to labour disputes in favour of newly established *industrial courts*. However, the high courts were granted one year to dispose of or decide all pending cases.

After South Africa and India, Nigeria was the third highest *HIV/AIDS*-infected country, with some 4 m persons living with the deadly virus. According to WHO, Nigeria topped the international polio list, with almost 1,000 cases in the northern part of the country. On 3 July, a five-day *polio immunisation* campaign in 11 endemic northern states was completed, but health officials were seriously concerned about the low turnout. Shortly thereafter, however, local health authorities, in collaboration with the UN, launched the 'Immunisation Plus' campaign to immunise 10 m people with the aim of eradicating the disease by the end of 2007.

The H5N1 *avian flu* virus reached Nigeria in January, causing health authorities to cull some 700,000 of an estimated 140 m poultry by October at a cost of more than $ 4 m. In early March, the government started to pay some compensation to poultry farmers, although 'backyard' poultry farmers accounted for an estimated 60% of business. On 29 March, however, the World Bank supported Nigeria's fight against the virus with a low-interest loan of $ 50 m.

In September, the *World Bank* emphasised that Nigeria was not a fragile state but had made rather good progress in addressing conflict and corruption. In December, the IMF commended the strong macroeconomic performance and the sustaining reforms in a difficult policy environment. In this context, the World Bank approved a $ 200 m loan for the Lagos metropolitan development and governance project on 6 July.

Nigeria in 2007

The April elections at federal and state levels dominated the political scene. The run-up to the elections soon became a legal battlefield, while the seriously flawed elections produced a large number of petitions before the election tribunals. Although the tribunal dealing with the petition on the presidential election had not reached its verdict by year's end, other tribunals had already declared some gubernatorial and National Assembly elections null and void. By the end of the year, there were additional indications that more governors and parliamentarians would be sacked the coming year. In the light of these decisions, the prospect that the elected president might suffer a similar fate was no longer unimaginable. Notwithstanding this situation, this was the first time in Nigeria's history that an elected government had taken over from a previously elected one, a circumstance that gave some hope of stabilising the still infant democratic system.

Domestic Politics

The salient issue over the course of the year was the *general election*, scheduled for 14 April (gubernatorial and state assemblies) and 21 April (presidential and National Assembly), and its aftermath. All eyes were fixed on the run-up to the elections, which was packed with drama. The Independent National Electoral Commission (INEC) could not meet the deadline of 30 January for completing the electoral register and had to extend the exercise for a third time, to 2 February. Eventually, the National Assembly amended the Electoral Act to allow the register, which included 61.3 million eligible voters, to be completed 60 days before the start of the elections, instead of 120 days. In addition, the amended act made it mandatory to display the voters' list 45 days prior to the election instead of 60.

© KONINKLIJKE BRILL NV, LEIDEN, 2017 | DOI 10.1163/9789004347410_005

On 15 March, the commission disclosed the list of presidential candidates. To the consternation of his followers and the public, the list of 24 names did not include that of vice president and Action Congress (AC) candidate Atiku Abubakar, on account of corruption charges by the anti-corruption agency, the Economic and Financial Crimes Commission (EFCC). Reacting swiftly, Atiku challenged the decision in court. Earlier, on 6 January, President Olusegun Obasanjo had already reversed the sacking of his vice president, whom he had removed from his post on 23 December the previous year, on account of a pending decision by the court of appeal on the case filed by Atiku on the matter.

On 20 February, the court of appeal ruled Atiku should remain in his post despite his defection from the ruling People's Democratic Party (PDP) to the AC. The *supreme court* confirmed the verdict on 24 April, taking the view that floor-crossing, though unethical, could not be grounds for the removal of a sitting vice president. He could, in fact, only be removed through impeachment by the National Assembly. Notwithstanding this, at the 11th hour the court handed down another landmark ruling on 16 April by deciding that INEC had no power to disqualify a candidate submitted to it by a political party, thereby setting aside an earlier judgment of the court of appeal and temporarily putting the poll in doubt. However, the many more than 100 candidates who had been screened by INEC and were subsequently dropped by the parties for alleged wrongdoing were no longer able to seek redress for their disqualification because events had overtaken them.

The presidential and National Assembly elections took place as scheduled on 21 April. Umaru Yar'Adua won a *landslide victory* with 24.6 million votes, well ahead of his two main rivals: retired Maj. Gen. Muhammadu Buhari of the All Nigeria People's Party (ANPP) won 6.6 million and Atiku Abubakar 2.6 million. The PDP, which had held power since the beginning of the democratic transition in 1999, consolidated its grip on power and won two-thirds majorities in both chambers of the National Assembly. The wins for the other candidates and parties were negligible. These results mirrored the voting patterns in the earlier gubernatorial and state assembly elections on 14 April. The ANPP held on to its strongholds in five predominantly Muslim states in the far north, while PDP won all but three of the other 31 states. Interestingly, the small Progressive People's Alliance (PPA) and its gubernatorial candidates, Theodore Orji and Ikedi Ohakim, won in Abia and Imo state in the Igbo heartland, decisively thwarting the ambitions of former Biafran leader Chukwuemeka Ojukwu and his All Progressive Grand Alliance (APGA). Last but not least, Lagos state was taken by the AC and its candidate Babatunde Fashola. However, according to independent observers, voter turnout for the presidential elections was 20%. Even allowing a 10% margin of error, that was still 25% less than the 55% turnout claimed by INEC.

Although Umaru Yar'Adua had already been declared the winner in the presidential elections by the chairman of the electoral commission Maurice Iwu on 23 April, INEC had to organise by-elections in several states for both state and federal constituencies and these took place on 28 April. Imo state, however, was the only one in which the poll for the governorship was re-run. Most foreign observers from Europe and the US, among them former US Secretary of State Madeleine Albright and EU parliamentarian Max van den Berg, as well as domestic observers, such as the transition monitoring group, the Catholic Church and – after the poll – opposition parties, vigorously criticised the handling of the polls, which cost some 200 lives. According to them, the polls lacked all credibility. They focused especially on the gubernatorial and presidential elections, which were marred by violence, widespread voter *intimidation*, seizure of ballot boxes, procedural irregularities, *fraud* and organised *rigging*, which caused observers to call for re-runs in the worst cases. While the Commonwealth was rather cautious and ECOWAS observers even declared the polls relatively free and peaceful, the two runners-up in the presidential election rejected the results and vowed to pursue the matter in court. Western governments, however, indicated their readiness to work with the new government and invited Yar'Adua to the forthcoming G8 summit in Germany.

On 29 May, Umaru Yar'Adua was sworn in as the first president to take power from a previously elected one through the ballot box. Goodluck Jonathan became vice president. In his inaugural speech Yar'Adua at least acknowledged the lapses and shortcomings in the electoral process and promised that future elections would meet international standards. As a result, he swiftly (22 August) inaugurated the *electoral reforms* committee comprising 22 eminent Nigerians, including former Chief Justice Mohammed Uwais as chair.

To save costs and ensure speedy justice, the presidential election petitions tribunal took over the petitions of Buhari and Atiku (16 October), but later declined a request by Atiku to subpoena certain witnesses, among them civil servants, foreign election observers and media chiefs, whose evidence he described as crucial. Consequently, on 27 November, he filed an appeal on this issue with the supreme court.

While state *election petitions tribunals* annulled the election of PDP governor Ibrahim Idris in Kogi state (10 October), PDP governor Saidu Dakingari in Kebbi state (20 October) and retired vice-admiral and former chief of naval staff, Governor Murtala Nyako of the same party, in Adamawa state (15 November), the supreme court handed down two further important verdicts on the elections. On 14 June, in a constitutionally and politically highly complex issue, the court unanimously decided that the newly inaugurated PDP governor Andy Uba in Anambra state should step down in favour of his predecessor Peter Obi of the All Progressive Great Alliance (APGA). The court maintained that there was no vacancy at government house when INEC conducted the gubernatorial election in that state. The judges supported the argument that Obi's four-year term of office began with the oath of office and the oath of allegiance, which he took on 17 March the previous year. Consequently, on 19 July the election tribunal nullified the gubernatorial election. However, Obi had been impeached by the state assembly in November 2006. The high court in the state capital of Awka declared the impeachment null and void, a ruling that was upheld by the court of appeal on 9 February. Thus, the new governor Virginia Etiaba handed back power to her former boss.

On 25 October, the highest court of the land voided the governorship of Celestine Omehia (PDP) in Rivers state and ordered that Rotimi Amaechi be sworn in immediately in Omehia's stead. The court held that Amaechi was wrongly substituted by the party and that the indictment on which his disqualification was based could not be upheld in law. Moreover, the immunity clause, which Omehia clung to in order to stay in power, was considered irrelevant since the case was a pre-election matter.

On 27 April, the supreme court put an end to the *impeachment saga* of the previous year and upheld the ruling of the court of appeal (8 March), which had declared the impeachment of Plateau state governor Joshua Dariye in 2006 to be unconstitutional.

During the elections, outgoing President Obasanjo renewed the *state of emergency* in *Ekiti* state on 18 April. He extended the tenure of sole administrator, retired Maj. Gen. Adetunji Olurin, until the end of his second term on 29 May to prevent any repeat of the violence that had erupted in the state after the gubernatorial election and its spread to neighbouring states. In a nationwide broadcast, Obasanjo justified the decision and accused impeached governor Ayodele Fayose of having instigated the crisis. Despite this decision, the National Assembly turned down Obasanjo's request to endorse the extension (24 April), thereby forcing the sole administrator to hand over power to the speaker of the state assembly, Tope Ademiluyi, who thus became acting governor.

At the senate's inaugural session on 5 June, re-elected PDP-senator David Bonaventure Mark from Benue state emerged as senate president, while Ike Ekweremadu (PDP) from Enugu state was elected as his deputy. The new senate president was a retired major general who had served as military governor, minister of communications and member of the Armed Forces Ruling Council under different

military regimes. Patricia Etteh (PDP) from Osun state was elected
speaker of the house of representatives, making her the *first woman*
to assume this position. Meanwhile, Babangida Nguroje (PDP) from
Taraba state became deputy speaker. However, by November, both
were removed from their posts following an in-house investigation
which revealed they had breached house rules in awarding contracts worth $ 5 m for the renovation of their official residences and
the purchase of several cars. On 1 November, Etteh was succeeded as
speaker by Dimeji Bankole (PDP) from Ogun and Nguroje as deputy
speaker by Usman Bayero Nafada (PDP) from Gombe state.

   The distribution of power among the top three positions in the
Nigerian political system was well balanced among the six *geo-political zones*. While these zones have never been formally entrenched,
implicit recognition of their relevance serves as a yardstick for securing a certain balance of power. With the exception of the northwest,
all the other zones were represented. However, despite the fact that
83 members of the senate and 271 of the house of representatives
had been elected for the first time, some of them were well-known
politicians. Seven former governors from the PDP and ANPP, who
had served the maximum of two terms and had not been indicted
for embezzlement at the time of nomination, used their local networks to secure election and featured most prominently in the senate: George Akume (Benue), Chimaroke Nnamani (Enugu), Ibrahim
Turaki (Jigawa), Ahmed Makarfi (Kaduna), Mohammed Adamu
Aliero (Kebbi), Bukar Abba Ibrahim (Yobe) and Ahmad Rufai Sani
(Zamfara). Two retired senior officers, Maj. Gen. Abubakar Tanko
Ayuba (Kebbi state) and Brig. John Nanzip Shagaya (Plateau state)
were also elected to the senate as PDP candidates. However, the latter was one of the first members of the National Assembly, along
with retired Major Satty Gogwin (AC), Ayogu Eze (PDP) and Patrick
Asadu (PDP), whose election was voided in December by election
tribunals.

   On 28 July, President Umaru Yar'Adua swore in his *cabinet*, reappointing four of his predecessor's cabinet members. In addition, he

retained the governor of the central bank, Chukwuma Soludo, chief of staff within the presidency Abdullahi Mohammed, and the national security adviser Sarki Mukhtar, both retired major generals. However, Yar'Adua assigned key portfolios to new staff with reasonable professional credentials: secretary to the government of the federation (Babagana Kingibe), justice (Michael Aondoakaa), finance (Shamsuddeen Usman), defence (Mahmud Yayale Ahmed), foreign affairs (Ojo Maduekwe), state security service (Afakriya Gadzama) and national intelligence agency (Emmanuel Imohe), while retaining the most important ministry, energy, for himself, the portfolio his predecessor had relinquished to Edmund Daukoru on 10 January. The finance minister, for example, was a former deputy governor of the central bank, while Kingibe was a well-known civil servant who had served under different military regimes and was the running-mate of the winner of the 1993 annulled elections, Moshood Abiola. Shortly thereafter, he changed sides and became foreign minister under military dictator Sani Abacha.

Just moments after he was sworn in, Yar'Adua replaced the inspector-general of *police*, Sunday Ehindero, with the most senior deputy inspector-general Ogbonna Onovo, an Igbo. Despite this decision, Onovo was removed three days later in favour of another deputy inspector-general, Mike Okiro from Rivers state, who soon undertook a major shake-up as a result of which at least 35 police commissioners changed positions.

The *military* also experienced far-reaching shake-ups during the year. Obasanjo had already retired 13 top-echelon officers in early May, and close to the end of his presidency he changed the command structure by promoting Lt. Gen. Owoye Andrew Azazi to be chief of defence staff and Maj. Gen. Luka Nyeh Yusuf to be chief of army staff. This action was necessary, since Azazi's predecessor General Martin Luther Agwai was about to take over the international peacekeeping force in Darfur. Both retained their new positions under the incoming government and were even promoted to general and lieutenant general respectively. Nevertheless, in late

July and early August, Yar'Adua retired some 40 top brass and re-deployed several key officers, such as commandants in the general command, military intelligence and logistics.

There were also changes in personnel in the *judiciary*, government agencies as well as parastatals. Idris Legbo Kutigi succeeded Alfa Modibo Belgore as chief justice on 18 January after the latter reached the mandatory retirement age of 70, and swore in 17 senior lawyers into the prestigious rank of senior advocate of Nigeria. While Obasanjo's spokeswoman Remi Oyo was appointed managing director of the news agency of Nigeria in July, the group managing director of Nigerian National Petroleum Corporation (NNPC), Funsho Kupolokun, was replaced on 10 August by one of the company's top directors, Abubakar Yar'Adua, the president's namesake, but not related.

One day before the gubernatorial and state assembly elections, the prominent Muslim cleric Sheikh Ja'afar Mahmud Adam and two of his followers were assassinated in a mosque in Kano, the biggest northern city. He was a strong advocate of strict shariah law and fell out with the governor, sharply criticising him for his allegedly cautious approach and even resigning from his post on the Hisbah Board. On 17 April, however, in the aftermath of the killings, *Islamist militants* stormed a police station and the office of the federal road safety commission, killing at least 13 people, most of them policemen. In addition, they attacked inhabitants of Panshekara suburb. Eventually, with the permission of then President Obasanjo, Kano state Governor Shekarau requested the military to cordon off the area. According to military sources, the soldiers killed 26 militants and arrested nine. An unknown number of militants escaped. In November, the state security service arrested Islamic militants in the three northern states of Kaduna, Kano and Yobe who had been found in possession of fertiliser and bomb-making devices and were suspected of having links to al-Qaida. As in previous years, however, Nigerian authorities could not provide substantive proof of an al-Qaida presence in the country. Mayhem broke out in the local government of Tudun Wada, home to a substantial Christian minority. An alleged blasphemy against the Prophet Muhammad caused Muslim youths to go on a rampage on Friday 28 September, burning churches and shops. At least nine people died and about 600 were displaced. For the umpteenth time that incident proved that Fridays have become potentially dangerous in the north for non-Muslims, who, for years, after noon prayers, have often been targeted by militants.

The case in Kano concerning the legality of *religious marshals*, known as 'Hisbah', took a surprising twist. The previous year, Kano state government had challenged the legality of a decision by the police inspector-general to outlaw Hisbah, which had been established under state law. The supreme court, however, dismissed the suit, pointing out that it lacked jurisdiction since there was no legal dispute between the federal government and the Kano state government. The court noted that jurisdiction in any such suit lay with the federal high court in Abuja. While Hisbah was still in evidence, in contrast to previous years its members were largely confined to barracks and assigned tasks such as directing traffic and helping sports fans to their stadium seats.

The Islamic spiritual centre Sokoto, home of the sultan, saw several *sectarian clashes* between mainstream Sunni Muslims and groups sympathetic to the Iranian revolution, and wrongly called Shiites. After high-profile Sunni cleric Umar Dan Maishiyya, well-known for his sermons against the Shiites, was shot on 18 July by four gunmen, the sect's headquarters were attacked by young Sunni men, who lynched one of the suspects. Two days later, the Shiite sect's leader Kasimu Rimin Tawaye and some 100 of his followers were detained and reportedly accused of assassinating the Sunni cleric. In the wake of the arrests, the state government ordered security forces to demolish the sect's headquarters; destroy a school, a clinic and some living quarters; and charged the detainees in court. In October, another three people were killed in what was believed to be an execution killing by members of the Shiite sect. Despite the latent sectarian tensions, the ceremony to inaugurate the spiritual head of Nigeria's Muslims took place in Sokoto on 3 March, when Sultan Muhammad Sa'ad Abubakar received his staff of office, thus formalising the government's recognition of his unique position.

The Niger Delta was the most volatile part of the country, although several other states also experienced violence, especially bloody communal clashes over the control of land. Even the conditional release of Mujahid Dokubo-Asari (14 June), leader of the illegal Ijaw Niger Delta People's Volunteer Force (NDPVF), who had been held on treason charges since 2005, did not improve the situation. While the supreme court had dismissed Dokubo-Asari's appeal to be released on bail on 8 June, describing him as a threat to national security, the federal high court in Abuja eventually changed its mind on medical grounds. Moreover, the court adjourned the trial until the accused was ready to stand. The federal government, however, did not intervene, indicating that the previous meeting of three Niger Delta governors with President Yar'Adua had paved the way for a political deal intended to boost a nascent peace process. Consequently, Dokubo-Asari met Vice President Jonathan in Abuja on 13 July, and maintained that abductions were not part of his struggle.

Notwithstanding this, violence in the Niger Delta reached new levels. As in the previous year, the crisis at times descended into open warfare, seriously affecting oil and gas production. Shoot-outs between militias and military personnel, *kidnapping* for ransom, armed robbery, killing innocent people and blowing up pipelines became the norm in the area. In the course of the year, several dozen foreign oil workers were taken hostage. In almost all cases, the hostages were released after some days, weeks or months, usually after a financial deal had been struck, thereby fuelling further hostage-taking as a lucrative and flourishing business. The Movement for the Emancipation of the Niger Delta (MEND) was the most visible group involved in this business, a business that gave rise to the constant proliferation of small armed groups.

For the first time, Chinese, Indian and South Korean workers were targeted, reminding the Nigerian public that these countries had become major economic players in Nigeria. On 5 January, five Chinese telecommunications workers were abducted at Rumuokunde, Emohua local government in Rivers state, but released on 18 January. A few days later, nine Chinese oil workers were taken hostage in Sagbama local government area in Bayelsa state after the kidnappers broke into the offices of a Chinese oil company, seizing cash as well. The hostages were set free after 11 days in captivity. Nine South Korean workers on a Daewoo oil facility were abducted on 10 January, but regained their freedom two days later. Another three Daewoo engineering workers, along with eight Filipinos, were taken at gunpoint from the Afam power plant northeast of Port Harcourt on 3 May. On 20 January, MEND had abducted 24 Filipinos from a cargo ship in Warri Southwest local government in Delta state; they spent 24 days in captivity. Only hours after they were freed on 8 May, armed men in speedboats seized four US citizens from a barge in Delta state, but they were released by the end of the month. However, the Indonesian Indorama Petrochemical Company in Eleme local government in Rivers state was one of those worst hit. On 19 May, seven Indians were rescued by a joint task force after a distress call from the company's residential quarters, but two were kidnapped and three Nigerians killed. On 1 June, militants stormed the residential estate again, abducting ten of the *expatriate workers* and killing two policemen attached to the place. The workers were released after more than two weeks.

In total, foreigners from at least another 16 countries in Europe, the Americas, Asia, the Pacific, the Middle East and Africa, working for international oil companies such as Shell, ChevronTexaco, Agip/ ENI, TotalFinaElf, ExxonMobil and others, were affected. In January, leading tyre manufacturer Michelin announced its decision to pull out of tyre production at its plant in Port Harcourt, but maintained its large rubber plantation.

Nigerians were even worse affected and several fell victim to the attackers, including policemen and soldiers. On 16 January, *gunmen* killed 12 people, including four local chiefs from the Kula kingdom in Rivers state. Late in the month (28 January), some 120 criminal suspects were sprung from two police stations by armed militants in Port Harcourt, among them Soboma George, a leading militant. There were casualties on both sides. Another prominent gang leader, Ateke Tom, however, a former ally of Dokubo-Asari, could operate almost unhindered. The attacks reached their climax when militants destroyed the house of Vice President-elect Goodluck Jonathan in Otuoke village and the police station in Ogbia in Jonathan's home state of Bayelsa (16 May). Three policemen died.

Despite the fact that the newly elected president took office towards the end of May and the conditional release of Dokubo-Asari, the overall situation did not improve. On 23 August, Emohua local government again experienced a serious incident when 20 locals were killed in Rumuekpe. On 20 October, three expatriates along with four Nigerians working for Shell were abducted in Bayelsa state, and the US company Wilbros was attacked in Bonny, Rivers state, on 27 November. Two policemen and a civilian guard lost their lives. On New Year's Eve, Ateke Tom's Niger Delta Vigilantes (NDV) geared up for another attack in Port Harcourt early the following morning.

The *counter attacks* by the military were somewhat counterproductive. Although they freed several hostages and killed dozens of militants, the military failed to ease the tensions, let alone stop the kidnappings. On 12 March, the joint task force rescued three Croatians in Ogbakiri, Rivers state. On 21 June, the task force recaptured an occupied Agip/ENI oil platform in Bayelsa state, killing 12 militants and freeing some 28 hostages. Two company staff and at least three soldiers lost their lives during the operation. In late August, 15 militants were killed in a security operation in Tombia, Degema local government in Rivers state, and seven lost their lives after a gun battle with navy personnel on 31 October. One naval officer was killed.

The Independent Petroleum Marketers Association of Nigeria (IPMAN) announced on 5 July that it had entered into a special arrangement with vigilante groups to protect pipelines. On 22 October, Col. Nanven Rintip replaced Brig. Lawrence Ngubane as commander of the joint task force. In addition, the paramount ruler of Evo kingdom in Rivers state, Eze Francis Amadi, admitted he had paid a ransom of naira 3 m (some $ 25,000) to free his kidnapped child. For the first time, the amount of the *ransom* was publicly acknowledged.

As in the previous year, close to 100 policemen lost their lives on duty – excluding those who fell victim to the violence in the Niger Delta and during the elections and the 28 mobile policemen who died in a road crash in Benue state. On 15 November, the inspector-general of police admitted that 785 suspected armed robbers had died in encounters with police and that almost 1,600 had been arrested the previous three months. During the same period, 62 officers lost their lives. Despite this, the police retained their poor reputation, as indicated by the findings of the UN special rapporteur on torture. After a week-long visit ending on 9 March, Manfred Nowak concluded that *torture* and *ill-treatment* in police custody were widespread and that torture was part and parcel of law enforcement operations in the country. Notwithstanding this woeful conclusion, Nowak thanked top police officials for opening up police facilities to unannounced visits.

The human and *civil rights record* was again mixed, although harassment of journalists decreased further. In addition, the federal high court in Abuja granted the detained Ralph Uwazuruike, leader of the banned militia Movement for the Actualisation of the Sovereign State of Biafra (MASSOB), three months of bail to accord his late mother a fitting burial (26 October). He had been arrested in 2005 and charged with treason. Courts in Enugu and Jos had earlier (in March and July) acquitted 29 MASSOB members. On 10 December, the court of appeal dismissed an appeal by the inspector-general of police to reverse a verdict voiding a Public Order Act, which made it mandatory to obtain a police permit before protest rallies. Nevertheless, the human and civil rights record was seriously tarnished on 17 December when the Kano state government admitted that seven convicts had been secretly executed the previous year outside the state. Only a little while before, the federal government had informed the UN that Nigeria had not carried out any executions in recent years.

While highway robbery decreased slightly, the number of bank raids and raids on bureaux de change again rose, leading to the deaths of several policemen and civilians. As in previous years, Lagos was the centre of armed *robbery* and *bank raids*, and in July the new AC state government approved naira 2 bn for the immediate expansion, reorganisation and upgrading of the state's rapid response squad. However, more and more banks in urban centres in the north were also affected, namely Abuja, Suleja, Kaduna, Katsina and Kano.

Premeditated *killings and assassinations* also increased. The traditional ruler Eze Davidson Okoro Anyanwu in Ahiazu-Mbaise local government in Imo state was gunned down on 1 May. Tunde Awanebi, chief security officer of the governor of Ondo state, was shot on 30 May, just hours after leaving office. Auwalu Jibril, former sole administrator of Minjibir local government in Kano state, was murdered on 19 June, while Mohammed Rabiu Yunus, deputy general manager of Kaduna Refinery and Petrochemical, was shot dead on 15 July. Retired Col. Lawrence Balogun was killed in Lagos on 23 July, the businessman Hamza Isa Kano in Abuja on 5 August and the Dutch businessman Tony Kouwenhoven in Port Harcourt on 2 September. More was to come. Olusegun Oladimeji, PDP member of the house of representatives, was assassinated in his home area in Oyo state on 14 September. The special advisor on revenue issues to the governor of Jigawa state, Alqasim Ahmad Gwaram, was hacked to death in Kano on 2 December and a prominent Kano Islamic scholar, Sani Naiya, was murdered on 17 December. As in preceding years, most well-known national and local victims were killed for political or personal reasons by hired assassins, as evidenced by the fact that victims were not robbed, suggesting that contract killing was becoming part of political and business life. It was estimated that contract killings could cost as little as naira 100,000 ($ 800). In fact, neither police nor other security agencies were able or willing to investigate. On rare occasions, such as the death in 2001 of Bola Ige, former justice minister and attorney-general, suspects were charged but eventually acquitted for want of evidence.

In December, Transparency International classified Nigeria the seventh most corrupt country in the world. The *anti-corruption campaign* did produce some positive results and there was a small ray of hope, when, on 26 July, former Bayelsa state Governor Diepreye Alamieyeseigha was found guilty of money laundering and sentenced to two years imprisonment. He also had to forfeit property in South Africa and Abuja as well as various bank accounts and was released from prison the following day, having already spent his term in detention. The case was in line with a decision by the supreme court, which in February affirmed that the anti-corruption commission EFCC could investigate state governments, considered to be the most corrupt institutions. With this ruling in mind, outgoing President Obasanjo approved another four-year term for EFCC chairman Nuhu Ribadu. The EFCC verdict was eventually confirmed on 25 October, when the court declined to nullify the EFCC Act of 2004.

Against this backdrop, EFCC went ahead with its investigation of 15 ex-governors on 6 June and arrested several of them, including Senators Nnamani and Turaki. The second *anti-corruption agency*, the Independent Corrupt Practices Commission (ICPC) disclosed on 2 July the launching in all 36 states of investigations codenamed Operation Hawk. By the end of the year, eight governors had been charged, all but one of them being freed on bail. Despite this, it was rumoured that the new justice minister and attorney-general, Aondoakaa, was obstructing the investigations – rumours given greater credence by the alleged temporary removal of the EFCC chairman at the end of the year to go on a special training course. Interestingly, late in the year it emerged that in February Obasanjo had approved two radio and two TV licences for himself as part of a pool of

38 new licences. However, on 13 November the UN Office on Drugs and Crime (UNODC) applauded the work of the EFCC and Nigeria's participation in the UNODC and World Bank Stolen Asset Recovery Initiative (StAR).

Foreign Affairs

Nigeria maintained good relations with the US, its biggest crude oil customer, and former colonial power Britain. It consolidated its relations with China, expanded its cooperation with India and was increasingly involved in peacekeeping missions in Darfur.

The launching of the US-Africa command, known as AFRICOM, which became operational on 1 October, brought mixed if guarded reviews. Thus, the Pentagon was careful to stress that the aim of the new command was to help struggling states with training and aid. The new Nigerian government, still under internal pressure on account of the flawed elections, was backed by the US when the deputy secretary of state, John Negroponte, and the assistant secretary, Jendayi Frazer, visited Nigeria on their West Africa tour (12–13 November). Negroponte pointed out that Nigeria was an important strategic partner and that the US was committed to maintaining a robust bilateral partnership, a commitment reiterated by the newly appointed ambassador Robin Sanders when she presenting her credentials in early December. Shortly beforehand, on 29 November, two senior command officials, Vice-Admiral Robert Moeller, deputy commander of the military, and Mary Carlin Yates, responsible for civil-military activities, mounted a charm offensive in Nigeria to dispel misgivings about AFRICOM. These statements and initiatives and Yar'Adua's subsequent official visit to the US, where he held talks with President Bush on 13 December, silenced critics of AFRICOM inside and outside the Nigerian government. Moreover, the Sultan of Sokoto's speech to the US Institute of Peace in Washington on Muslim-Christian relations in Nigeria (13 November) was aimed at silencing Nigerian Muslims critical of the US.

However, in its annual report on terrorism published at the end of April, the US mentioned Nigeria as a country where some individuals and groups had ties with possible *terrorists* in Sudan, Iran and elsewhere, and suggested that international terrorist groups had operated and recruited in Nigeria. Nevertheless, in May the US financial crimes enforcement network removed Nigeria from the list of non-cooperating countries in the fight against money laundering and set aside $ 15 m to support electoral reforms over a three-year period. In December, Delta Airlines started daily direct flights between Atlanta and Lagos. On 26 September, Yar'Adua gave his maiden speech at the UN General Assembly.

Chinese investments continued to increase despite the dangers for Chinese citizens in the Niger Delta. On 13 May, China Great Wall Industry Corporation, acting as the international cooperation platform for China Aerospace Science and Technology Corporation, launched into orbit Nigeria's communications satellite NIGCOMSAT-1 using a 'Long March' 3-B rocket. This was the first time that a foreign customer had purchased both a Chinese satellite and a Chinese launching service. The satellite is supposed to remain in operation for 15 years, offering broadcasting, broadband internet and phone services and control of it was eventually passed to the federal government in July. Both governments tried to strengthen military cooperation, indicated by the meeting of then defence minister Thomas Aguiyi-Ironsi with his counterpart in Beijing on 5 April. Xu Jialu, special envoy of Chinese President Hu Jintao, attended Yar'Adua's inauguration. Shortly afterwards, the new president held bilateral talks with his Chinese counterpart in Berlin on 7 June in the run-up to the G8 summit in Heiligendamm. Financial cooperation between the two partners received a boost when the United Bank for Africa, one of Nigeria's top banks, entered into a partnership arrangement with the China Development Bank in October.

Nigeria's strong orientation towards Asia was underlined by the three-day state visit of India's Prime Minister Manmohan Singh (14–16 October). It was the first time since Jawaharlal Nehru's visit in 1962 that an Indian prime minister had come to Nigeria, which is now India's biggest African trading partner. Indeed, India had become the second biggest importer of Nigerian oil after the US. Singh's address to the National Assembly highlighted the need for and desire to set the stage for an *Indo-Nigerian strategic partnership.* Against this background, the Abuja Declaration was signed. It includes several agreements, including direct flights, closer defence cooperation, double taxation avoidance, protection of investments and mutual legal assistance. In early November, the Indian Oil Corporation, the leading oil and refinery company on the subcontinent, made a request to raise Nigeria's annual crude oil export from 2 to 3 m tonnes.

To an extent, *relations with Britain* were influenced by the corruption investigations against Nigerian ex-governors who owned assets and properties worth millions of dollars, particularly in Greater London. In addition, the Nigerian government requested the return of funds looted by ex-Governors Dariye and Alamieyeseigha and still held in Britain. Former Delta state Governor James Ibori's legal battle in British courts over his assets outside Nigeria worth $ 35 m reminded the British public that Nigerians constituted by far the biggest part of the African diaspora. Africans have become Britain's fastest-growing minority and number up to one million, of whom 80% live in the London area alone. Immigrants of Nigerian origin have been by far the most successful, only slightly lagging behind those from the US, thanks to the reasonably good Nigerian education system in the 1970s and 1980s. This diaspora continues to provide a large part of the estimated $ 4 bn in annual remittances worldwide. Against this background, Theresa Nkoyo Ibori, wife of ex-governor James Ibori, was arrested at Heathrow airport on 1 November in connection with an ongoing money laundering inquiry. The information made public revealed that in the early 1990s he had been convicted in Britain of credit card fraud and fined for theft, along with his wife and then girlfriend. In April, Joyce Bamidele Oyebanjo, an accomplice of Dariye, was sentenced to three years imprisonment for laundering the proceeds of his loot.

On the political front, Prime Minister Tony Blair maintained that Britain would work with the next government of Nigeria, despite widespread rigging in April's elections, but stayed away from Yar'Adua's inauguration and sent Baroness Royall of Blaisdon instead. Earlier, on 1 February, Lord David Triesman, in charge of African and Commonwealth issues, had held talks with the Nigerian government on the forthcoming elections, in which it was maintained that the process was on course. At the end of August, Britain's new under-secretary of state for international development, Shriti Vadera, paid a two-day visit to Nigeria to assess the ambitious plans of the British government's aid agency, Department for International Development (DFID). At the Commonwealth summit in Uganda in November, the president asked new British Prime Minister Gordon Brown for help in reorganising Nigeria's police force.

Against the background of the flawed elections, the political relationship with the EU cooled somewhat. Several members of the EU parliament demanded that the EU freeze its aid to Nigeria until free and fair elections were held, recalling that over the past five years the EU had spent more than € 500 m on projects including good governance, water supply and health. However, the EU commission was against cutting aid, arguing that such action would harm the Nigerian people rather than the government. In November, Nigeria was accused of being one of the obstacles in the path of the new Economic Partnership Agreements (EPAs) between African states and the EU. Notwithstanding this, Yar'Adua attended the second African-European summit in Lisbon (8–9 December).

As to relations with other African states, Nigeria focused on the crisis in Darfur, the Bakassi peninsula conflict with Cameroon, the AU summit in Accra and ECOWAS summit in Abuja, both in June, and a meeting of the Gulf of Guinea commission in Abuja in July. Additionally, Yar'Adua toured *key African countries*, including Ghana and South Africa, immediately after his election, in a shrewdly judged show of leadership in a politically crucial situation. The visits, at short notice, paid off, as indicated by the attendance of Thabo

Mbeki (South Africa) and John Kufuor (Ghana) at Yar'Adua's inauguration. Their attendance helped to endorse Nigeria's leadership under the new president.

Nigeria's peacekeeping efforts in *Darfur* were recognised on 24 May when General Martin Luther Agwai was appointed as the new force commander of the AU peace mission, AMIS, and the subsequent AU/UN hybrid operation, UNAMID. Agwai had served as deputy commander of the peacekeeping mission in Sierra Leone and deputy military advisor in the UN peacekeeping department in New York. However, Nigerian forces suffered several casualties, many more than in previous years. During two attacks by rebel militias in May and September, 11 soldiers lost their lives. Despite these setbacks, another contingent of 680 soldiers left for Sudan in early October.

The *Bakassi conflict*, supposed to have been resolved the previous year, re-emerged on the political agenda. On 22 November, the newly elected senate passed a resolution repudiating the 2006 agreement between Nigeria and Cameroon, in terms of which the Bakassi peninsula was ceded to Cameroon. The senate questioned the validity of the agreement, claiming that then President Obasanjo had failed to bring the treaty before the National Assembly for ratification. It was subsequently revealed that his letter seeking ratification had been read on 14 June 2006, although due process had not been followed for either the letter or the agreement. On 28 November, Bola Ajibola, Nigeria's representative on the Nigerian-Cameroon mixed commission, countered the senate's claim by asserting that his government would not renege on the treaty and ruled out any possibility of reopening the Bakassi issue.

However, tension increased when at least 21 Cameroonian soldiers were killed in a cross-border raid on 12 November. The Nigerian military denied involvement in the attack, blaming the Nigerian militants who had also attacked Nigerian naval forces in the coastal town of Ibeka in the same area. An observer team, made up of the UN, Cameroon and Nigeria, was put together under the auspices of the UN in New York on 8 December. The team was supposed to visit the Bakassi peninsula in early 2008 to assess the challenges faced by those displaced in the wake of the International Court of Justice verdict on Bakassi.

Socioeconomic Developments

The oil price rallied to new heights and Nigeria's high quality crude rose from $ 60 per barrel at the start of the year to close to $ 100 by the end of November, before falling slightly towards the end of 2007. In spite of the permanent upheaval in the Delta region, which forced oil companies to cut oil and gas production, Nigeria accumulated more than $ 50 bn in foreign reserves by year's end. Thus, newly elected President Yar'Adua inherited the healthiest balance sheet of any new head of state since independence. This included the *annual budget*, which for the first time since 1999 was already in effect at the beginning of the financial year, which coincided with the calendar year. His predecessor and the previous National Assembly had passed the 2007 budget totalling naira 2.3 trillion ($ 18.2 bn). A deficit of naira 579 bn had been projected, based on the benchmark of $ 40 per barrel and an exchange rate of naira 125:$ 1. The naira, in fact, appreciated against the US dollar from 132:1 at the beginning to 116:1 by year's end. Security and public works got the highest allocation, 12% each, followed by education (10%) and health (7%), while power and water supply each received 6%.

Nigeria was able to settle its *debts* with the London Club of creditors. The government bought back promissory notes worth about $ 500 m, due in 2010, and settled oil warrants of some $ 400 m. Thus, the accumulated external debts owed by the federal government and the 36 federal states stood at $ 3.3 bn. Nevertheless, internal indebtedness grew to almost naira 1.9 trillion. In January, the AfDB successfully launched its first bond issue denominated in naira, with a maturity of one year. The issue had a face value of naira 127.80 m and a fixed coupon rate of 9.25%. In November, the debt management office issued new three-year and 10-year bonds worth naira 50 bn and with a yield of more than 9%.

The phenomenal growth in Nigeria's *telecommunications sector* continued as the number of subscribers skyrocketed to more than 46 m towards the end of the year. That number translated into 27 mobile phones per 100 people. Against this background, at the end of May British Telecom (BT) entered into a lucrative partnership with the Nigerian wireless telecommunication firm 21st Century Technologies, which was to manage the Nigerian end of the connection to BT's global platform for a new generation of internet protocol. Shortly before, BT pulled out of the technical services agreement with Transcorp, the majority shareholder of NITEL (Nigerian Telecommunication Limited), which had been privatised the previous year. The pull-out followed the termination of John Weir's appointment as head of the mobile subsidiary M-TEL over serious in-house disagreements over the selection of equipment suppliers. NITEL and M-TEL still had estimated debts of about naira 29 bn and a generally poor reputation, which worsened their competitiveness in an otherwise profitable market.

The *privatisation programme* slowed down again, after the local Bluestar Oil Services consortium pulled out of its purchase of 51% equity in the state-owned Kaduna and Port Harcourt refineries in July. The consortium had emerged as the preferred bidder days before the new president took power. He soon indicated that he might cancel the deal, allegedly due to pressure from labour unions. As in previous years, Nigeria depended on the importation of petroleum products because the National Petroleum Corporation (NNPC) could not revamp the four ailing refineries in order to meet the high demand, thereby causing permanent nationwide fuel shortages. In addition, the power situation went from bad to worse, even though at least $ 5 bn had been spent since 1999 to improve the sector. Licences were issued to five new independent power producers, bringing the total to 20. At the end of November, however, government agreed to review all privatisation deals approved by the former president.

On the eve of handing over power, Obasanjo increased the pump price of one litre of petrol by naira 10 to naira 75 and the value added tax from 5% to 10%. On assuming office, Yar'Adua was confronted with a *nationwide strike*, which began on 20 June. The labour unions and civil society groups under the umbrella of the Joint Action Forum wanted the measures reversed, including the sale of two refineries. After four days, the unions resolved to call off the strike after both sides agreed to fix the petrol price at naira 70, provided there were no further hikes for 12 months. The government also eventually suspended the new VAT rate.

The spread of HIV/AIDS continued unabated and Nigeria retained its position as the third most infected country, with some four million people living with the virus. The megacity of Lagos topped the infection rate with over 500,000, including 100,000 children. While, with 380,000 new cases, tuberculosis was on the increase, the fight against polio gained momentum and the number of cases decreased by 80%. In October, however, authorities were combating the outbreak of a rare vaccine-derived form of polio in the far north, where 69 children caught the paralysing *disease* from others who had already been vaccinated.

The deep-seated suspicion of any form of *immunisation* programme in the Muslim north was illustrated by two lawsuits in Abuja and Kano, in which the federal and Kano state governments sued the international pharmaceutical company Pfizer for damages and compensation for the families of those who had died or suffered serious side-effects. The lawsuits stemmed from an unregistered drug test in Kano state in 1996 during an outbreak of meningitis. Some 200 children took part in the trials of a new anti-meningitis drug. In 2001, a medical panel reviewing the drug trial concluded that the experiment was an illegal trial of an unregistered drug. According to government officials, more than 50 children had died in the experiment, while many others had developed mental and physical deformities. Pfizer dismissed those claims, maintaining that the trials were lawful and only 11 had died. In December, the $ 8.5 bn lawsuits were adjourned until February 2008.

On 3 March, Newton Aduaka's film 'Ezra' won the Yennenga Stallion prize, the top prize at the 20th Panafrican Film and Television Festival of Ouagadougou (FESPACO) in Burkina Faso, while the celebrated author Chinua Achebe was awarded the Man Booker International Prize on 13 June for his contributions to world literature. The previous week, his former pupil Chimamanda Ngozi Adichie won the prestigious Orange Broadband Prize for Fiction for her novel 'Half of a Yellow Sun'. Last but not least, Nigeria won the fourth FIFA U17 world cup in South Korea for the third time, defeating Spain 3–0 on 9 September.

Nigeria in 2008

The legal aftermath of the 2007 general election dominated domestic politics for most of the year. While the supreme court finally endorsed the election victory of Umaru Musa Yar'Adua towards the end of the year, the court of appeal declared some gubernatorial results null and void and several other cases were still before the court at the year's end. Over much of the year, the president enjoyed limited legitimacy and authority. This was compounded by his health situation, a contentious issue in the public perception and one that to an extent further undermined his leadership. It soon became apparent that Yar'Adua was on shaky political ground. However, he did everything possible to reinforce his position against his predecessor Olusegun Obasanjo, who saw himself as having the right to maintain influence. Against the background of this silent struggle, some long overdue socioeconomic projects and programmes, particular in the energy and power sector, lost momentum, thereby putting the economy almost on hold. The situation in the Niger Delta remained deadlocked.

Domestic Politics

The two main rivals and runners-up in the presidential election, retired Maj. Gen. Muhammadu Buhari of the All Nigeria People's Party (ANPP) and Atiku Abubakar of the Action Congress (AC), had challenged the outcome of the election in 2007, won by Umaru Musa Yar'Adua. Notwithstanding serious allegations of widespread voter intimidation, procedural irregularities, seizure of ballot boxes, fraud and organised rigging, the presidential election petitions tribunal unanimously dismissed the petitions on 26 February. Other petitions were struck down on the grounds of alleged incompetence. Without delay, both defeated main rivals filed notice of appeal in the *supreme court*, which has the final say on presidential elections. On 12 December, the highest court of the land, in a narrowly split 4–3 decision, rejected Buhari's final challenge to the presidential election. The majority of judges were convinced that the appellant had not proved that the non-serialisation of the ballot affected the outcome of the election. In Atiku's case, the court ruled 6–1 in favour of the incumbent.

More was to come because the *tribunals* and the courts had to deal with other petitions concerning almost all gubernatorial and several National Assembly election results, which in some cases led to a re-run. Senate president David Bonaventure Mark (People's Democratic Party, PDP), a retired major general, was the most prominent figure in parliament to (almost) fall victim to this trend. His election had been voided on 23 February by the election petitions tribunal in Benue state, which ordered a partial re-run. However, on 15 July the court of appeal set aside the nullification, thereby upholding his election in April 2007. The same applied for retired Brig. John Nanzip Shagaya (Plateau state) on 15 December, when the Independent National Electoral Commission (INEC) had to issue him a certificate of return for the senate. Major Satty Gogwin's defeat in the tribunal, however, was upheld by the court of appeal, but the AC-candidate for the Plateau central senatorial constituency eventually got back into the senate by winning the re-run on 26 July. There were comparable cases in other federal states, two of which in Anambra were noteworthy. On 11 July and 19 December respectively, the supreme court ordered two PDP members of the House of Representatives, Obinna Chidoka and Linda Ikpeazu, to surrender their seats and for Gozie Agbakoba and Charles Chinwendo Odeda to be sworn in in their place. According to the court, the latter two were denied their right to be validly nominated after the PDP primaries. It was only because this was a pre-election matter that the supreme court got involved.

The fiercest legal battles, however, took place on the gubernatorial front where organised rigging, fraud and intimidation during the 2007 elections had been most obvious. Consequently, almost all the results were challenged in the tribunals and subsequently in the *court of appeal*. The tribunals had already annulled the elections of the governors of Adamawa, Kebbi and Kogi states the previous year and voided more results during 2008 (Abia, Bayelsa, Cross Rivers, Edo, Enugu, Ondo, Sokoto). In Edo and Ondo states, they even declared the runners-up Adams Oshiomhole (AC) and Rahman Olusegun Mimiko of the Labour Party duly elected. Notwithstanding these verdicts, the court of appeal overruled the nullifications in Enugu and Kebbi, thereby upholding the election of Sullivan Chime and Saidu Dakingari respectively. On 12 November, it confirmed the tribunal's ruling and declared the AC-candidate and former president of the Nigeria Labour Congress Oshiomhole to be the governor of Edo state. The court had already upheld the other nullifications and ordered a re-run. As widely expected, Ibrahim Idris (Kogi) in March, retired Vice Adm. Murtala Nyako (Adamawa) in April, Timipre Sylva (Bayelsa) and Aliyu Wammako (Sokoto) in May, Liyel Imoke (Cross River) in August, all PDP-frontrunners who had already won the gubernatorial elections in 2007, reclaimed their respective governorships. While the court of appeal had confirmed the tribunals' rulings in favour of almost half the elected governors, the petitions concerning Abia, Delta, Ekiti, Imo, Kaduna, Katsina, Kwara, Niger, Ogun, Ondo, Osun and Oyo states were still pending at year's end.

However, the court's verdicts raised more questions than provided answers about Nigeria's *constitutional law*. The supreme court in an important ruling the previous year on the power struggle in Anambra state, took the view that Governor Peter Obi's four-year term of office began with the oath of office and the oath of allegiance in 2006 after he had won a protracted legal contest with then PDP Governor Chris Ngige over the outcome of the election in 2003. The gubernatorial election in Anambra state in 2007 therefore had to be nullified because the court maintained there was no vacancy at government house when INEC conducted the election. As a result of that case, governors whose elections had been null and void but had won the re-run elections had longer tenures than all the other duly elected incumbents. Indeed, these candidates could even benefit from a fraudulent election in which they might at least have been indirectly involved. Interestingly, though the legal wranglings and the political power struggles were very fierce, not a single actor, party or public institution involved dared to sue a rival or a candidate for committing a breach of the law in the run-up to and during the election.

Shortly after the April 2007 elections and against the background of the ensuing political and legal wrangling, the *electoral reforms committee* under former Chief Justice Mohammed Uwais was inaugurated. On 11 December, the committee eventually submitted its report. Its most important recommendation was that the INEC chairperson and deputy should be of different gender and should be appointed by the national judicial council instead of the president. Chairman Uwais admitted that some recommendations would require constitutional amendment to ensure their implementation.

Ever since the *1999 constitution* came into force, it lacked full legitimacy, having been imposed by the outgoing military regime of General Abdulsalami Abubakar on the eve of his handing over power to the newly elected president, retired General Olusegun Obasanjo. Efforts by the National Assembly to at least correct some of its deficiencies and contradictions had failed in the past, highlighting the extreme difficulty if not impossibility of amending the constitution under the current federal system. The obstacles are very considerable because in addition to the required two-thirds majority of all the members in both chambers of the National Assembly, any amendment has to be approved by not less than two-thirds of the state assemblies. In some cases even a four-fifths majority is required in the National Assembly to get a proposal approved. In this context, it is only the supreme court that is capable of amending and revising the constitutional order.

Towards the end of March, the health minister, Adenike Grange, and her minister of state, Gabriel Aduku, were the first cabinet members to resign, after they were accused by the anti-corruption agency (the Economic and Financial Crimes Commission or EFCC) of embezzlement. That decision heralded the beginning of a *massive reshuffle* within the cabinet, the police and armed forces and a rather quieter restructuring within the presidency, indicating the ultimate goal of eliminating Obasanjo's continuing political influence. On 2 June, the chief of staff to the president, retired Maj. Gen. Abullahi Mohammed, who had served the president's predecessor, was forced to resign and on 18 August the office of chief of staff was formally scrapped. While another retired major general, Sarki Mukhtar, kept his position as national security advisor, on 8 September the president sacked Babagana Kingibe, secretary to the government of the federation, and immediately replaced him with then Minister of Defence Mahmud Yayale Ahmed. Shortly afterwards, Yar'Adua restructured several ministries and created the ministry of Niger Delta. In the end, the splitting of several portfolios increased their number from 19 to 28, manned by 42 ministers.

The long-awaited *cabinet* reshuffle by President Yar'Adua took place on 29 October with the removal of 20 ministers, among them a dozen ministers of state. However, it took the leadership several weeks before the new appointments were announced and subsequently cleared by the senate, and it was only during the second half of December that the reshuffle could be completed. While retaining the ministers of justice (Michael Aondoakaa) and foreign affairs (Ojo Madueke), the president assigned other key portfolios such as finance (Mansur Mukhtar), petroleum (Rilwanu Lukman), defence (Shettima Mustapha) and Niger Delta (Ufot Ekaette) to well-known politicians and technocrats. While Ekaette had served as secretary to the government of the federation under the previous administration, Lukman had been secretary general of OPEC in the 1990s and Mustapha, a former minister, was the pioneer treasurer of the ruling party PDP. The latter appointments raised public concern over the ages of the appointees and, in the case of Lukman, even over his frail health.

In addition to the cabinet reshuffle, the president had already assigned new personnel to various public institutions. Hamman Kajoli Ahmed replaced Jacob Gyang Buba as comptroller general of customs; Mrs. Ama Inyingiala Pepple took over from Mrs. Ebele Okeke as the new head of the federal civil service; and Oba Abdulraheem became chairman of the federal character commission, an executive body established to implement and enforce fairness and equity in the distribution of public posts and socioeconomic infrastructure. The sensitive position of chairperson of the anti-corruption agency EFCC was eventually assigned to Mrs. Farida Waziri, a retired assistant inspector-general of police, thereby finally confirming the contentious and in some ways dishonourable removal of EFCC chairman Nuhu Ribadu the previous year. On 8 March, Vincent Ogbulafor emerged as the new national PDP chairman at the party's special national convention, while Usman Baraje was elected national secretary of the party. All in all, these appointments cautiously achieved a considerable *power shift* towards the far north, close to President Yar'Adua's home area.

For the second time under the new administration, *the military* experienced far-reaching shake-ups. On 20 August, only days after he had scrapped the office of chief of staff in the presidency, Yar'Adua appointed new service chiefs. Maj. Gen. Abdulrahman Dambazau, an indigene from Kano state, replaced Lt. Gen. Luka Yusuf as chief of army staff. Rear Adm. Ishaya Iko Ibrahim took over from Vice Adm. Ganiyu Adekeye as chief of navy staff, while Air Marshal Paul Dike was made chief of defence staff, replacing General Andrew Azazi. Air Vice Marshal Oluseyi Petinrin took over as chief of air staff. Shortly thereafter, all the appointees were promoted a rank and their predecessors retired. The real impact of the shake-ups, however, was caused by a wave of retirements and promotions, the more so because more than 40 top-echelon officers had to leave the service in July and August, most of them mandatorily, and more than 500 officers in all the services were promoted at the beginning and the end of the year.

In January, 15 military men, amongst them six field officers, faced court martial over the disappearance of fairly significant quantities of arms and ammunition. The weapons were allegedly stolen from an armoury in the northern city of Kaduna and subsequently traced to militias in the Niger Delta. According to the court, the arms were sold through Sunny Bowei Okah, brother to Henry Okah, a leader of the Movement for the Emancipation of the Niger Delta (MEND) who was extradited from Angola in February and was standing trial in a federal high court for alleged *gun running* and treason. In November, the court-martial eventually sentenced six culprits to life imprisonment while two were demoted. This trial brought to mind the proceedings in 2005 against high-ranking officers who were convicted of oil theft in the Niger Delta. Both trials clearly indicated the existence nationwide of sophisticated criminal networks in respect of the unstable situation in the Niger Delta.

As in previous years, the oil producing Niger Delta was the most volatile part of the country, with the number of attacks and counter attacks by militias and security forces definitely exceeding those in the previous year. While the crisis developed into open warfare on several occasions, it was also characterised by a sophisticated propaganda and counter-propaganda campaign, in which local and international media as well as improved communications methods were used. The most visible militia group MEND, which was behind the worst attacks on the oil and gas infrastructure and abductions, dubbed its campaign 'Hurricane Barbarossa', declaring war on the oil industry and announcing and calling off ceasefires. Government security forces called for all-out action against the militias, adopting labels such as 'Operation Flush Out III'.

Given the frequent unreliability of figures, it is difficult or impossible to verify facts, claims and counter-claims about the number of attacks, acts of sabotage, victims as well as fatalities on both sides. In the course of the year, however, more than 44 foreign oil and construction workers, engineers and businesspeople from at least a dozen countries in the Americas, Asia, Europe, the Middle East and

Africa were kidnapped by different *militia groups* in Akwa Ibom, Bayelsa, Delta and Rivers state. All but two Britons, who had already been held captive for three months at year's end, were released almost unharmed. As in previous years, however, Nigerians – including civilians, policemen and soldiers and even toddlers – were again the worst affected and fell victim to attackers and hijackers. When, for example, gunmen kidnapped a staff member of a German construction company in Port Harcourt on 4 March, the Nigerian driver and two soldiers escorting him were killed. The German was released several hours later. In another incident near the major oil city on 11 July, two other German staff were kidnapped and an armoured vehicle was blown off the road with dynamite, leaving one soldier in the convoy dead. The two Germans were released on 14 August.

Njo Amadi, abducted in Port Harcourt on 24 February, was not so lucky, being killed by the *kidnappers* after they had collected a naira 2 m ransom. The list of Nigerian kidnap victims grew longer by the day and the cold-bloodedness of the hostage-takers increased significantly. In extorting money from the victims' families, the criminals targeted their victims carefully, some of the best-known being Seinye Lulu-Briggs, wife of an oil magnate (6 February), Dorothy Otele, wife of a Bayelsa state assembly member (18 March), Margaret Idisi, wife of the manager of a drilling company (13 April), Norum Yobo, elder brother of Everton football player Joseph Yobo (5 July) and Paul Edemobi, younger brother of the then director general of the national agency for food and drug administration and control, Dora Akunyili, who shortly thereafter became minister of information (1 December).

Apart from the numerous attacks, victims and deadly disputes over control of stolen oil between rival armed gangs, the major cause for concern for the federal government, its security forces and the oil companies was the fact that in June the militias proved for the first time that all facilities were within their reach, even offshore. These had previously been considered safe from attack. On 19 June, militants claiming to be members of MEND raided Shell's flagship project, the Bonga installation with a capacity of 220,000 bpd and lying some 120 km off the coast. On their way back, they kidnapped a US worker from a separate vessel. Despite the arrest of some 200 militants in September and of Sabomabo Jackrich, a leading member of MEND, in Rivers state on 28 December, security forces could not prevent further *offshore attacks*. On 4 and 19 December, oil services ships were attacked by speedboats off the coast of Akwa Ibom state and at least two persons killed. The Soku gas plant in Rivers state, which provided the biggest liquefied gas plant (Nigeria Liquefied Natural Gas or NLNG) in Bonny with some 40% of its requirements, was shut down on 27 November after militants attacked and damaged the pipeline several times. Given the current unlikelihood of resolving the Niger Delta issue, Shell entered into an arrangement with local communities called 'Community and Shell Together' (CAST). This approach was directed at local people in communities in which pipelines were laid in order to protect oil and gas facilities from vandalism. It clearly indicated that ultimately a sustainable solution is only possible with the local people, including most of the militias.

Notwithstanding the dangerous increase in violence, raids and the blowing up of pipelines and flow stations, the federal government called for a Niger Delta summit under the contentious auspices of Ibrahim Gambari, a former minister, undersecretary general and special envoy of the UN. His appointment as chairman of the steering committee did not go down well with the targeted stakeholders in the Niger Delta, who pointed to his role as Nigeria's representative in New York during the military dictatorship of Sani Abacha. In early July, the president backed down. Even the nomenclature for the proposed talks was changed from summit to dialogue, and the Niger Delta Technical Committee was inaugurated on 8 September with Ledum Mitee as chair. This was the umpteenth half-hearted initiative and from the very beginning there were strong indications it was meant to fail, feeding widespread suspicion that neither the federal nor state governments in the Niger Delta region were really interested in resolving the deep-rooted crisis at this time. The 40-person committee submitted its report to the president before the year's end.

The Middle Belt, where deep political, ethnic and religious division prevailed, was the second most volatile area. There were, in relative terms, minor incidents in the form of communal, sectarian and political clashes in Anambra, Taraba, Kano and Ogun state. However, Plateau state and its capital Jos once again experienced a wave of violence. More than 400 persons were left dead and several thousand homeless sought refuge in local mosques, churches and army and police barracks. On 27 November, local elections took place in all 17 local governments in the state. In these elections, control over a portion of Nigeria's oil revenue, no matter how small, was at stake. Skirmishes between rival political gangs started late that night in Jos North local government, an area always hotly contested by the mostly Christian indigenous inhabitants and the predominant Muslim Hausa-Fulani settler communities. Supporters of the mostly Hausa-Fulani-backed ANPP allegedly became violent when rumours spread that their candidate was to be declared runner up, although in their opinion he was leading the mostly Christian-backed PDP candidate. The following day, more violence erupted and several persons were killed, forcing police to impose a dusk-to-dawn curfew and in some areas even a 24-hour curfew, and causing Governor Jonah Jang to issue a shoot-on-sight order. However, no sooner had the state election commission declared the mostly Christian-backed governing PDP the overall winner on 29 November than demonstrators of the Muslim faith and strong supporters of the ANPP took to the streets to protest the results.

Within hours, the protest spread to other parts of the populous city, leading to mayhem and killing. Churches and mosques were torched as mobs from the Muslim Hausa-Fulani community as well as from mainly Christian ethnic groups went *on the rampage*. Police forces were overwhelmed and soldiers were eventually deployed to restore a measure of calm. In addition, some 500 people were arrested, among them allegedly some 50 non-indigenes dressed in military and police uniforms and armed with guns. The federal government set up a commission of inquiry on 24 December, chaired by retired Maj. Gen. Emmanuel Abisoye. This decision reminded the public of the bloody riots in 2001 and 2004 in which several thousand people died or were injured. The judicial commission of inquiry at that time under the chairmanship of the well-known Justice Niki Tobi produced a report, which was never released. The then government simply issued a white paper and eventually brought this tragic chapter to a close. This action now prompted speculation that the forthcoming inquiry would meet a similar fate.

As in previous years, the southern parts of the country were particularly crime-ridden, but the number of assassinations and killings of policemen declined slightly. Even so, the number of civilians injured or killed mainly by bank robbers increased dramatically to more than 100, while at least 40 policemen lost their lives. Raids on banks and bullion vans were executed by well organised gangs using automatic rifles, modern cars and communication devices, indicating that former and active police and military must have taken some part in the raids. One of the most spectacular robberies took place in Lekki, Lagos state on 21 November, when criminals clad in police and military uniforms approached a bank in the lagoon area, killed two staff and made their getaway in a speed boat. The highest civilian casualties, however, were sustained in *bank robberies* in Ilesha, Osun state (11 February) and Abakaliki, Ebonyi state (12 February): at least ten people died in the first incident and 11 in the second, several others were wounded and some naira 15 m was taken. Several persons were killed along the Enugu-Port Harcourt expressway when a gang of about 30 in military camouflage attacked a bullion van on 11 June and got away with an unknown amount of money. Prior to this, six gunmen on motorcycles had overpowered the security personnel of another bullion van in Port Harcourt on 26 March and carted away about naira 60 m. This was one of the rare armed incidents in which no one was killed. On 15 December, a gang of 20 robbers laid siege to the ancient city of Ile-Ife, Osun state and simultaneously raided three banks and a micro-finance institution, killing more than half a dozen people and injuring 30 to 40. In Adamawa state, in the east of the country, 11 persons were shot and a huge amount of money stolen on 20 September at the Ganye cattle market, a hub for traders, including from neighbouring countries. Even places of worship, at least those considered to be wealthy, were targeted. One example was the Church of the Living God of God's Kingdom Society in Warri, Delta state, which was raided on 28 November. For more than two hours thugs held the community hostage, killing two pastors and two laypersons and extorting money and valuables from residents and worshippers. However, at least 90 armed robbers lost their lives while perpetrating their crimes. According to the Ogun state commissioner of police, 66 died in this southwestern state alone.

Vice President Jonathan Goodluck launched 'Operation Yaki', meaning 'operation war', on 26 March, an initiative mounted by the Kaduna state government in an effort to end *political killings*. The reality on the ground was different. For instance, Alih Ayegba, PDP chairman of Ankpa local government, Kogi state, was murdered at his residence in the presence of his wife on 23 March. In late June, three motorcyclists shot Lawrence Anosike, head of service of Ikwuano local government, Abia state. Salomon Azande, a senior staff member in the office of the federal accountant general, was gunned down in Abuja on 14 August. A member of the editorial board of the nationwide daily 'This Day', Paul Abayomi Ogundeji, was killed in Lagos on 17 August and Ephraim Audu, a colleague from the Nasarawa Broadcasting Service, was shot dead in Lafia on 17 October. Last but not least, the traditional ruler in Nkanu West local government, Enugu state, Igwe Uche Nwachime, was abducted from his hotel in Enugu on 29 November and his corpse was found at a refuse dump two days later. This list is incomplete. The fact that the security forces could not track down the culprits revealed once again the degree of incompetence on the part of the authorities, as well as their lack of human resources, money and political support.

Against the background of the still poor security situation, the record on *human and civil rights* was again mixed. The US State Department in its report maintained that the overall human rights record was poor and that government officials at all levels continued to commit serious abuses. The American journalist and filmmaker Andrew Berends and his Nigerian escort Samuel George were arrested by the joint military taskforce on the Nembe waterfront in Rivers state on 31 August and handed over to the state security service for taking shots for a documentary on the Niger Delta. On 12 April, their US colleagues Sandy Cioffi, Tammi Sims, Cliff Worsham and Sean Porter, along with their Nigerian counterpart Joel Bisina, who had been working on the project for years, were taken into custody for several days. All of them had entered Nigeria legally in early April with permission to complete the film. However, the filmmakers were interrogated by Nigerian security forces for lengthy periods. No formal charges were brought and they were ultimately deported.

On 16 September, the state security service shut down the fairly popular private station Channels TV and arrested managers and senior staff after it reported that President Yar'Adua would step down due to poor health. The broadcast was a hoax attributed to the News Agency of Nigeria (NAN), which denied putting out the report and maintained that a false e-mail address had been used. Nevertheless, more staff were arrested the following day and the suspension of its transmission announced by the national broadcasting commission. Sharp criticism from within the National Assembly, unions and civil society forced the commission to lift the suspension several days later (19 September) and the detained staff were released the same day.

Ever since Yar'Adua took power, there has been widespread speculation about his health. Rumours gained further momentum when on 8 November the 'Leadership' newspaper, belonging to Leadership Newspapers Group, published a report on the president's allegedly failing health. According to the paper, he had fallen critically ill and had been unable to attend a number of public functions. Hardly had the story been published than the police and state security service interrogated all senior editors, and in the subsequent edition the newspaper apologised for the offensive publication. However, the president sued Leadership Newspapers for *libel* and shortly afterwards the police charged the chairman and three staff members with defamation, injurious falsehood and the sale of material containing defamatory information. On 27 November, however, the Abuja magistrate court granted bail to the accused, who had already been out on police bail. Once again, security forces had overreacted corroborating claims that harassment of journalists and civil rights activists whenever the government saw fit was still part of its political agenda. At the same time the whole affair revealed an increasing and accelerating decline in professional journalism in both private and state media. In short, the *Nigerian media*, with its many publications and programmes, developed more and more into public relations agencies, predominantly serving dubious lobbyists as well as corporate and political interests.

On 22 January, a mild drama was played out at the state police commissioner's office in Owerri, Imo state, when the police declined to take Ralph Uwazuruike back into custody. The leader of the banned militia Movement for the Actualisation of the Sovereign State of Biafra (*MASSOB*) had turned himself in after burying his late mother in October the previous year. In addition, the federal high court in Abuja turned down a request by the federal government to return him to prison (5 March) and in June granted him a further three months of bail for post-burial rites. The court case was still pending at year's end. On the other hand, some 80 members detained in May were charged with treason in the Enugu federal high court. However, it transpired that as early as June a deep rift had opened up within the MASSOB leadership.

In February, Nigeria's official news agency NAN revealed that six men in the northern state of Bauchi were awaiting death by stoning, while 46 others were awaiting amputation. In Katsina, Kebbi and Sokoto state, *shariah courts* passed death sentences by stoning for adultery and pregnancy out of wedlock. So far, no stoning verdict has been carried out but on a few rare occasions convicted persons have been punished by amputation. In this context, the relationship between the religious marshals in Kano, known as 'Hisbah', and the Nigerian police force was still tense, the result of the unresolved and contentious legal issue of state recognition. Last but not least, according to AI, as of February 736 people were on *death row*. About 200 had been awaiting hanging for over 10 years and some for more than 20.

Some progress was made towards achieving *gender equality* when the comptroller general of immigration announced in August that a letter of consent from husbands would no longer be a requirement for a wife's passport. However, women were still required to submit copies of their marriage certificates.

Despite TI's view that Nigeria's *corruption* perceptions ranking had improved significantly, the anti-corruption campaign in fact slowed. In most cases, the anti-corruption agency EFCC, mainly financed by Western donors, failed to secure conviction of charged ex-governors and former ministers and chairpersons of parastatals. Many of the trials had stalled. The disclosure by the new EFCC chairperson that a probe would commence into more than 550 local government chairmen accused of embezzling most of the statutory allocations for years, illustrated that corruption was rooted within all three tiers of government and that the prospect of alleviating or eradicating it were bleak. On occasion, one or the other defendant was arrested, only to be released on bail shortly after. The former Delta state Governor James Ibori, detained in December the previous year, was granted bail in February. He and his wife Theresa Nkoyo Ibori became prominent figures in a legal battle in British courts over assets and money laundering. However, while his wife had been re-arrested and granted bail in London in May, the court of appeal in Kaduna ordered the release of his passport in July. Eventually in December, the London court of appeal upheld Ibori's stance against the EFCC that the legal material used against his wife and him by the London police had come out of Nigeria unlawfully. On 18 December, Lucky Igbinedion, ex-govenor of Edo state, became the only governor convicted so far. He paid a fine of $ 25,000 rather than spend six months in prison for the embezzlement of $ 21 m while in office. He also had to repay $ 3.5 m and forfeit three of his properties. The EFCC, however, filed an appeal against the verdict in the court of appeal, maintaining that such fines were no deterrent.

Foreign Affairs

Despite the fact that most African countries, including Nigeria, had forced AFRICOM, the US-Africa command, to drop its plans to locate its military headquarters in Africa and to keep them in Germany, the close *US-Nigeria* relations were predominantly shaped by security issues. This was underlined by Todd J. Moss, US deputy assistant secretary of state, bureau for African affairs, who pointed out that Nigeria was a partner in the promotion of sub-regional security, democracy and economic growth (26 January). In this context, retired Brigadier Oluwole Rotimi was appointed ambassador to the US. On 25 March, US and British military and intelligence officers and Nigerian security chiefs met in Abuja as part of the Gulf of Guinea Energy Security Strategy, to which a small number of other European countries, Canada and major donor agencies such as USAID, DFID and UNDP also belonged. In February, a one-week joint Nigerian-US military exercise 'Maritime Safari' took place off the Lagos coast. On 16 July in Abuja, 225 military communications experts from 23 countries and representatives from the AU and ECOWAS took part in another one-week exercise, 'Africa Endeavour 2008', sponsored by the US European Command. On 3 December, the senate committee on defence and the army met a high-ranking US congress delegation led by Senator James Inhofe to explore new ways of strengthening defence relations between both countries. Earlier, the 3rd THISDAY Townhall meeting on financial and stock markets was held in Abuja and attended by Lawrence Summers, former US secretary of the treasury, and by Steve Forbes of 'Forbes Magazine' together with top managers from Nigeria's financial institutions (3 October). Their presence complemented the US Eximbank's decision in June to double its Nigerian bank facility to $1 bn due to rising demand for long-term financing for infrastructure and transport projects.

The importance of security to relations with *Britain* was reflected in a joint offshore security seminar aboard HMS Albion in mid-June, but bilateral relations had a far wider political scope. On 17 May, an overwhelming majority of councillors elected the Nigerian-born Ezekiel Obasohan as mayor of the London borough of Barking and Dagenham. He thus became the first African to hold such a position of responsibility. This election confirmed the increasing political relevance of the African and *Nigerian diaspora* for British domestic policy, a trend further underlined by the visit of the Lord Mayor of the City of London, David Lewis, at the head of a business delegation to Nigeria in May. President Yar'Adua paid a visit to Britain on 15–18 July, holding talks with Prime Minister Gordon Brown on how to tackle the fast growing criminal rackets and the large-scale theft of crude oil in the Niger Delta. They agreed to establish a security training force to help Nigeria suppress the lawlessness in the region. This approach was reaffirmed by Britain's energy minister, Malcolm Wicks, who during his visit in late August offered additional assistance in restructuring the ailing energy and power sector.

Over the years, Nigeria has been a focus for the activities of DFID. This year, it earmarked £ 100 m in favour of a new six-year HIV/AIDS project and £ 50 m for combating malaria. This support was underscored by the visits of Ivan Lewis, minister for international development (November) and Gillian Merron, parliamentary under-secretary of state for international development (July). The five-day official visit of the spiritual head of the Muslim community, the Sultan of Sokoto, Alhaji Sa'ad Abubakar III, to Britain in March underlined the special relations between Britain and Nigeria, particularly the northern region. However, towards the end of the year, the British NGO Female Prisoner's Welfare Project Hibiscus put the number of Nigerian women convicted in Britain of drug trafficking and other related offences and serving varying prison sentences at 165.

While President Umaru Musa Yar'Adua visited *China* for four days (27 February– 1 March), PetroChina aborted its bid for an offshore oil block offered by Shell a few months after the China National Offshore Oil Corporation had withdrawn its bid for the block. Nevertheless, the Chinese government, through its export guarantee agency SINOSURE, offered President Yar'Adua export guarantee facilities of $ 40 bn to $ 50 bn to encourage investment in Nigeria as part of a clear strategy to woo Africa's second biggest oil and gas producer. In addition, China opened its first Confucius Institute in Nigeria at the Nnamdi Azikiwe University, Awka on 7 March, the sixth in Africa, and financed the teaching of Mandarin in a private boarding school in Ota, Ogun state. In July, one of China's top engineering firms, China Harbour Engineering Company, the major international operating division of China Communications Construction Company, signed a MoU with the African Finance Corporation, a private sector-led investment bank and development finance institution, to build a six-lane ring road worth some $ 1 bn around the volatile oil city of Port Harcourt. However, the Nigerian government in May rejected a $ 2.5 bn loan to finance high-speed rail lines from Lagos to other parts of the country. Nigeria's suspension in November of a $ 8.3 bn contract, agreed in 2006, to modernise a north-south rail route, threatened to sour bilateral relations and compounded the situation faced by China Railway Construction Corporation, whose shares in Hong Kong had fallen 18% on 4 November.

On 14 August, the chapter on the disputed *Bakassi peninsula* was finally closed when the Nigerian flag was lowered and that of Cameroon raised, thus implementing the Green Tree agreement of 2006. At short notice, the venue of the handover was changed due to serious security concerns and shifted from Abana on the peninsula to the Nigerian city of Calabar, where the solemn ceremony took place under the auspices of Nigeria's justice minister, Aondoakaa, and Cameroon's deputy prime minister, Ahmadu Ali. Troops from both countries were placed on high alert after the little-known, self-styled Nigerian group Niger Delta Defence and Security Council attacked Cameroonian gendarmes twice in June and July, killing several persons. On 31 October, the militants seized a French oil supply vessel, kidnapping 10 crew members. These French, Tunisian and Cameroonian nationals were, however, released unharmed on 11 November. Last but not least, three communities in Sardauna local government in Taraba state – Kan Iyaka, Tamiya and Dorofi – were ceded to Cameroon (14 December), in line with the International Court of Justice verdict on Bakassi and the common border.

For the first time the government and National Assembly publicly acknowledged that Nigerian nationals living in South Africa had been victims of the violence, humiliation, crime, xenophobic attacks and extra-judicial killings directed against immigrants. There was no proof that Nigerians had lost their lives during the fast-spreading riots against foreigners in June, an issue which threatened to cool bilateral relations further. Yar'Adua's first state visit to South Africa (2–4 June), which included addressing parliament and attending the Nigerian business forum, was therefore an exercise in mending fences, with the president reminding South Africans that Nigeria had been the biggest African donor in the fight against apartheid. Notwithstanding this, 450 Nigerians were deported between January and September and the consul general in Johannesburg admitted in October that about 40 Nigerians were being deported each month.

Quite a few Nigerians were deported from other countries as well, a fact that highlighted the number of Nigerians living abroad and the number of them accused of committing *crimes* or violating immigration rules. Libya deported 150 in February and 163 in May. In August, 40 Nigerians suffered a similar fate in Saudi Arabia, while the US had already deported 95 and Canada 10 in January alone. On 26 June, two Nigerians convicted of drug smuggling were executed in Indonesia and in September the Indonesian supreme court confirmed the death sentences on ten others for similar offences. The situation in the EU was not very different, as indicated by the arrest in January of more than 60 Nigerians for human trafficking. The arrests were the result of close collaboration between European police and the National Agency for the Prohibition of Traffic in Persons and Other Related Matters in Nigeria. In April, Spanish police, in a coordinated operation with the FBI, arrested 87 Nigerians suspected of defrauding Europeans and US citizens of millions of euros in a postal and internet lottery scam.

Poor health prevented President Yar'Adua from addressing the annual plenary debate of the UN in September and caused him to miss the formal commissioning of the Nigerian cultural centre in Salvador da Bahia in Brazil at the end of August. Instead, he spent almost three weeks in Saudi Arabia receiving medical treatment, which led to wild speculation back home. However, he attended the *G8 summit* in Japan in July and made an official visit to France (11–13 June), where he signed an accord promoting cooperation in developing civilian nuclear energy. He joined the AU summit in Egypt (30 June–1 July) and at the end of July received his Ghanaian counterpart John Kufuor and concluded arrangements to establish a Nigeria-Ghana chamber of commerce. On 7–9 November, German President Horst Köhler chaired the fourth German-Africa forum, which this time took place in the capital Abuja. During the 35th ordinary session of ECOWAS in Abuja, Yar'Adua was elected chairman for a one-year term (19 December).

As part of the AU/UN hybrid operation UNAMID, *Nigerian peacekeeping forces* once again suffered casualties. While only two soldiers were killed in action, 45 soldiers who had just returned from Darfur were killed in a fatal road accident in Nigeria's northeastern state of Borno (21 May). In recognition of Nigeria's leading role in UN peacekeeping, Lt. Gen. Chikadibia Isaac Obiakor, force commander of the UN mission in Liberia, was appointed by the UN secretary general as military advisor for peacekeeping operations (28 May). However, the military did not escape accusations of corruption. In September, five army officers were arrested and accused of illegally withholding the allowances of peacekeeping personnel who had openly protested in Akure, Ondo state, on 4 July. Unsurprisingly, quite a number of the latter were subsequently charged with mutiny.

Socioeconomic Developments

The international oil and gas price reached new heights and Nigeria's high quality crude rose from $ 90 a barrel at the start of the year to $ 147 in July before crashing to $ 40 in December. At mid-year, Nigeria had accumulated $ 62 bn in *foreign reserves*. However, the slump in prices, partly triggered by the meltdown on Wall Street and in other major financial markets from August, as well as by a shortfall in oil production of not less than 20%, quickly eroded the ample reserves, which stood at $ 52 bn at the end of the year. This trend continued while, at the same time, the naira began to depreciate against the dollar to 140:$ 1, with the central bank's intervention on the interbank foreign exchange market in early December leading to another revival of the parallel market.

After weeks and months of bickering over spending increases, the federal government and National Assembly agreed on the 2008 *budget* totalling naira 2.748 trillion ($ 20.8 bn), which Yar'Adua eventually signed into law on 14 April. The budget was based on a benchmark of $ 59 a barrel, above the $ 54 initially proposed by the government, and an exchange rate of 117:$ 1. A supplementary budget of naira 683 bn became law in November. At that time the bickering over the benchmark and the 2009 budget resumed. On 2 December, the president presented his budget proposal totalling naira 2.87 trillion while acknowledging the federal government's inability to fully implement the current one. While the senate passed its increased version of naira 3.049 trillion (17 December), the House of Representatives deferred its deliberations to January 2009.

For most of the year, Nigeria was a nation in darkness, since the average *power supply* dropped to an all-time low. On 19 February the president set up a task force for the accelerated expansion of the country's power infrastructure, aimed at reviving the theoretically installed capacity of some 6,000 MW within 18 months. In spite of this, the output of the state-owned power holding company of Nigeria was far below 2,000 MW in May. In a televised address on 29 May, marking his first year in office, Yar'Adua acknowledged that Nigeria would not be able to generate the required electricity for its citizens until at least 2015. Before his election, however, the president had promised to take swift action on power. Against this background, in August the government admitted that even the mid-term goal of 10,000 MW in 2010 was no longer feasible and for the umpteenth time the target date was shifted, this time to 2011. In this context, a preliminary agreement on a Nigerian-German energy partnership was signed in Abuja on 19 August, involving the German energy giants E.ON, EVONIK, Siemens and the KfW IPEX-Bank, to help boost the power supply in years to come. On 14 January, the sixth unit of the country's biggest liquefied gas plant NLNG, estimated to have cost $ 1.6 bn, was inaugurated, lifting the annual shipment to 22 m tonnes. While Nigeria exported all its gas to customers abroad, three finished gas-fuelled power stations lay idle.

As in previous years, this bleak situation, which swallowed billions of dollars due to the costly and often overpriced importation of generators and diesel, sharply contrasted with the sustained and almost explosive growth of the *telecommunications sector*. According to the Nigerian communication commission, this sector absorbed more than $ 11 bn in investment over the preceding six years and Nigeria had become one of the world's fastest growing telecom markets with a penetration rate of 30%. The market leader, MTN from South Africa, alone had an annual turnover of about $ 3 bn and the Swedish mobile network manufacturer Ericsson announced on 18 December that it had signed a deal to provide a nationwide residential fibre-optic broadband network. However, the ambitious Nigerian satellite project suffered a serious setback when the NIGCOMSAT-1 satellite, built and launched into orbit the previous year by a Chinese company, was shut down in November due to solar power problems. According to telecom experts, the satellite project was a 'white elephant in space' and the whole exercise a debacle from the start.

On 13 February, the IMF concluded Article IV consultations with Nigeria and commended it for its strong macroeconomic performance with a generally positive outlook. Shortly afterwards, its managing director, Dominique Strauss-Kahn, during his trip to four African countries, paid a visit to Nigeria (27–28 February).

In July, the *World Bank* approved two credits totalling $ 450 m to support the federal and state governments in the fight against poverty. Of this, $ 250 m was dedicated to the rural area project Fadama III, while the balance was assigned to community and social development projects. Meanwhile, the first of three projects to upgrade urban facilities in nine Lagos districts, approved by an IDA credit facility of $ 200 m in 2006, eventually took off in May. In June, Nigeria sold $ 411 m in five year and ten year bonds in a step to restructure its domestic debts, estimated at some $ 18 bn, and to fund part of its budget deficit.

The spread of HIV/AIDS continued unabated while the fight against polio lost momentum. The number of polio cases increased sharply from 279 to more than 800 cases at the end of the year, revealing that Nigeria was the only African country battling a *polio epidemic*. Two lawsuits in Abuja and Kano, in which the federal and Kano state governments sued the international pharmaceutical company Pfizer for damages and compensation, dragged on in the courts. The lawsuits stemmed from an unregistered drug test in Kano state in 1996 in which several children had died, while others had developed mental and physical deformities. However, out-of-court settlement talks broke down in early July when the governments and representatives of the victims' families turned down an offer of $ 10 m in compensation. Talks between plaintiffs and the respondent on an out-of-court settlement resumed in November, but at year's end no agreement had been reached.

During the *Olympic games* in Beijing, Nigeria's flag was hoisted three times. The national football team was narrowly defeated 1–0 by Argentina in the final, thereby winning the silver medal, while the 4 × 100 m women's relay team and the long-jumper Mrs. Blessing Okagbare won bronze. Much to the delight of Nigerians, the 2000 Olympic gold medal for the 4 × 400 m relay event was re-awarded to the country, after the executive board of the International Olympic Committee subsequently disqualified the US team for testing positive for drugs.

Nigeria in 2009

The ill-health of President Umaru Yar'Adua and his physical absence during the last weeks of 2009 exacerbated the power struggle within the ruling People's Democratic Party (PDP) and the federal executive council. Brinkmanship, manipulation and deliberate misinterpretation of various constitutional provisions prevented the seemingly hapless Vice President Goodluck Jonathan from immediately assuming presidential powers, so that towards the end of the year a military coup seemed possible. With some delay, the international financial melt-down also reached the Nigerian economy, although the serious banking crisis, which forced the central bank to inject huge amounts of money to avert a systemic crisis, was almost entirely home-made. In the wake of an unprecedented increase of violence, attacks and counter-attacks by security forces and the militias in the Niger Delta, the government eventually offered an amnesty programme, thereby making a surprising political U-turn in an effort to break the long-lasting deadlock in the oil and gas producing region.

Domestic Politics

When President Umaru Musa Yar'Adua travelled to Saudi Arabia on 23 November for follow-up medical checks, nobody thought that he would not be back by the end of the year. Ever since he had become governor of Katsina state in 1999, a position he occupied twice, it was common knowledge that he suffered from recurring *health problems*, but he was nevertheless elected president in 2007 and went abroad on several occasions for temporary medical treatment. This time, however, the situation was different because, when he arrived in a Saudi Arabian hospital in Jeddah, it was announced that he had acute pericarditis, or inflammation of the lining around the heart. His ill-health then became the focal point of domestic politics for the rest of the year, raising serious legal and constitutional issues in respect of the president's powers.

During the month of December, continuing doubts surrounding Yar'Adua's ill-health led to a period of great uncertainty, as scheming politicians and godfathers outside of government and parliament prepared for the possibility that he might be too sick to remain in office. Unfortunately, although Vice President Goodluck Jonathan had presided over cabinet meetings, articles 144, 145 and 146 of the 1999 *constitution* prevented him from assuming executive powers, a situation which led to questions over the legality of government decisions. According to the Constitution, the vice president assumes the role of president if the president sends a written declaration to the president of the Senate and the speaker of the House of Representatives, indicating that he is going on vacation or that he is otherwise unable to discharge his office, until such time as he sends a written declaration to the contrary. Moreover, the president or vice president ceases to hold office if a resolution passed by a two-thirds majority of all members of the executive council of the federation declares that the president or vice president is medically incapable of discharging his office. This declaration must be verified by a five-man medical panel, appointed by the Senate president, of whom one should be the personal physician of the office-holder concerned.

By the end of the year, however, the president had sent no such written declaration to the Senate leadership nor had the executive council of the federation passed any resolution, thus creating a serious power vacuum in which rumours of an imminent military coup were rife. Throughout December, while published opinion called for Yar'Adua's resignation, the cabinet unanimously and vigorously maintained its view that there were no grounds on which to seek his resignation. Against this background, it became apparent that the ruling PDP was engaged in a quiet power struggle, horse trading behind closed doors and grappling with the question of whether to transfer executive power to Vice President Jonathan to make him acting president. Interestingly, while this *power vacuum* brought politics at the federal level almost to a standstill, the state governors consolidated their position, forcing the National Assembly to work on a modus operandi that would empower Jonathan to become acting president, thereby preventing a possible military coup.

The controversy over the vice president's constitutionally weak position took a further twist when the chief justice of the federation, Idris Legbo Kutigi, was expected to retire at the end of the year, having reached the mandatory retirement age of 70, with his successor, Alloysius Katsina-Alu, already having been confirmed by the Senate. On 30 December, the president's absence and the vice president's lack of powers forced the outgoing chief justice to conduct the swearing-in ceremony of his successor himself, breaking with the tradition that all previous chief justices had been sworn in by the head of state. This situation prompted further scathing remarks from legal practitioners and the public concerning the *state of the nation*. On 12 March, Kutigi had already sworn in two new supreme court judges, among them a woman, Olufunmilola Adekeye, bringing the number to 17. She thus became the court's second female justice after Aloma Mariam Mukhtar. Isa Ayo Salami became president of the court of appeal, the second highest court in the land.

Despite his ill-health, President Yar'Adua made several *strategic appointments*. In a minor cabinet reshuffle, the minister of interior, retired Maj. Gen. Godwin Abbe, swapped his portfolio with the minister of defence, Shettima Mustapha (14 July). On 23 July, Ogbonnaya Okechukwu Onovo, an ethnic Igbo, became inspector-general of police in place of Mike Okiro, whose tenure had expired. This appointment, however, reminded the public of Onovo's rather dishonourable demotion to his former rank as deputy inspector-general after just three days in charge of the police force in 2007. At that time, in a contentious move, the new president had revoked his previous decision in favour of Okiro. In June, the managing director of First Bank, Sanusi Lamido Sanusi, replaced Chukwuma Soludo as governor of the central bank, and Steve Oronsanye, permanent secretary at the ministry of finance, became head of service of the federation, succeeding Ms Ama Inyingiala Pepple, who had reached the mandatory retirement age of 60. Soon after taking over, Oronsanye implemented new rules within the federal civil service, which provide for a four-year tenure renewable only once for permanent secretaries and an eight-year tenure for directors. In August, the new comptroller-general of the Nigeria customs service, Abdullahi Dikko, took over from Bernard-Shaw Nwadialo, who had been in charge only since January. Christopher Uloneme Anyanwu emerged as new director-general of the privatisation agency Bureau of Public Enterprises on 10 March, succeeding Irene Chigbue. In October, Samuel Ukura became auditor-general of the federation. Timi Alaibe became special presidential adviser on the Niger Delta, while on 8 August Mudashiru Atoyebi was appointed executive secretary of the Nigerian press council. In addition, the president approved new boards for several parastatals and agencies, such as the Nigerian Television Authority, Federal Radio Corporation of Nigeria, the News Agency of Nigeria, Airports Authority, Civil Aviation Authority and the Niger Delta Development Commission, to mention only the most important, paving the way for hundreds of lucrative positions within the public sector. Within the Nigeria Electricity Regulatory Commission, however, the chairman Ransom Owan and his commissioners were sacked in February, following allegations of corruption.

Within the *military*, Maj. Gen. Babagana Monguno assumed command of the defence intelligence agency (10 July), while his predecessor Musa Sa'id retired after 36 years' service. In October, the army promoted 261 majors and lieutenant colonels to their next rank, and in November the air force followed suit, promoting another 105 officers with the rank of squadron leader, equivalent to major, to air commodore, equivalent to brigadier. To avoid any discontent among non-commissioned officers, the military leadership also promoted more than 9,600 soldiers to their next rank. A number of army officers, implicated in the non-payment of allowances to 27 soldiers on the peace-keeping mission in Liberia the previous year, were demoted in January after they were found guilty of diverting more than $ 68,000 meant for peace-keeping troops to another military unit. Eventually, they suffered the consequences and were compulsorily retired. The soldiers, however, who had been openly protesting in Akure, Ondo state, the preceding year, were subsequently charged with mutiny and sentenced to life imprisonment by a court-martial on 27 April. On 29 August, the army headquarters commuted the sentences to seven years' imprisonment and eventually released the records of proceedings in the cases to the convicts and their counsels, who appealed the sentence at the court of appeal.

The legal aftermath of the 2007 elections was still taking its toll, although all but five of the pending gubernatorial election appeals (Ekiti, Delta, Imo, Ogun and Sokoto states) were closed at the appeal court in favour of the incumbents. On 17 February, the court of appeal sacked Olusegun Oni, governor of Ekiti state, ordering him to hand over to the speaker of the state house of assembly and ordering fresh elections in ten out of the 16 local government areas. The re-run between the candidate of the Action Congress (AC), Kayode Fayemi, who had successfully filed an appeal against the ruling of the *election petitions tribunal*, and the formally declared winner, Olusegun Oni of the PDP, was won by the latter on 25 April. The runner-up, however, again challenged the outcome at the tribunal, which was still out on a decision at year's end.

Apart from the gubernatorial elections, the courts still had to deal with petitions regarding the *National Assembly* election results in various senatorial districts and federal constituencies in Ekiti, Anambara and Oyo states. Interestingly, as in the previous year, not a single actor, party or public institution dared to sue a rival or a candidate for committing a breach of the law in the run-up to, or during, the election. However, bye-elections in Ondo for the Senate and in Adamawa state for the House of Representatives were won by the candidates of the Labour Party, Debo Olugunagba, and the PDP, Abubakar Mahmud Wambai, respectively.

To the great surprise of public and legal experts, the *supreme court* ordered the presidential election petitions tribunal to establish a fresh panel of justices to hear, *de novo*, the election petition filed by Ambrose Owuru, the candidate of the Hope Democratic Party, a rather small political grouping (27 March). It accepted his appeal and set aside the tribunal's ruling, which had dismissed the petition on the grounds that it lacked merit, although the same court, by a narrow decision of 4–3, upheld the tribunal's ruling that the challenge by Chukwuemeka Ojukwu, presidential candidate of the All Progressive Grand Alliance, was incompetent (24 April). On 17 November, however, the newly established tribunal, like the previous one, struck out the petition filed by Owuru.

After months of fierce fighting, attacks and counter-attacks by militias and security forces in the oil producing Niger *Delta*, Yar'Adua offered a presidential pardon and an amnesty programme to gunmen in the area, trying to end years of bloody unrest that had cost billions of dollars in lost revenues (24 June). The previous day, a high-ranking government delegation, led by retired Maj. Gen. Godwin Abbe and the then inspector-general of police, Mike Okiro, paved the way by meeting prominent militia leaders to discuss the amnesty terms. These included setting up 27 collection and reintegration centres for disarming the fighters, mostly in Bayelsa, Delta and Rivers states, where the violence had been at its worst. In addition, the disarmed militants would be paid 20,000 naira ($ 135) a month during the rehabilitation programme, along with a daily 1,500 naira for food. Such action had been strongly recommended by the Niger Delta Technical Committee the previous year and the fixed time frame of 60 days, from 6 August to 4 October, was supposed to offer a small window of opportunity to break the vicious circle of organised violence, crime and human rights abuses. In addition, the federal government was ready to release from prison a leader of the Movement for the Emancipation of the Niger Delta (MEND), Henry Okah, who was standing trial in a federal court for alleged gun-running and treason.

On 13 July, soon after the announcement, Okah accepted the *amnesty offer* and was set free, despite the fact that MEND had set fire to the 'Atlas Cove Jetty' in Lagos the previous day, leaving five workers dead and endangering the fuel supply to other depots. On 19 October, he was even received by the president. On 7 August, more than two dozen MEND militia members led by Victor Ben Ebikabowei met the president, who had also agreed to a dialogue with other militia leaders, such as Ateke Tom, Farah Dagogo and Government Ekpemupolo, alias Tompolo. At the end of October, Yar'Adua approved the sum of $ 1.3 bn in federal funding to build roads, hospitals and schools in the Niger Delta. Despite these good intentions and the *voluntary disarmament* of some 15,000 militia members, by early November, the promised rehabilitation and reintegration camps being set up to receive the fighters were not ready to process them. Furthermore, the ill-health of the president and his subsequent absence almost brought the peace and reconciliation process to a standstill. Notwithstanding, on 16 December, the government, represented by the vice president, inaugurated a presidential committee and four sub-committees on the Niger Delta. Shortly thereafter, however, MEND claimed to have attacked a major pipeline in Rivers state as a 'warning strike', a claim which security forces and oil companies denied. Furthermore, in Yenagoa (Bayelsa state), and Warri (Delta state) heavily armed police forces were deployed to disperse former militants protesting over the non-payment of amnesty allowances (22/23 December), claiming that they had been promised some $ 2,000 each in return for laying down their weapons earlier in the year, but that the government had failed to pay.

Prior to that, there were strong indications that this volatile situation, exacerbated by *hostage-taking* and piracy, was about to get completely out of hand, causing a further serious shortfall in oil production and revenues and leading to the deaths of dozens of security personnel, militia members, oil workers and civilians. In addition, the growing crisis had led to a massive increase in security expenditure, the oil companies having spent an estimated $ 3.7 bn the previous year. As before, the main oil companies such as Shell, Chevron and Agip, operating in a joint venture with the Nigerian National Petroleum Corporation (NNPC), had been the main target of organised attacks and had to shut down oil and gas production several times. In addition, within the first seven months of the year more than 500 people from Nigeria and countries such as Britain, Russia, Lebanon and Lithuania were taken hostage. Most of them were released almost unharmed after militants and criminals had collected ransoms from the companies or extorted money from the victims' families. Some of the hostages were freed by security forces. Virtually all of the kidnappings took place in the southeast and the Niger Delta. Two Britons, Robin Barry Hughes and Matthew Maguire, who had been taken hostage in September the previous year, were released by MEND on 20 April and 12 June respectively.

In a major reorganisation of the security forces in the Niger Delta, 'Operation Flush Out III' was merged with 'Operation Restore Hope' in March. Led by Maj. Gen. Yakin Bello and his deputy, Brigadier Nanvem Rintip, the more centralised task force eventually started a large-scale *military assault* in May, killing dozens of militants and destroying a number of strongholds, such as the notorious Camp 5. The principal militant groups, however, declared an 'all-out war', and several military personnel fell victim to their counter-attacks. At this time, the federal government back-pedalled and presented its amnesty programme, which, however, did not convince local analysts.

On 8 June, Royal Dutch *Shell* agreed a $ 15.5 m out-of court settlement in the Ogoni case, initiated 13 years earlier in the US. Shell had been due to go to trial, accused of complicity in the show trial and subsequent execution of human rights activist Ken Saro-Wiwa and eight of his comrades-in-arms in Nigeria in 1995. Moreover, at year's end, a district court in The Hague in the Netherlands ruled that it was competent to handle a case brought against Royal Dutch Shell and its Nigerian branch by Nigerian farmers in the Niger Delta and the environmental group Friends of the Earth Netherlands, who were suing for compensation for alleged damage caused by oil spills.

While the proposed amnesty and disarmament exercise in the Niger Delta brought the violence at least temporarily to a standstill, the Muslim north and the eastern part of the Middle Belt experienced a wave of *sectarian clashes* between security forces and Islamic sects such as 'Boko Haram', 'Kalo-Kato' and the 'Nigerian Muslim Brothers', also known as the 'Islamic Movement in Nigeria', sympathetic to the Iranian revolution but wrongly called Shi'ites. On 26 July, violence broke out in Bauchi, the capital of the state of the same name, when some members of 'Boko Haram' were arrested on suspicion of plotting to attack a police station. Within 48 hours, the unrest had spread to the sect's stronghold in the Borno state capital, Maiduguri, and to Yobe and Kano states, where the sect clashed with police forces, leaving dozens of militants and several policemen dead and a police station burnt to the ground. More was to come, and security forces including army personnel were deployed to quell the uprising, which turned Maiduguri into a battlefield for days, leaving at least 700 people dead and thousands homeless. The leader of the sect, 39-year-old Mohammed Yusuf, and scores of his followers, including former state commissioner for religious affairs and the sect's alleged financier, Buji Foi, were killed while in custody, highlighting the fact that extrajudicial killing was still practised by the security forces. A high-ranking delegation, led by the justice minister and attorney-general Michael Aondoakaa, hypocritically apologised to the UN in Geneva for the killings and promised to punish those responsible. By year's end, no investigation, let alone any punishment, could be reported.

The 'Boko Haram' *sect* had been fighting for the implementation of strict Islamic law for years and was known to the security agencies under various names. Its leader Mohammed Yusuf, thought to be a theology undergraduate drop-out from the Islamic University of Medina, was considered a charismatic preacher. He attracted illiterate and jobless youths, as well as educated people and school and university drop-outs, who felt betrayed by mainstream Islam. In November of the previous year, he, along with some of his followers, was arrested for public incitement through preaching and charged in court in the capital Abuja but, on 20 January, they were granted bail. In 2006, the federal government had charged Yusuf with belonging to an international terrorist network, but the charges never reached court.

On 21 February, the 19th *Shehu of Borno*, Mustapha Umar Ibn El-Kameni, died at the age of 85 in an Egyptian hospital in Cairo and was buried in his palace in Maiduguri. His successor, 51-year-old Abba Kyari Abubakar Ibn Umar Garbei El-Kanemi, was turbaned on 4 March and received his staff of office on 30 May, formalising government recognition of his unique position, which traces its authority back to the ancient Kanem-Borno Empire.

Towards the end of the year, in the city of Bauchi, the Islamic sect 'Kala-Kato', which rejects modernity, Western education, radio and television, and adheres only to the Qur'an, clashed with security forces, who had intervened in an intra-sectarian power struggle. Some 40 persons died during the two-day *uprising*, including security personnel. The incidents around the 'Boko Haram' and 'Kala-Kato' sects recalled the Maitatsine uprising in 1980, which left several thousand people dead. The remnants of the movement, founded by the self-proclaimed prophet Mohammed Marwa Maitatsine (meaning 'the one who curses'), were thought to have kept alive his ideas, which are inspired by Mahdism.

In the aftermath of the clashes with 'Boko Haram', a puritanical Darul-Islam community near Mokwa in Niger state came to limelight. It had been founded some 16 years previously to live and practise pure Islam. Although there was no proof that the community had any relationship with the sects mentioned above, the federal and state governments sacked the settlement in a joint action and dispatched the approximately 4,000 members to their respective states of origin or home countries.

On 11 September, the 'Nigerian Muslim Brothers' under the leadership of its founder Ibrahim El-Zakzaky were marking the annual

Quds (Jerusalem) day in their stronghold Zaria, in Kaduna state and in other northern cities, in solidarity with the plight of the Palestinians. The procession in the ancient *city of Zaria*, however, clashed with police forces who opened fire, killing at least two people and injuring three. According to police sources, armed members of the group had shot at police, confirming the suspicion that the radical Islamic group was in possession of weapons. Ever since the group was founded in the late 1980s, its aim had been to establish a theocratic state, by force if necessary, and the number of its followers had grown steadily. In the meantime, it had established a formidable network all over the country's far north, rejecting the formal introduction of shariah law as half-hearted.

As in previous years, there were several violent *communal clashes* in a number of states. In Gada and Kasanga village in Mashegu local government (Niger state), at least half a dozen people were killed in February in a clash over the relocation of the village market. At least four people lost their lives and almost a dozen were injured at the end of March in a controversy between pastoralists and farmers in Marke and Boyoni villages in Miga and Kaugama local governments (Jigawa state). In Okene (Kogi state), the army had to help restore peace in early July following the inability of the police to bring under control a crisis that had claimed no fewer than eight lives and involved the destruction of several properties. For years, Okene had been plagued by recurring violent clashes arising from political differences and disagreements between clans. In mid-July, a crisis broke out between the Nyieva and Uyough communities in Kwande local government (Benue state), leaving six people dead and hundreds displaced. In mid-August, five people were killed as a result of a boundary dispute in villages along the administrative border between Abia and Akwa Ibom states. And in December, fighting between cattle herdsmen and peasants in Udeni village in Nasarawa local government (Nasarawa state) led to the death of some 30 people.

In most of these clashes the culprits were not brought to book. The violent unrest in Jos in November of the previous year, however, in which more than 400 people were left dead, saw not less than six *investigations*, examining both the immediate and indirect causes. While the federal government inaugurated the nine-member panel of inquiry on 5 February, chaired by retired Maj. General Emmanuel Abisoye, the Plateau state governor had already set up another panel in January, chaired by the former attorney-general of the federation Bola Ajibola. In addition, both chambers of the National Assembly, as well as the house of Plateau state Assembly and the defence headquarters, set up their own inquiries behind the scenes. The ex post review and the question as to who had the authority to probe such an issue, said much about how the Nigerian political elite ran public affairs. This case proved for the umpteenth time that, in the still unstable Nigerian political system, the elite could set aside almost any rule and pursue different agendas whenever it saw fit. While Ajibola submitted his as yet unpublished report on 27 October, within the period under review, the Abisoye panel could not wind up its sittings until the year's end.

When Jacob Gyang Buba, former comptroller-general of customs, became the fourth Gbong Gwom of Jos, the paramount ruler of the Berom Kingdom in Plateau state (1 April), it underlined once again how more and more high-ranking officers were cleverly occupying the positions of traditional leaders, which offered the possibility of utilising for their local political interests an institution corrupted and discredited by successive military regimes. His predecessor, the late Victor Dung Pam, had been a retired deputy inspector-general of police.

The *anti-corruption campaign* slowed down again, partly reflected in the poor ranking of TI, which placed Nigeria 130th of 180 countries in the corruption perception index. Most of those charged were released on bail or even had their cases dismissed. Only in a few instances did the court sentence respondents to imprisonment. For example, Attahiru Bafarawa, former governor of Sokoto state, was granted bail in December, soon after he had been arrested. The same applied to former comptroller-general of customs, Hamman Bello Ahmed, in August. The trials of the Rivers state chief of staff, Nyesom Wike (17 July), the ex-chairman of the police equipment foundation, Kenny Martins (24 November), and the former health minister, Adenike Grange, and her ex-minister of state, Gabriel Aduku (10 December), as well as that of the former governor of Delta state, James Ibori (17 December), were even quashed, indicating that the Economic and Financial Crimes Commission (EFCC), mainly financed by Western donors, generally lacked the competent and independent personnel to provide sufficient evidence. In the cases of Martins and Ibori, however, the commission appealed the verdict.

Bode George, former chairman of the Nigerian ports authority and ex-vice-chairman of the PDP, was sentenced to two years in prison along with five other board members (26 October). They were found guilty of inflating contracts and abusing public funds worth some $ 500 m. Bode George's was the highest profile conviction since Yar'Adua had taken office in 2007. The EFCC was also able to hand over assets worth naira 44 bn, including a hotel in Abuja, to the Bayelsa state government (9 July) as part of the property recovered from the state's former governor Diepreye Alamieyeseigha, who was briefly jailed for *corrupt practices* in 2007. The judicial annulment of the right of occupancy of a valuable piece of land in Port Harcourt reminded the Nigerian public that the family of the late military dictator, Sani Abacha, still owned property and a lot of money, siphoned off while he was in power. The supreme court revoked the unlawful occupancy and returned the land to the original owner. In addition, Abba Abacha, a son of the deceased, was convicted in Switzerland of being a member of a criminal organisation and had assets worth $ 350 m seized (20 November). Switzerland had already returned some $ 700 m to Nigeria during Obasanjo's presidency. Against this background, it became clear in March that the former subsidiary of the US construction company Halliburton,

Kellog, Brown and Root (KBR), had been bribing Nigerian officials in connection with the construction of liquefied natural gas facilities in the Niger Delta between 1995 and 2004. While Halliburton and KBR agreed to pay heavy fines in the US, at year's end the Nigerian authorities had not brought any charges.

As in previous years, in most states, including the Federal Capital Territory, Abuja, *security* generally deteriorated and the number of policemen and civilians killed increased significantly, although the figures did not include those who fell victim to the violence in the Niger Delta. Well over 100 policemen lost their lives on duty and Abuja and other urban centres in the far north became new hubs of organised crime. On 19 March, gunmen raided a foreign exchange office in the Kano metropolis, killing six policemen in the Wapa area, where hundreds of moneychangers do business. In Kabba, Kogi state, three policemen were shot dead on 6 August; two local government chairmen were also kidnapped, but were freed two days later. In the city of Kaduna, a Canadian, Julie Mulligan, was kidnapped on 16 April while visiting Nigeria for a conference. She was released after two weeks and the ring-leader of the kidnap gang was arrested soon afterwards. This was one of the rare occasions when the police arrested a member of an organised criminal gang. On 3 April, a Sokoto state civil servant, Mustapha Isa Tela, was murdered, and on 7 July in Bauchi state, businessman Michael Ogboh was killed by unknown assailants.

In the southern parts of the country, the *crime* rate continued to be high. In two incidents in Edo state alone, 15 policemen lost their lives. On 11 February, a gang of robbers killed seven policemen and, on 25 March, eight policemen attached to the convoy of the Delta state commissioner of police also fell victim to armed robbers. In October, the president approved a joint military/police patrol in the state in response to the extraordinarily high crime rate. In Abia state, five policemen died on 30 June when a gang attempted to abduct expatriates working for a bottling company in Aba and, on 8 October, the Delta state police command lost five of its staff in an attack by a kidnap-syndicate operating within and outside the state. Many more people were killed during raids on long-distance buses and bullion vans and others were assassinated or kidnapped. But the killing of football star Abel Tador, captain of Bayelsa United, which had just clinched the Nigerian championship, caused a nationwide outcry (14 June). Two other famous stars were luckier and escaped death after being kidnapped. 'Nollywood' star Pete Edochie was taken hostage on 16 August in Anambra state but was set free unharmed two days later, while retired Capt. Elechi Amadi, the author of the famous 'The Concubine' and other novels, was kidnapped on 5 January in Rivers state but released shortly after. On 20 September, Bayo Ohu, editor of the 'Guardian' newspaper (Lagos), was shot dead in his apartment in Lagos. On 21 November, Charles Nsiegbe, who was close to the Rivers state governor, died from gunshot wounds in Port Harcourt and, on 20 December, the former ambassador to the Ukraine, Hakaire Ignatius Ajuru, fell victim to highway robbers in Abia state. In July, against the background of the *worsening security* situation the police service commission approved the recall of almost 1,600 police officers who had unilaterally and without due process been sacked in 2008.

With regard to *human and civil rights abuses*, the situation improved slightly. A court in Abuja adjourned *sine die* the criminal defamation suit initiated by the president against the 'Leadership' newspaper the previous year (18 June). Moreover, a law that had forced hospitals to withhold emergency treatment for victims of gunshot wounds until a police report had been filed was lifted in October. On 8 April, the verdict against Lateef Sofolahan and Aminu Mohammed, who were given long prison sentences for conspiracy and the attempted murder of the late Afenifere, Abraham Adesanya, reminded the public that a number of well-known people close to the late Sani Abacha, such as former chief security officer Hamza Al-Mustapha, were still on trial, proceedings having begun in 1999. On 5 September, Gani Fawehinmi, one of the most outspoken human rights lawyers and democratic activists, died at the age of 71. Under military rule, he had defended many political dissidents and been arrested, detained and charged more than 30 times.

Foreign Affairs

Since Yar'Adua came to power in 2007, Nigeria's close relationship with the *United States* had cooled considerably. This relationship was not helped by the flawed elections in 2007, or by the fact that new US President Barack Obama snubbed the Nigerian leadership on his first African trip as president (10–11 July) by visiting Ghana rather than the sub-region's leading country. The critical remarks by Secretary of State Hillary Clinton during her two-day visit to Nigeria (12–13 August) about its reputation for corruption aggravated the situation and were subsequently strongly condemned by leading politicians. In addition, the Nigerian president's absence from the annual meeting of the UN General Assembly in September was seen as a deliberate diplomatic protest against the attitude of the US, which the federal government considered to be unfair. This discomfort had been reinforced by the rejection of the newly appointed ambassador to the US, Tunde Adeniran, a retired professor of political science and former education minister and ambassador to Germany. He was meant to succeed retired Brigadier Oluwole Rotimi, who had been recalled in February for gross insubordination. The US-government's refusal to accept Adeniran's appointment was said to hinge on the arrest of his son, who lived in the US and had been charged with having raped a girl in Baltimore a short time before. As a result, shortly before he left for Saudi Arabia for medical treatment, Yar'Adua nominated Adebowale Adefuye, who had served as deputy high commissioner in Jamaica and Britain. But bilateral relations almost hit rock bottom when, on 25 December, 23-year-old Nigerian Umar Faruk Abdulmutallab attempted to blow up a Delta Airlines flight on its final approach to Detroit. The suspect's close relations with al-Qaida in Yemen soon came to light and the anchorless Nigerian embassy was weighed down by the challenge of handling the case in accordance with international diplomatic conventions.

Despite diplomatic irritations, the assistant secretary of state for Africa, Johnnie Carson, pointed out in May that Nigeria remained a *strategic partner*, supplying the US with almost 50% of its oil and a significant amount of liquefied gas. Furthermore, US investment in Nigeria was well in excess of $ 15 bn. This statement was mirrored in the ongoing efforts to boost maritime security in the Gulf of Guinea, which was plagued by raids on oil facilities, piracy and drug smuggling. To this end, the US navy was holding training courses on board the USS Nashville, including in hand-to-hand combat and intelligence gathering, for partners from around the Gulf within the framework of the 'Africa Partnership Station', a naval component of the US-Africa command AFRICOM. The exercises in Nigerian coastal waters took place in March and June, and Rear Admiral William Loeffler visited Lagos in March as part of his Africa tour. In early September, chiefs of naval staff from Ghana, Kenya and South Africa met in Uyo, Akwa Ibom state, for a conference on maritime security. Towards the end of the year, Nigeria and São Tomé and Príncipe agreed to set up a joint maritime military commission. On 11 June, Delta Airlines started twice-weekly flights between Abuja and New York, the first direct route between the Nigerian capital and the US. On 3 June, the former secretary of state, Colin Powell, attended a conference to celebrate ten years of democracy in Nigeria and, in October, Nigeria was given a clean bill of health for its drugs control programme.

Over the years, Nigeria has been a focus of the activities of the UK's DFID. In February, the department confirmed its former commitment and unfolded a six-year development agenda worth £ 500 m to aid development targets and comprehensive health schemes and to combat malaria. The focus of bilateral relations during the year turned on the question of repatriation of the more than 800 Nigerians serving various terms in British jails for sex, drugs, immigration and various minor offences. Nigerians were second only to Jamaicans in the numbers of foreign inmates. Britain was even willing to refurbish Nigerian prisons in order to allow Nigerians to serve out their sentences at home. However, Nigerian law would have to be amended to allow prisoners to be transferred without the individual's consent.

On 19 November, the *European Union* signed an agreement worth € 677 m for the period 2009–13, which was designed to help Nigeria tackle development challenges in three main areas. The fund, financed through the EDF, was intended to be distributed as follows: € 166 m for peace and security; € 297 m for governance and human rights; € 105 m for energy and regional integration; € 99 m for miscellaneous issues such as facilitating health, cultural and technical cooperation. In addition, the EU sponsored the anti-corruption agencies, the EFCC and the Independent Corrupt Practices and Other Related Offences Commission, to the tune of some 85% of their annual budget, but threatened to cut funding the following year should the government fail to produce clearer results in its fight against corruption.

Relations with *China* focused on resuming ambitious technical projects. In February, the 'China Great Wall Industry Corporation' finally agreed to replace the communication satellite NIGCOMSAT 1, which had disappeared in space in 2008 after being launched into orbit by a Chinese company in 2007. In addition, and after a lot of bickering, the federal government eventually gave the go-ahead to continue with the contract, worth $ 8.3 bn, to modernise the north-south rail route, which had been suspended the previous year. When, in early October, Sinopec (China Petroleum & Chemical Corporation) acquired the Canadian Addax Petroleum Corporation through its subsidiary 'Mirror Lake', China eventually made its long expected move into the direct exploitation of Nigeria's oil and gas fields. On 28 November, the Nigerian ambassador to China acknowledged that Nigerians accounted for about 90% of the crimes committed by Africans in China. At that time, more than 100 Nigerians were serving various jail terms and more than 300 were awaiting deportation. Some were even on death row. More than two dozen had died in jail or had been executed. However, an estimated 20,000

Africans were believed to be living in Guangdong province, many of them students and traders from Nigeria.

When *Russia*'s President Dmitry Medvedev visited Nigeria in June and Gazprom and the NNPC agreed a joint investment of at least $ 2.5 bn, it became obvious that another heavy-weight global player in the energy sector had finally arrived in the country (24 June). The new company, Nigaz, a 50/50 joint venture, proposes to build pipelines, refineries and gas power stations in various parts of the country. Moreover, the planned giant gas pipeline across the Sahara, agreed by Nigeria, Niger and Algeria on 3 July, also offered long-term perspectives for Russian capital. Yet another global player, *Brazil*'s state-run Petrobas, which owned 20% of the deep offshore oilfield Akpo, revealed that plans were under way for long-term investments in Nigeria second only to those in the Gulf of Mexico. The increasing economic cooperation was underlined politically by a three-day state visit by President Yar'Adua (29–31 July) to Brazil. At the second Africa–South America Summit in Caracas, Venezuela, in late September, however, he was represented by the vice president. Finally, in June, the Indian energy giant ONGC Mittal Energy announced its readiness to start exploration of its own deepwater block.

As for relations with African states, Yar'Adua chaired an ECOWAS meeting in Abuja on 15 October amidst concern over the crises in Guinea and Niger, which resulted in an arms embargo on Guinea on 17 October and the suspension of Niger on 20 October. In July, the president had already taken part in the 15th summit of the Non-Aligned Movement in Egypt, but was conspicuously absent at the AU summit in early February and at a follow-up summit in July in Libya, where nearly half of Africa's leaders were discussing a proposed 'African government'.

As in previous years, Nigeria was heavily engaged in the crisis-ridden *Darfur* region and continuously involved in training courses for several hundred military personnel and police forces at the peacekeeping centre Jaji, in Kaduna state. Shortly before his term ended on 31 August, the outgoing commander of the joint UN/AU

UNAMID force, Nigerian Martin Luther Agwai, said he believed that the Darfur region was no longer in a state of war. He maintained that the conflict was of low intensity and had descended into banditry, reflecting the increasing fragmentation of the rebel groups. On 29 October, the 15-member AU Peace and Security Council met in Abuja to consider the report on Darfur by a team of African 'wise men' led by Thabo Mbeki. The Sudanese government was represented by its vice president, after President Omar al-Bashir had had second thoughts and decided to stay away, thus avoiding possible arrest following the issue of a warrant by the ICC. Despite Agwai's rather optimistic view, UNAMID staff were still experiencing rebel attacks, kidnapping and killings by rebels and, on 2 December, the controversial Nigerian diplomat Ibrahim Gambari was appointed as the new head of the UNAMID mission and expected to take up his post on 1 January of the following year.

Ever since Nigeria's independence, relations with *Israel* have been controversial, with diplomatic ties having been broken off in 1973 and restored only in 1992. However, for Nigerian Christians a pilgrimage to Israel or Rome is seen as the equivalent of the Islamic hajj, and Nigerian military and intelligence services have made use of Israel's competence in these fields for years. In addition, more than 100 Israeli companies have been doing business in Nigeria. In that context, Avigor Lieberman, who doubled as deputy prime minister and minister for foreign affairs, visited Nigeria in early September as part of his Africa tour; he met his counterpart and the vice president and signed a trade agreement. The two governments also concluded a deal for the manufacture and delivery of patrol boats worth some $ 25 m.

Last but not least, on 15 October, Nigeria was elected to serve on the UN *Security Council* for the period 2011–12, and in July the president attended the G-8 summit in Italy.

Socioeconomic Developments

The international oil and gas price recovered over the course of the year to some $ 77 per barrel at the end of December, up from $ 40 at the beginning of the year. Foreign reserves, which stood at $ 52 bn in January, fell by some $ 10 bn by December, mainly triggered by the aftermath of the international financial melt-down the previous year and a shortfall in oil production during the first six months caused by the unrest in the Niger Delta. By early February, the naira had depreciated by more than 20% within two months. As a result, regulators announced tighter controls on the more than 1,100 bureaux de change (25 February), to which the central bank makes a weekly sale of some $ 200 m. They were eventually split into class A and class B sections to allow easier supervision. Class A was allowed to import and transfer foreign exchange provided they had a minimum paid-up capital of naira 500 m at all times and a minimum deposit of $ 200,000 with the central bank, while class B was permitted to sell a maximum of $ 5,000 per transaction. Despite these actions, the local currency fell to naira 188:$ 1 on the *parallel market* within two weeks before recovering to naira 160:$ 1 towards the end of March. Shortly before the end of his five-year term on 29 May, however, central bank governor Soludo announced that the bank would lift the restrictions and would return to a fully liberalised foreign exchange market within three months. At year's end, the naira rebounded and was trading at 150:$ 1.

Against the background of these controversial regulations, the president finally signed the 2009 *budget* into law on 10 March. The budget, totalling naira 3.101 trillion ($ 21.2 bn) had eventually been approved by both chambers of the National Assembly on 18 February. However, the budget left key benchmarks unchanged, despite the reality on the ground. While the assumed exchange rate was put at naira 125:$ 1, the projected oil price per barrel was $ 45 and the expected oil output 2.3 m barrel a day.

On the eve of his departure to Saudi Arabia for medical treatment, Yar'Adua presented a 2010 budget proposal of naira 4.079 trillion, an increase in spending of 31.5%. A supplementary budget, however, passed by parliament shortly thereafter, did not come into force because the vice president refused to sign it into law, having taken the position that he would not sign anything that required the president's approval. Despite this issue, which could have raised sensitive constitutional problems, the 2009 budget was not fully implemented until March of the following year, highlighting the fact that in early November the government had only implemented some 30% of the budget, underlining its own lack of competence in handling this central political issue.

In an unprecedented move, the central bank, under its new governor, Sanusi Lamido Sanusi, injected naira 400 bn ($ 2.6 bn) into five undercapitalised banks on 14 August and sacked their top management in an effort to prevent a systemic *banking crisis*. While the 24 Nigerian banks accounted for more than 60% of the market capitalisation of Nigeria's stock exchange, the five affected banks accounted for as much as 40%. On 2 October, the central bank intervened again, providing yet another naira 200 bn ($ 1.3 bn) to four more banks expected to face a grave liquidity crisis, and dismissed their chief executives and some of their staff. Hardly had they been removed from their posts than the EFCC arrested and detained all those it could get hold of, and prosecuted them on multiple fraud charges. Within a rather short period of time, the EFCC recovered some $ 300 m of bad debts, but an estimated $ 10 bn were still outstanding. In mid October, the central bank released a list of major bank debtors, including such powerful people as former vice president Atiku Abubakar, who owed $ 730,000. However, towards year's end all detainees were granted bail and set free. Despite the banking crisis and its legal implications, the external *debt* portfolio was kept stable at some $ 3.75 bn, while domestic debts rose to the enormous amount of some $ 17 bn. In November, however, the World Bank estimated an inflow of almost $ 10 bn of foreign exchange from Nigerian citizens abroad, representing 4.7% of Nigeria's GDP and making the country the sixth highest recipient of diaspora remittances of all developing nations.

The growth of the *telecommunications* sector continued and the number of mobile phone subscribers was put at some 67 million. Notwithstanding the sector's success story, the saga of the former state monopoly, Nigerian Telecommunication Limited (NITEL), took a new twist when, on 1 June, the government resumed control of the fixed line operator and its mobile subsidiary M-TEL, of which a majority stake had been taken over by the local Nigerian Transnational Corporation Limited in 2006. The government justified its action by citing lack of investment and unpaid debts and tried to find a new investor. On 8 December, however, it extended the deadline for a third time, allowing another month for prospective bidders after two previous deadlines had lapsed without any bids being made.

The government totally failed to reverse the disastrous trend in the *power* sector, which produced less than 3,000 MW instead of the promised 6,000 MW. Moreover, it continued to subsidise fuel, mostly imported, to the tune of some $ 4 bn and put the oil sector reform bill on hold.

In July, US-based Nigerian writer E.C. Osondu won the 'Caine Prize for African Writing', and in early November the two-day 'African Media Leaders Forum' took place in Lagos, with some 100 publishers from almost all countries participating. Shortly before, 50 years of television in Nigeria had been celebrated, recalling the introduction of the new media on 31 October 1959 by the government of the then Western Region. These minor achievements contrasted sharply with the surprise defeat of Nigeria, the defending FIFA U17 champion, by the maverick Switzerland in the final in Abuja on 15 November.

On 30 July, after years of litigation, the Kano state government signed an out-of-court settlement worth $ 75 m with US pharmaceutical company *Pfizer* over an unregistered drug test in 1996, in which several children had died, while others had developed mental problems and/or physical deformities. $ 30 m were to go to the victims and their families and the same amount was to be used to provide health projects in the state. $ 10 m were to pay for litigation and $ 5 m for settling sundry expenses. This settlement did not affect charges against Pfizer filed by the federal government, which was seeking billions of dollars in damages. In November, however, Pfizer insisted on DNA tests to ensure that the real victims benefited from the settlement, thereby shifting the responsibility for the payment to a settlement team led by retired supreme court judge Abubakar Wali, and delaying full payment till at least 2010.

Nigeria in 2010

The ill-health of President Umaru Musa Yar'Adua, which for months caused a serious leadership and constitutional crisis, the unconventional resolution of that crisis and the subsequent death of the ailing president in early May dominated politics for quite some time. The aftermath of the crisis resulted in an unprecedented amendment of the constitution, the first amendment by a democratically legitimised institution in the history of independent Nigeria. In addition, the law makers passed a new electoral act and the new and highly respected chairman of the electoral commission, Attahiru Jega, a professor of political science, committed himself to establishing a new electoral register and to the running of fair and impartial elections. All eyes of the political actors, however, were on the forthcoming elections in early 2011, and the incumbent President Goodluck Ebele Jonathan cautiously prepared the ground for becoming the candidate of the ruling if somewhat weakened People's Democratic Party (PDP). The re-appearance of the former military dictator and twice presidential candidate, Muhammadu Buhari, heralded a fierce and initially unexpected open battle for the highest office. The general security situation deteriorated, with a significant increase in assassinations and killings.

Domestic Politics

By early February, the ill-health and physical absence of President Yar'Adua had brought politics at the federal and state levels almost to a standstill and, after the failure of the president's appointed cabinet ministers to declare the president unfit to rule, as required by the constitution, a high percentage of the 36 locally powerful state governors urged the National Assembly to pass a resolution enabling the vice president to act as president. Eventually, on 9 February, parliament almost unanimously resolved that the vice president should, as acting president, discharge the functions of the office of both president and commander-in-chief of the armed forces of the federation. A BBC interview with Yar'Adua, allegedly speaking from his sickbed in Saudi Arabia, had been broadcast on 12 January and served as the basic argument for the implementation of section 145 of the constitution. Furthermore, the parliamentarians used a common law rule, the 'doctrine of necessity', to support their move, which was without precedent and was not explicitly backed by the constitution. Nonetheless, Vice President Jonathan's appointment as *acting head of state* was eventually backed by law. The very next day, 10 February, Jonathan chaired his first cabinet meeting and, in his first major decision, immediately demoted the powerful justice minister and attorney general, Michael Aondoakaa, to minister of special duties. He had been among the group of ministers working with the ailing president's wife and his closest aides who had held out most strenuously against formally transferring power to the vice president during Yar'Adua's absence of more than two months. To seal his authority, Jonathan made a wide-ranging broadcast to the nation on the same day, in which he pledged to prioritise peace in the Niger Delta, punish those behind religious unrest and work towards credible national elections in 2011. However, the majority of the cabinet still maintained that there were no grounds for declaring Yar'Adua unfit to govern, thereby prolonging Jonathan's period as acting president.

On 24 February, President Yar'Adua returned home secretly from Medina, Saudi Arabia, triggering renewed uncertainty over the leadership. But the ailing president was not seen in public and neither did Jonathan or any of his senior staff meet with him before he passed away late on 5 May. Groups of clerics had been invited to meet with the president on his sickbed in the state house. While the acting president was *sworn in* as president the next day by the chief justice, Umaru Musa Yar'Adua was buried according to Muslim rites in his northern hometown of Katsina, paving the way for the forthcoming elections in 2011 – the most hotly contested since Nigeria's democratic restart in 1999.

On 1 March, Jonathan set up an advisory panel headed by the highly respected retired Lieutenant General Theophilus Danjuma, who had been chief of army staff on the eve of the Second Republic and defence minister during elected President Olusegun Obasanjo's first term in office. In addition, on 11 February, Jonathan had already sworn in 17 top civil servants in a clear-cut sign of government business returning to normal. Within the following weeks and months, he made several *strategic appointments*. Retired Lieutenant General Aliyu Gusau, who had already served in the same capacity under former President Obasanjo, replaced national security adviser, retired Major General Abdullahi Sarki Mukhtar on 8 March, and soon after, on 17 March, Jonathan dissolved his cabinet. He eventually announced the new federal executive council on 6 April, reappointing several of his predecessor's cabinet members, such as Adetokunbo Kayode and Mrs Diezani Alison-Madueke, who took over the ministries of defence and petroleum respectively. Other vital portfolios were assigned to new personnel: finance to Olusegun Aganga, former Goldman Sachs executive in Britain, and justice to Mohammed Bello Adoke.

The controversial chairman of the *Independent National Electoral Commission* (INEC), Maurice Iwu, had to step down at the end of April, and in June the president's nominee, Attahiru Jega, a political scientist, was approved by the council of state and ultimately confirmed by the Senate. He had made a name for himself as a fierce leader of the union of university academic staff during the military regime of Ibrahim Babangida and as a respected vice chancellor of Bayero University Kano, in a situation threatened by Islamic fundamentalism. On 18 May, both chambers of the National Assembly confirmed the appointment of Kaduna state Governor Namadi Sambo, an architect and an ethnic Hausa-Fulani of Muslim faith, as vice president, thereby endorsing the geo-political and religious balance between north and south. Sambo, a relative newcomer to national politics, was succeeded by his deputy Patrick Ibrahim Yakowa, the first Christian politician to govern Kaduna state, which is deeply divided between a predominantly Muslim north and a Christian south. On 12 May, presidential spokesman Olusegun Adeniyi, who was appointed by the late president Yar'Adua, had resigned and accepted a Harvard University fellowship. He was succeeded by Ima Niboro. Mike Oghiadomhe was named chief of staff to the president, Hassan Tukur principal secretary and, in a surprising move, President Jonathan relieved Shehu Ladan, the group managing director of the Nigeria National Petroleum Corporation (NNPC), of his duties just seven weeks after his appointment and assigned this prestigious position to Austin Oniwon on 17 May.

Other appointments followed and, in August, the president eventually appointed Mrs Bolanle Onagoruwa as the substantive director general of the privatisation agency, the Bureau of Public Enterprises, replacing Christopher Anyanwu, who had been suspended in March. Mrs Precious Kassey Garba was named chief economic adviser and Barth Nnaji head of a special task force for the dilapidated power sector. In mid-September, the national security adviser, retired Lieutenant General Aliyu Gusau, resigned, allegedly planning to seek the ruling party's nomination to run in the presidential elections in early 2011. Retired Colonel Kayode Are temporarily took over the position until a former chief of defence staff, retired General Andrew Azazi, emerged as the new security adviser on 4 October. In December, former inspector-general of police Mike Okiro became chairman of the newly formed private public partnership outfit NATFORCE, established in July, whose purpose was to support the efforts of security agencies to combat the importation of small arms, ammunition and light weapons into the country. Femi Ajayi was appointed director general of the National Drug Law Enforcement Agency.

On 8 September, the *security services* experienced far-reaching shake-ups. Within the military, President Jonathan retired all service chiefs but one, making the chief of the air staff, Air Vice Marshal

Oluseyi Petinrin, chief of defence staff. Major General Onyeabor Azubike Ihejirika was appointed as chief of the army staff, the first ethnic Igbo to hold the highest post in the most powerful branch of the armed forces since the civil war. Rear Admiral Ola Sa'ad Ibrahim emerged as chief of the naval staff and Air Vice Marshal Mohammed Dikko Umar chief of the air staff. All the appointees were promoted a rank. In addition, Assistant Inspector-General of Police Hafiz Ringim replaced the incumbent inspector-general, Ogbonna Onovo, causing the retirement of all six deputy inspector-generals, and Ita Ekpeyong succeeded Afakriya Gadzama as director general of the state security service. The real impact of the shake-ups, however, was caused by a wave of retirements, promotions and redeployments, because top-echelon staff had to leave the service in dozens, several of them against their will. Towards the end of September, the army carried out a posting exercise that resulted in the redeployment of all five general commanding officers and the appointment of several new principal staff officers. In late October, the air force and navy announced similar exercises, with the posting, appointment and redeployment of more than 130 senior officers. On 12 December, the army council pardoned the 27 soldiers who had been sentenced to seven years' imprisonment the preceding year for openly protesting in Akure (Ondo state) two years earlier against the failure to pay their peace-keeping mission allowances. Initially, a court-martial had sentenced them to life imprisonment.

The police force followed suit in December, promoting and redeploying some of its top officers and elevating more than 200 officers, ranging from superintendents to commissioners. In addition, some 2,500 policemen, allegedly sacked illegally, were called back and their dismissals reviewed. This decision, however, was basically seen as a frantic attempt to strengthen the still *fragile police force* in anticipation of the forthcoming elections in 2011. Against this background, it emerged that, at regular intervals, hundreds of policemen were trained by security personnel from Israel, brought in by the private security firm Vic-Phranc Nigeria. Interestingly, retired General

Martin Luther Agwai, once the commander of the joint UN/AU peacekeeping force in Darfur, was the firm's chief executive officer.

In June, President Jonathan directed the immediate payment of naira 23 bn pension arrears to more than 100,000 military pensioners; this had remained unresolved for some years. Earlier, the retired army, navy and air force officers' club had called on the federal government to re-think the role of *retired military personnel* in development projects. It reminded the public of the existence of a nationwide organised network of high-ranking retired officers, whose retirement encouraged them to become more involved in domestic politics.

After Goodluck Jonathan was sworn in as president on 6 May, he acted with caution in respect of his running for president. He was well advised to behave in such a manner because an unwritten agreement on a policy of rotating and zoning within the PDP was at stake, which in practice meant that the presidency had to switch between the predominantly Muslim north and the largely Christian south every two terms. Had he accepted this agreement, Jonathan would not have been able to decide to stand. Against this background, he did not inform the PDP governors of his decision to run in the presidential poll with Vice President Sambo as running mate until early September. Towards the year's end it became apparent that the battle for nomination at the ruling party's convention in the forthcoming weeks had narrowed down to the incumbent president and his main challenger, the extremely controversial Atiku Abubakar, who had twice been vice president during Obasanjo's terms in office. At the end of the year, however, the political re-appearance of former military dictator Muhammadu Buhari, as well as of the erstwhile chairman of the anti-corruption agency Nuhu Ribadu, heralded a *broadening power struggle* for the highest office. Buhari, a former presidential candidate and strict Muslim from the north, made his bid on the platform of the Congress for Progressive Change, while Ribadu sought to become the candidate of the Action Congress of Nigeria (ACN), formerly called the Action Congress (AC) and only recently re-named.

Against the background of the constitutional and leadership crisis, the *National Assembly* and the state assemblies amended the relevant section 145 of the constitution as follows: "In the event of the president failing or being unable to transmit a written declaration to the president of the senate and speaker of the house of representatives within 21 days, declaring that he is proceeding on vacation or is otherwise unable to discharge the functions of his office, the National Assembly shall by a resolution made by a simple majority in both chambers mandate the vice president to perform these functions as acting president. This mandate is valid until the president conveys by letter that he is available to resume office." The same procedure was to be applied to the governors' offices and section 190 was amended accordingly. *More amendments* followed, such as fixing presidential and gubernatorial elections to be held 120–150 days prior to the expiry of the tenure of the incumbents, as well as a clause ruling that the tenure of a sitting president or governor who wins a re-run election after the annulment of his previous election victory may not be extended beyond the original four-year term. Thus far, governors whose elections had been nullified but who had won the re-run had longer tenures than all the other duly elected incumbents.

To the surprise of all, however, on 19 September, the electoral commission called for a *postponement of the elections* scheduled to take place in January 2011. The majority of the 63 registered parties immediately agreed with INEC that the elections should instead be held in April because the original timetable had been too tight and could not be complied with. On 27 September, a joint parliamentary committee accepted the need to postpone the elections in order to iron out logistical problems, particularly that of voter registration. By 26 October, the National Assembly had fast-tracked the necessary constitutional amendment, thereby postponing the elections to April 2011 and requiring that voting take place not later than 30 days prior to the 29 May hand-over date. Despite the innovative nature of these decisions, the amendments were challenged in court by legal experts who insisted that they be signed by the president, an argument rejected outright by the legislative arm of government. Nevertheless, the federal government demanded that the supreme court make a pronouncement on the matter; the case was still pending at year's end.

The *legal aftermath* of the 2007 elections dragged on into 2010 and took its toll. In the months of October and November, the appeal court finally sacked the incumbent PDP governors Olagunsoye Oyinyola (Osun), Segun Oni (Ekiti) and Emmanuel Uduaghan (Delta) and declared Rauf Aregbesola and Femi Kayode duly elected for Osun and Ekiti respectively. Both had stood for the ACN, then known as the AC. Moreover, the court directed INEC to conduct fresh elections in Delta state within 90 days, with the date fixed for 6 January 2011. It should be borne in mind that the partial re-run in Ekiti state the previous year was, according to the electoral commission, won by the incumbent. However, the outcome was challenged in court by the runner-up and was finally decided in the latter's favour. Prior to that, on 6 February, the gubernatorial election took place in Anambra, one of the country's most politically turbulent states. The incumbent, Peter Obi of the All Progressive Grand Alliance, was declared the winner in an election that was again marred by widespread irregularities. Apart from the gubernatorial elections, the courts still had to deal with some petitions regarding the National Assembly and, last but not least, on 5 July, the supreme court struck out the petition filed by Ambrose Owuru of the Hope Democratic Party challenging the outcome of the 2007 presidential election for lack of jurisdiction. It was the second time that the party had appealed to the supreme court on this matter.

Over the course of the year, it became increasingly obvious that the PDP was losing coherence, which had initially seemed unlikely. Court verdicts that removed more sitting PDP governors in the ethnic Yoruba heartland were a serious blow and the arrest on 30 December of PDP senate leader Teslim Folarin for his alleged involvement in the murder of the trade union activist Lateef Salako in Ibadan merely added more fuel to the flames. The issues that raised even more questions about the party's status and the president's leadership were the *deepening internal divisions* and increasing wrangling in the party, as well as Obasanjo's dubious role in the background and the careless handling of security during the golden jubilee celebrations of the 50th anniversary of Independence on 1 October.

Although both domestic and foreign intelligence services, in particular the British, had passed on information about an impending terror attack, the government intensified security only half-heartedly. Eventually, on Independence Day, two bombs exploded in Abuja near a parade of top government and foreign officials, killing more than a dozen people. The blasts occurred only about one hour after an alleged faction of the Movement for the Emancipation of the Niger Delta, which seemed to be frustrated by the aftermath of the amnesty deal the previous year, had issued an email bomb warning, saying it had planted several devices at the parade and warning people to evacuate. Militants in the central Niger Delta region had already detonated two car bombs outside a government building in Warri on 15 March and one in Yenagoa on 2 May. On 3 November, a blast hit a government guest house in Asaba. The *deadly explosions* presaged more trouble, threatening to put the whole Niger Delta amnesty programme on hold, despite the fact that most of the militias and their leaders had accepted the amnesty offer and laid down their arms. Some arrests were made in the wake of the blasts, including that of Charles Okah, brother of Henry Okah, one of the main beneficiaries of the amnesty deal, who had subsequently moved to South Africa. Interestingly, his house in Johannesburg had been raided by police the previous day at Nigeria's behest and he was arrested soon after the blasts and put on trial on terrorism charges. On New Year's Eve, another terrorist attack rocked the capital Abuja, when a bomb exploded at the crowded Mammy Market, killing at least ten people and injuring more than a dozen. For the time being, no one claimed responsibility for this assault.

Over much of the year, it became clear that the promised post-amnesty programme of rehabilitation and reintegration of the 20,000 or so militia members was not working well. Several attacks by relatively unknown factions targeted mainly Agip's, Chevrons's and Shell's oil pipelines and flow stations. Moreover, the *kidnapping* of foreigners and affluent locals for ransom went on unabated. On 31 January, former director-general of the national youth service, retired Major General Edet Akpan, was abducted during a church service in Nsit Atai local government in Akwa Ibom state. His two personal guards and a worshipper were killed during the raid; he was released shortly after an unknown amount of ransom money had been paid. Four journalists and their driver were abducted in Abia state on 11 July while returning to Lagos after an executive meeting of the union of journalists in Uyo in Akwa Ibom state. A week later, they were set free unscathed. Even schoolchildren were targeted, and the hijacking of a school bus carrying 15 nursery and primary school children in Abia state on 27 September enraged the general public. Three days later, however, they were rescued unharmed by security forces.

Niger Delta stakeholders such as Ledum Mitee, chairman of the defunct Niger Delta Technical Committee, sharply criticised widespread mismanagement of the rehabilitation and reintegration programme and, in early July, more than 1,000 *aggrieved ex-militants* suddenly showed up in Abuja protesting against the federal government's alleged inaction. Most of the well-known leaders such as Government Ekpemupolo, alias Tompolo, Ateke Tom, Tony Uranta and Dokubo-Asari, who were among the main beneficiaries of the amnesty deal and openly supported President Jonathan, distanced themselves from the protesters, maintaining that the programme was basically on course. They even paid a solidarity visit to the president soon after the first blasts in Abuja.

Notwithstanding these conflicting statements, *heavy fighting* broke out in the Niger Delta on 17 November, when a faction of the Niger Delta Liberation Force under the leadership of self-proclaimed

'General' John Togo engaged with a military unit of the Joint Task Force in Delta state. Eight soldiers and an unknown number of militia members and civilians died. This fatal incident exposed the fragility of the amnesty programme. Soon after, on 20 November, armed forces arrested more than 60 militia members and their leader Obese, whose real name was Tamunotonye Kuna. He admitted having gone back to the creeks because he was disillusioned about the amnesty. Prior to that, Sobama George, a one-time militant leader who had also accepted a government amnesty, had been gunned down in the oil hub of Port Harcourt in Rivers state on 24 August. On 2 December, the military began raiding three camps close to the Ayakoromo and Okrika communities in Delta state in a series of related operations following the release of 19 local and foreign hostages on 17 November. According to local community reports, at least nine civilians lost their lives during the raid, which culminated in a gun battle between some militia members and the security forces. By contrast, on 6 December, Nnimmo Bassey from the Niger Delta was among those who received the 'Right Livelihood Award' (or 'Alternative Nobel Prize') from the Swedish foundation of the same name for revealing the full ecological and human horrors of oil production. On 22 April, the president had signed into law the Nigerian Oil and Gas Content Development Bill, which was aimed at promoting Nigerian companies and contractors dealing with the oil and gas sector, as well as increasing training and employment for Nigerians in this field.

Despite the incidents in the Niger Delta, it was in fact the Middle Belt and particularly *Plateau state* that was the centre of serious political and socioeconomic conflict throughout the year. This concerned the local political power structure, rights over fertile farmlands, and housing. These issues had a quite noticeable ethnic and sectarian undercurrent. The general public was reminded of the bloody riots of late 2008, in which several hundred people died and many more were injured. Plateau state is made up of a predominantly Christian Berom majority, who claim to be the indigenous inhabitants, and a Muslim minority of ethnic Hausa-Fulani and Fulani. In most cases, it was almost impossible accurately to verify the number of victims of the violence or identify those who triggered it. Communal violence started as early as 17 January in the state capital Jos and in nearby villages and went on for four days, leaving close to 400 people dead and some 24,000 displaced. Despite a military presence in the area and the setting up on 1 February of a presidential advisory panel on sectarian violence, which submitted an interim report towards the end of March, more was to come. On 7 March, Muslim Fulani pastoralists killed 400–500 ethnic Berom in Dogon Na Hawa, Ratsat and Jeji villages in Jos South local government, apparently in reprisal for the January attack. The discovery of the dumped body of a Muslim man sparked another act of revenge on 24 April, when a rampage by Muslim youths in the city of Jos led to the deaths of at least half a dozen people, among them Sunday Gyang Bwede and Nathan Dabak, two journalists with the monthly newspaper 'The Light Bearer', published by the Church of Christ. Despite the military presence, the *wave of violence* in the state went on unabated in the months that followed, causing the death of dozens of people of both faiths, among them the wife of the special task force commander, Mrs Rifkatu Umaru, who was killed on 5 December. In addition, numerous mosques, churches and houses were set ablaze. Although the police had made dozens of arrests, on 16–17 December, the federal high court in Jos eventually sentenced only 17 individuals involved in the disturbances earlier in the year to various jail terms ranging from seven to ten years. On Christmas Eve, in the aftermath of the trial, two bomb blasts in Gada Biyu and Angwan Rukuba in Jos North local government area killed 32 and critically injured more than 100, an event which triggered mayhem and unrest in the city of Jos the next day.

Neighbouring Bauchi and far away north-eastern Borno state again experienced a wave of *sectarian clashes*, particularly between security forces and remnants of the Islamic sects 'Boko Haram' and 'Kalo-Kato'. In Maiduguri, which was rocked by a Boko Haram's uprising the previous year, a dozen policemen were killed between August and December by snipers believed to be members of the militant sect. Even civilians, such as the Islamic scholar Sheikh Bashir Mustapha, the local ANPP politician Awana Ngala, and Bulama Hassan, ward head of the suburb Bulabulin-Alajiri, were deliberately shot or lost their lives in crossfire. The Islamic scholar had condemned the radical sect in a radio discussion the previous day, and the politician was related by marriage to the state governor, Ali Modu Sheriff. Assassinations went on in the state capital and, on Christmas Eve, a group of armed suspected sect members attacked the Victory Baptist Church Alamderi and the Sinimari Church of Christ in Nigeria, killing six. In early November, security forces paraded some 25 suspects believed to have been involved in the Borno serial killings. On New Year's Eve, they captured Buna Wakil, an alleged Boko Haram financier, and some 90 other people following a four-hour gun battle with suspected sect members.

In *Bauchi state* and the capital of the same name, the situation was slightly different. In addition to the killing of some policemen in October/November and the ward head Tukur Ahmed on 23 October, members of the sect stormed Bauchi prison on 7 September, killing some staff and setting more than 700 inmates free. Some 150 of the inmates were awaiting trial following their arrest after the Boko Haram uprising the previous year. The police could only re-arrest a small number, while some 120 finally returned voluntarily, but inmates torched part of the building on 8 October, a month after the jailbreak.

There were changes at the top of the *religious hierarchies*. The Most Reverend Nicholas Dikeriehi Orogodo Okoh, a retired lieutenant colonel and former military chaplain, became the fourth primate of the Anglican Church in Nigeria on 25 March. After a crucial vote, a Pentecostal pastor, Ayo Oritsejafor, replaced the incumbent Catholic Archbishop John Onaiyekan as president of the Christian Association of Nigeria on 5 July. The Chief Imam of the Abuja National Mosque, Ustaz Musa, was removed on 10 August by the Supreme Council for Islamic Affairs, along with the entire management committee.

As in previous years, security deteriorated in almost all parts of the country and the number of *assassinations and killings* of policemen and civilians increased significantly, although the security forces arrested suspected bank robbers and kidnappers by the dozen. In addition, several criminals were gunned down by police and military forces. One of them was Obioma Nwankwo, popularly known as Osisikwankwu, who was shot on 12 December; he was the alleged leader of several notorious kidnapping gangs in Abia state. On 25 March, the assistant inspector-general, in charge of zone 7 police command, comprising the Federal Capital Territory Abuja, Niger state and Kaduna state, acknowledged that 150 policemen had lost their lives over the previous 15 months in this zone alone. In the course of the year, more than two dozen fell victim to criminals, including those killed by alleged Boko Haram members and, for the first time, the Economic and Financial Crimes Commission (EFCC) was targeted and some high-ranking officers were assassinated, among them Edoga Eze in Imo state on 18 March and forensic chief Abdullahi Muazu in Kaduna state on 14 September. Only the day before, Garba Bello, an assistant director of the state security service, together with his wife and three of their children were slaughtered in Kano. In addition, an investigator of the federal inland revenue service and former staff of EFCC, Danjuma Mohammed, was shot in Abuja on 20 February.

Similarly, the number of murdered or assassinated civilians and officials increased dramatically. The former correspondent of African Independent Television, Efenji Efenji, was murdered in Abuja on 14 February, and Edo Sule Ugbagwu, working for 'The Nation' newspaper met his death in Lagos on 25 April. The US-based physician, Charles Ndulue, was gunned down in Benin City on 28 March, and on 19 September, Stanley Ude, a medical doctor and proprietor of a hospital in Aba, was killed after being abducted, despite a *ransom* of 30 m naira being paid. In Port Harcourt, gun-men assassinated Anthony Egobueze, head of the Rivers civil service commission on 11 June. Jimmy Omogberem, chieftain of the state chapter of the Delta Peoples' Forum, was murdered in Kaduna on 18 September and Adol Nwachukwu, a retired assistant corps marshal of the federal road safety commission, was shot in Ehime-Mbano local government in Imo state on 29 October. The killings went on unabated and, on 15 December, Tafida Umar, PDP chairman of Mubi North local government in Adamawa state, was shot dead in his home town, while the human rights activist Chidi Nwosu was killed in his compound in Arochukwu, Abia state on 29 December.

This list is nowhere near complete. In the light of the general security situation, the *human and civil rights record* worsened significantly. In terms of abuses by government agencies and security forces, however, the situation improved slightly. In Warri in Delta state, for example, a total of 47 prisoners on death row had their cases reviewed by the state government. On 30 September, seven were released while the remaining condemned men had their verdicts commuted to life imprisonment. Soon after, the state's chief judge, who was to review more than 400 cases seeking to address the problem of congested prisons, freed 20 inmates awaiting trial.

On 21 December, a Lagos high court discharged and acquitted chief security officer Hamza Al-Mustapha, who had served under the late dictator Sani Abacha, and three others, who were all standing trial for the attempted murder of Alex Ibru, publisher of 'The Guardian' (Lagos) newspaper. The protracted proceedings had begun as early as 1999. While former police commissioner James Danbaba and Zamfara state military administrator Jubrin Bala Yakubu were set free, Al-Mustapha and former head of the Aso Rock anti-riot police, Rabo Lawal, were detained on remand because of another pending trial related to the murder of the famous Mrs Kudirat Abiola in 1996.

The *anti-corruption campaign* produced some positive results, despite the poor ranking by TI, which placed Nigeria 134th of 178 countries in the corruption perception index. Apart from corruption charges against international companies such as Julius Berger, and Halliburton's former subsidiary Kellog, Brown and Root, as well as Siemens, and quite a number of high-profile politicians, the EFCC tried to lay hands on former Delta state governor James Ibori. In previous years, he had been rather successful in battling the EFCC in Nigerian and British courts, but in April, when the agency again declared him wanted over a fresh $ 290 m fraud and other corruption charges, he slipped out of the country and took refuge in Dubai. Soon after, however, he was taken into custody after Interpol had issued an international arrest warrant. He was also wanted for questioning in Britain. Despite taking legal action, which lasted for months, on 13 December, Ibori finally lost an appeal against his extradition to the UK, although it had still not been carried out by year's end. Meanwhile, Ibori's sister, Christine Ibori-Ibie, and his mistress, Udoamaka Onuigbo, were each convicted by a London court of laundering $ 20 m on behalf of James Ibori and sentenced to a five-year jail term on 1 June. Furthermore, on 22 November, his estranged wife, Theresa Nkoyo Ibori, was found guilty of the same offence, and received the same sentence. As a result of a settlement agreement, on 8 October, a Lagos court sentenced Mrs Cecilia Ibru, former CEO of Ocean Bank, to six months' imprisonment for fraud and ordered her to hand over some $ 1.2 bn in cash and assets. She was one of a number of executives who had been held in connection with the non-disclosure of several toxic assets following the near-collapse of nine banks the previous year. The Ibru family ran several big businesses and had even been allowed to keep 10% of the bank's equity. Finally, staff of the national drug law enforcement agency had for years been assumed to have abused their office. Eventually, former chairman Bello Lafiaji and his personal assistant Usman Amali were tried and sentenced on 21 June to four years and three years imprisonment respectively for conspiracy and for the diversion of more than € 160,000 from a suspected drug baron.

However, as far as the above mentioned international companies were concerned, an out-of-court deal led to all charges against them being dropped, with the companies agreeing to pay fines to the federal government, ranging from almost $ 30 m by Julius Berger to nearly $ 40 m by Siemens and $ 250 m in the case of Halliburton, thereby saving its former CEO Dick Cheney from possible prosecution.

Last but not least, on 15 December, Anthony Enahoro died at the age of 87. He was one of the last surviving influential veteran politicians who had fought for Nigeria's independence.

Foreign Affairs

The generally good relations with the US were temporarily strained when Nigeria was placed on a terror watch list. Nevertheless, the country's main crude oil customer played an unprecedented role in resolving the leadership crisis and in reinforcing President Jonathan's position, thereby noticeably enforcing bilateral ties. On 8 February, the day before Jonathan became acting president, Assistant Secretary of State Johnnie Carson held bilateral talks with the then vice president. This was the beginning of strategic discussions and negotiations between the US government, represented by the then ambassador Mrs Robin Sanders, and the unfolding new leadership. According to Wikileaks' published cables, she must have been a regular visitor to the presidential villa, giving advice on how to proceed and offering substantial support.

On 6 April in Washington, Secretary of State Hillary Clinton and the secretary of the Nigerian government, Yayale Ahmed, signed the framework for the establishment of the *US-Nigeria bi-national commission.* Shortly after, Acting President Jonathan paid a four-day working visit to the US, where he attended the nuclear summit in Washington on 12–14 April. He met Barack Obama at the White House on 11 April and held talks with members of the Black Caucus on Capitol Hill on 14 April. On 12 April, Jonathan also had a closed-door meeting with World Bank President Robert Zoellick on how to revamp Nigeria's ailing power sector.

Barely a week after Jonathan's visit to the US, on 24 April, Under-Secretary of State for Political Affairs William Burns made a stop-over in Abuja on his seven-nation tour of Africa. The full impact of the strengthened ties came to light when *FBI instructors* commenced a two-week training programme for operatives of the anti-corruption and drug law enforcement agencies, the police and the state security services on 30 August. Also in August, Nigerian airlines had gained the right to fly their own planes to the US, though Arik Air was the only carrier certified and able to afford services there. Furthermore, Nigeria was removed from the major illicit drug production and drug trafficking list for the year 2011 and, on 28 September, both countries agreed to update their existing letter of agreement on counter-narcotics cooperation. In early November, the New York law enforcement authorities announced the seizure of 10,000 counterfeit DVDs of Nigerian movies after complaints by 'Nollywood' about rampant piracy. However, prior to that, in September, a New York court declined to hear a lawsuit in which ethnic Ogoni Nigerians, relatives of those executed by the then military regime in the mid-1990s, sought to sue Shell for acts committed abroad, arguing on the basis of a law dating back to 1789, known as the 'Alien Tort Claims Act'.

Britain joined the US in praising the unique transfer of executive powers to the then vice president and offered its full support. This was in line with deepened bilateral relations over the previous years, which had an even wider political and legal scope. The Ibori court case was only one of many that demonstrated that Nigerian and British legal issues were becoming more and more intertwined. This trend gained further momentum with a divorce case. On 10 March, the supreme court passed a landmark ruling in the divorce proceedings of a Nigerian-born couple with British citizenship. In essence, the court ruled that the plaintiff, who was unhappy with the settlement awarded to her by a Nigerian court, was eligible to receive a much higher lump sum payment. In this particular case, the London court awarded the plaintiff £ 275,000 instead of the

£ 21,000 the Nigerian court had considered appropriate. Although the number of Nigerians serving various prison sentences in Britain had dropped to slightly more than 750, the issue of the transfer of prisoners to Nigeria was still hotly discussed. Despite some efforts, the awaited bill had not yet been passed by the National Assembly, and the *prisoners' transfer deal* between Nigeria and Britain was still pending at year's end.

At the end of June, London, the hub of the *Nigerian diaspora*, saw the arrival of numerous members of the Nigerian political and economic elite to commemorate and celebrate the 50th anniversary of Independence. The two-day so-called business summit was also meant to attract foreign investors. However, only a small number of the latter appeared; they were unimpressed and most were even disappointed by the way Nigeria was presented as a country trying to attract foreign private investment. Thus, the meeting prompted scathing remarks from opposition parties and the Nigeria Labour Congress, who branded the golden jubilee summit a wasteful, irrelevant jamboree and a national disgrace. Even President Jonathan eventually shunned the event, pointing out that he had already met Prime Minister David Cameron at the recent G-8 summit in Canada on 25 June. A strange incident occurred earlier, on 17 June, when the Metropolitan Police raided the London home of a Nigerian diplomat, thinking it was a cannabis factory. No drugs were found and, within hours, the Foreign and Commonwealth Office apologised to the Nigerian government, regretting that the police had mistakenly entered the diplomat's residence. In April, the BBC broadcast a critical documentary entitled 'Welcome to Lagos', which caused a lot of controversy. The programme portrayed the city as a slum and the Nigerian government had asked the BBC not to show it, but to no avail.

As in previous years, however, Nigerians, most of them claiming refugee status, were deported in dozens from the UK. Towards year's end, three Nigerians, including a solicitor, were given long prison sentences after they were found guilty on 14 December of setting up fake educational institutions named the 'Academy College of Education' and the 'Academy of Training and Recruitment', which were nothing more than bed-sits to help *illegal immigrants* remain in Britain. At the end of June, the EU inaugurated a project worth € 1.2 m to assist in curbing human trafficking between Africa and Europe. The project was to run for two years and to be implemented by the ILO and the Italian counter trafficking commission. While some 60 Nigerians were deported from Spain on 7 July, it was reported that, within the previous two years, some 8,000 illegal migrants from Nigeria had had their residence regularised.

Relations with *China* focused on deepening existing technical and commercial relationships and attracting more direct investment. According to Chinese officials, the government had invested more than $ 7 bn in the previous year and Chinese companies were employing more than 30,000 Nigerians. On 13 May, the Nigerian state-run oil company NNPC and China State Construction Engineering Corporation agreed to seek $ 23 bn in funding to build three refineries in Lagos, Bayelsa and Kogi state and a petrochemical complex at a still unspecified location. The project was expected to be funded largely by a consortium of Chinese banks and China's Export and Credit Insurance Corporation. No time frame was given, but it became apparent on 5 July that the first $ 8 bn oil refinery was to be built in the Lekki free trade zone in the eastern part of Lagos state. While Lagos would provide land and infrastructure, the NNPC would cover 20% of the cost and its Chinese counterpart 80%. In addition, the China Great Wall Industry Corporation agreed to spend $ 230 m to replace Nigeria's failed satellite NIGCOMSAT 1. The launching was scheduled for the second half of 2011. On 23 December, the finance minister announced that Nigeria had been given a $ 900 m loan from the China Import-Export bank to finance the Abuja-Kaduna railway and the national public security communications project. The interest rate was put at 2.5% with maturity at 20 years.

In the course of the year, Nigeria deliberately reached out to the Middle East, hosting the 7th Developing-8 (D-8) summit in Abuja on 8 July, which was even attended by Iranian President Mahmoud Ahmadinejad and Turkish President Abdullah Gül. The D-8 is a group of eight countries with substantial Muslim populations that aim to further economic cooperation among member states. In November, the 4th Joint Commission meeting between Nigeria and Turkey, with Deputy Prime Minister Cemil Çiçek attending, was concluded in Abuja. The improved relationship with *Iran* became strained later in the year, however, after intelligence staff intercepted an illegal arms shipment in the port of Lagos at the end of October and Nigeria reported Iran to the UNSC. Iran's foreign minister immediately flew to Nigeria on 11 November, promising to cooperate with the investigation. He even allowed Nigeria to interview an Iranian citizen inside the embassy in connection with the seized shipment, which was allegedly destined for Gambia. Eventually, the Iranian and three Nigerians were charged in court. Soon after, on 19 November, the anti-drugs agency discovered a consignment of 130 kg of heroin concealed in auto parts shipped from Iran.

As for relations with African states, on 1 February, Nigeria was elected for a three-year term to represent West Africa in the Peace and Security Council of the AU at the summit in Addis Ababa. At the *ECOWAS* summit in Abuja on 16 February, the then Acting President Jonathan was elected chairman, thereby extending Nigeria's leadership for another year. In this capacity, he joined the Franco-African summit in Nice on 31 May–1 June, and he also attended the 15th ordinary AU summit in Kampala on 25–27 July. In contrast to reasonably normal relations with countries in the sub-region, relations with Libya were temporarily tense. In March, Nigeria recalled its ambassador after Kadhafi suggested that Nigeria would be better off being split into separate Muslim and Christian countries as a way of resolving its sectarian and religious problems. At the end of August, however, the ambassador returned to Libya. According to Libyan sources, several convicted foreigners, including Nigerians, were executed in Libya at the end of May. Furthermore, Nigerians were deported in dozens, particularly from South Africa, Sudan and

Mali. In November, Nigeria for its part deported some 700 migrants originating from neighbouring countries around Lake Chad as part of a security crackdown on the Boko Haram sect.

Nigeria had been elected onto the *UNSC* the previous year, and so President Jonathan attended the Council's summit-level meeting on 'Maintaining International Peace and Security' on 23 September. On the same day, he addressed the General Assembly. In recognition of Nigeria's contribution, the Nigerian army peacekeeping centre in Jaji, in Kaduna state, was endorsed by the UN on 6 May as a centre for the UN's training activities and efforts in the promotion of peace-keeping throughout the world.

Socioeconomic Developments

The international oil and gas price increased once again and Nigeria's high quality crude rose from $ 77 a barrel at the start of the year to more than $ 90 at year's end. Foreign reserves, however, fell significantly to some $ 33 bn, mainly triggered by the excessive spending of the windfall oil savings against the background of the forthcoming elections.

On 22 April, President Jonathan signed into law the *2010 budget*, totalling naira 4.6 trillion ($ 31 bn), assuming an average oil price of $ 67 a barrel, crude production of 2.35 m b/d, an exchange rate of naira 150 : $ 1 and deficit spending of naira 1.5 bn or some 6% of GDP – an undertaking which was intended to be financed by mas-sive domestic and foreign borrowing. In respect of the shortfall, the central bank issued medium- and long-term bonds and short-term treasury bills almost by the month, worth more than $ 7 bn. In July, however, a supplementary budget of naira 645 bn ($ 4.3 bn) finally exposed the reckless spending of the political class in all three tiers of government. To appease local critics and international donors, the initial budget was eventually trimmed by naira 200 bn against the background of lower than expected oil prices and crude output.

Moreover, central bank governor Sanusi Lamido Sanusi paved the way for getting Islamic banking started in the year to come.

The *debt profile* provoked controversy, despite the finance minister's estimating Nigeria's debt to GDP ratio at some 16%, which is low compared with the internationally acceptable benchmark of 40% for developing countries. As of September, however, the debt stock had increased to $ 4.5 bn external and some $ 28 bn domestic debt. During the year, Nigeria received $ 1.5 bn in international development aid alone, the bulk of the grants and credits being given by the World Bank and its subsidiaries for agriculture and social projects and for the ailing power sector.

The federal government took some strategic decisions in the financial sphere, trying to restore confidence in the *banking sector*. The turmoil on the Nigerian Stock Exchange, caused by alleged corruption, mismanagement, a drastic fall in share values and the unprecedented removal of its president, Aliko Dangote, and its long serving director general, Mrs Ndi Okerere-Onyiuke, was temporarily put to rest in early August. On 5 August, the Securities and Exchange Commission appointed Emmanuel Ikazoboh, a former top Deloitte accountant, as interim manager to run Africa's second-biggest equities market and, on 26 August, he downsized the staff by one-third. On 30 August, Mustafa Chike Obi, formerly an investment banker in the US, was assigned to run the infant Asset Management Company of Nigeria or 'Bad Bank'. The company had been established the previous month with a projected lifespan of ten years to absorb the non-performing loans of nine banks rescued in a $ 3.9 bn bail-out the previous year. The toxic assets were to be exchanged for seven-year bonds or other debt instruments issued by the 'Bad Bank' and guaranteed by the finance ministry. On 8 November, the central bank withdrew all existing licences for class 'A' bureaux de change as one of a number of measures to stem gross abuses of the enhanced category 'A' in line with the central bank's avowed commitment to eradicate money laundering. The previous year, the bureaux de change had been split into classes 'A' and 'B' to further liberalise the foreign exchange market, to enhance its allocative efficiency and at the same time allow easier supervision, but the implementation of this measure ultimately proved to be extremely difficult.

On 2 December, in its efforts to reduce widespread poverty, the federal government launched a $ 500 m loan facility for *small and medium sized businesses* run by the bank of industry and the bank was also mandated to manage a special entertainment fund of $ 200 m to promote the flourishing 'Nollywood' cinema industry, believed to be second only to India's 'Bollywood' in terms of the number of films produced.

The *mobile phone market* continued to expand. However, the on-going saga of the state-owned Nigerian Telecommunication Limited, which had been running for at least nine years, went on. On 12 October, the president approved the planned $ 2.5 bn sale, reviving a process that had repeatedly stalled. Although an international consortium made up of three companies from China, Dubai and Nigeria was the preferred bidder, serious doubts about their financial capacity soon emerged. Not surprisingly, the consortium failed twice to pay the bid security sum of $ 750 m and the issue remained unresolved at year's end.

In the course of the year, Nigeria experienced heavy rains and flooding and the worst *cholera outbreak* for nearly two decades. The latter cost the lives of some 1,500 people, while some 40,000 were infected. The north of the country was particularly affected, but this region also saw impressive progress in the fight to eradicate the once endemic polio.

On 30 June, President Jonathan suspended the *national soccer team* from international competition for two years following a poor showing at the FIFA World Cup in South Africa. On 2 July, FIFA threatened to suspend Nigeria from world football, unless the president reversed his decision within three days. The Nigerian government eventually backed down on 5 July, but at the same time the Nigerian Football Association's executive committee sacked three top officials. Only on 25 August did Aminu Maigari emerge as the association's new president, but internal legal wrangling over the leadership continued and FIFA suspended the association on 4 October. Four days later, however, it provisionally lifted the ban to enable the soccer team's African Nations Cup qualifier to take place in Guinea. FIFA fully lifted the suspension on 29 October, but more was to come: Amos Adamu, Nigeria's representative on the FIFA board, was accused of involvement in corruption related to influencing the choice of venue for the 2018 world tournament. He was suspended for three years and fined 10,000 Swiss francs by the FIFA ethics committee on 17 November.

The *Commonwealth Games* in India in October were overshadowed by failed drug tests, and Nigerian athletes were in the forefront. The 100 m. gold medal winner, Ms Damola Osayemi, the runner-up in the 400 m., Ms Folashade Abugan, and the women's 400 m. relay quartet, which came second and had Abugan as one of its members, were stripped of their medals. Samuel Okon, who was sixth in the 110 m. hurdles, also tested positive.

On 16 December, the 62 year old musician, Fuji legend Ayinde Barrister, passed away in a London hospital.

Nigeria in 2011

The April elections at federal and state levels dominated the political scene and confirmed the incumbent Goodluck Ebele Jonathan as president, giving him a very strong political mandate. An improved election commission conducted the most credible elections yet in Nigeria's history, despite continuing widespread shortcomings and lapses. However, the country experienced an unprecedented wave of political and sectarian violence, evoking the political turmoil and ethnic violence on the eve of the civil war. Although the political class had demonstrated its willingness and ability to continue to stabilise democratic institutions, it failed to understand the dynamics and structures underlying sectarian violence, suicide bombings and organised crime, so that the president and his government gave the impression of being rather helpless. Furthermore, they continued to ignore the microeconomic level as well as the persistent, grinding poverty in the far north. Thus, the government somehow managed to return to the brinkmanship politics of the past, exacerbating the north-south dichotomy and the nationwide youth violence.

Domestic Politics

Over the course of the year, the most striking issues were the *general elections*, scheduled for 2 April (National Assembly), 9 April (presidential) and 16 April (gubernatorial and state assemblies), and the threat of Boko Haram. All eyes were fixed on the run-up to the elections, in which the incumbent President Goodluck Ebele Jonathan, a Christian from the Niger Delta, eventually emerged as the front runner of the ruling People's Democratic Party (PDP). On 13 January, almost 80% of the more than 3,500 delegates voted in favour of the incumbent at the PDP primaries in Abuja, thereby, in all probability, heralding a strong mandate. While Goodluck Jonathan kept his vice president, Namadi Sambo, a Muslim from the north as running mate, the former military dictator and twice presidential candidate, Muhammadu Buhari, was endorsed by the Congress for Progressive Change (CPC) as the main challenger.

At the start of the year, however, it became obvious that the *Independent National Electoral Commission* (INEC) would not meet the deadline for completing the electoral register. Reacting swiftly, the National Assembly on 25–26 January amended the electoral act No.6 of 2010, reducing the time INEC had to complete the registration of voters before a general election from 60 to 30 days. In the end, the electoral register comprised 67 m eligible voters, and the lists went on display at the 120,000 polling stations in mid-February. In early March, however, INEC updated the number to about 73.5 m.

Twenty presidential and dozens of gubernatorial candidates, as well as more than 50 parties, contested the elections. Soon after parts of the electorate had cast their vote in the parliamentary election on 2 April, and to the consternation of most Nigerians, the well respected INEC chairman, Attahiru Jega, aborted the whole exercise at the eleventh hour after it turned out that voting materials had failed to arrive on time in large parts of the country. As a result, the elections were postponed for one week.

To the surprise of many Nigerians, as well as international observers, the delayed ballot for the bicameral National Assembly on 9 April passed off with far fewer hitches and some notable improvements, despite the chaotic run-up, which was marred by legal wrangling and localised violence that left some 100 people dead. Despite its successes, INEC had to postpone parliamentary polls for 15 senatorial and 48 federal constituencies, where ballot papers had printing errors or had already been used during the aborted election. The PDP maintained its grip on power and won a two-thirds majority in the 109-member senate and an absolute majority in the 360-member house of representatives. The Action Congress of Nigeria (ACN) did reasonably well and came second in both chambers, winning more than a dozen seats in the senate and some 60 seats in the house of representatives, thus confirming its strong stand in the ethnic Yoruba dominated south-west. As in previous elections, several results were subsequently challenged at the *election tribunals*; some were reversed while others were annulled and fresh elections conducted. A small number of cases were still pending in the appeal courts at year's end.

Given the fact that Jonathan had a level of resources no other candidate could hope to match, the ACN and the CPC tried to form an alliance to unseat him. This strategy failed, however, making the result of the *presidential election* a foregone conclusion. Jonathan polled close to 59% of the some 38 m valid votes cast and the runner-up, Buhari, almost 32%. However, against the background of the run-up to the election, local observers and even members of Buhari's inner circle had had no expectation that Buhari would achieve such a respectable result. Interestingly, apart from securing the majority of votes, only Jonathan fulfilled the second constitutional requirement for winning an election, that is to say, to win at least a quarter of the votes cast in 24 states and in the Federal Capital Abuja (FCT). In fact, since Jonathan exceeded this requirement, with 32 states and the FCT, the electorate had given him a mandate stronger than any previously elected head of state or government. Shortcomings and lapses notwithstanding, most international observers and Nigerians saw the poll as the *most credible* in Nigerian history. When the head of INEC officially declared Goodluck Ebele Jonathan the winner on 18 April, he immediately accepted the mandate. Buhari for his part rejected the poll result but refrained from challenging it at the election tribunal. Instead, his party, the CPC, went to the tribunal, but the petition was dismissed on 1 November and, on 28 December, in a unanimous decision, the supreme court confirmed the tribunal's verdict.

However, in some northern parts of the country, a wave of violence unparalleled since the eve of the civil war erupted in the aftermath of the elections. No sooner was it known that Jonathan would definitely win the election than organised gangs, mostly of youths angered by the incumbent's victory, went on the rampage in northern urban centres, particularly in the cities of Kaduna, Kano, Bauchi, Yola and Azare. The apparently well orchestrated protest gathered momentum in the days that followed, and threatened to spiral out of control. Polling stations and INEC offices were vandalised, churches, mosques, houses and police stations set ablaze, up to *1,000 people killed* and thousands of innocent citizens forced to flee their homes before security forces finally checked the spreading violence. According to the national Muslim and Christian leaders, the vast majority of those killed were Muslims, but some 200 Christians suffered a similar fate.

Kaduna state, which on 18 April imposed a two-day 24-hour curfew, suffered the greatest level of destruction and recorded the highest number of deaths. A less rigid curfew in the state lasted until 26 July. Against this background, it emerged that, in the run-up to the general election, INEC's chairman, Attahiru Jega, had sidelined large numbers of staff and had instead entered into close partnership with the *national youth service corps*, which comprised tens of thousands of youths completing their one-year national service outside their home states. This move was aimed at avoiding, or at least significantly reducing, malpractices at the polling stations, an operation which the corps members were able to implement quite successfully. However, ten of them, all but one from southern states, fell victim to the violence in Bauchi state and, soon after, several hundred members originating from the South were evacuated from the North back to their respective states. The slain corps members were given a national burial and the families generously compensated by the government.

On 21 April, Jonathan addressed the nation and vowed that, despite the violent incidents, the final round of elections would go ahead as planned. He also indicated his reluctance to declare a state of emergency in any part of the country.

At the state level, all assembly seats were contested, but of the powerful *gubernatorial mandates* only 26 of the 36 eventually went to the vote. Apart from five sitting governors – three affiliated to the ACN; one to the All Progressive Great Alliance (APGA), and one to the Labour Party (LP) – whose tenure had not yet expired, the legal end of the tenures of five sitting PDP governors in Adamawa, Bayelsa, Cross River, Kogi and Sokoto states was highly contentious. All had reclaimed their governorships in a 2008 re-run, after their victories the previous year had been annulled, so their tenures had started later than all the other duly elected incumbents. In 2010, a constitutional amendment had resolved the contentious tenure issue, and it was on the basis of this amendment that INEC tried to push through the implementation of gubernatorial elections in the five states in question. For their part, the governors argued in court that the case came under pre-amendment regulations. On 15 April, after a fierce legal battle, the appeals court affirmed the judgement of a lower court, which had made the point that constitutional changes could not be applied retrospectively and barred INEC from holding the said ballots. In the case of the re-run in Delta state on 6 January, however, the amended rules were applied, although an appeal by INEC to the supreme court was still pending at year's end. Emmanuel Uduaghan reclaimed his governorship by a considerable margin and abided by the appeals court's verdict, contesting the gubernatorial elections held on 26 April.

Uduaghan and 17 other PDP front runners finally triumphed, while the ACN and the All Nigeria Peoples Party (ANPP) won three and the APGA, LP and CPC one governorship each. In other words, the PDP, despite minor losses, continued to dominate politics at state level. The ACN consolidated its power in the south-western Yoruba region, ANPP kept its position in the north-eastern Kanuri area and the APGA in the Igbo heartland in the south-east. At year's end, all *elected governors* were still in power. Most petitions had been dismissed with only very few exceptions, such as in Borno state where, on 23 December, the appeals court ordered that the petition by the PDP candidate be heard afresh at a different tribunal. The incumbent ANPP governor, Kashim Shettima, challenged this verdict at the supreme court, which was now entitled to deal with the outcome of gubernatorial elections. On 3 December, Kogi state was the first of the five controversial states to conduct a gubernatorial election in accordance with the appeals court's verdict of 15 April. This election was eventually won by PDP candidate Wada Idris.

Thanks to the amended deadline of 21 days for filing petitions and another 180 days for the tribunal's verdict, only some 400 cases involving election disputes were reported, compared with more than 1,200 after the previous general election. However, on 11 May, in the immediate aftermath of the election, a 22-man *investigation panel* on election violence and civil disturbances was inaugurated. The panel was chaired by Sheikh Ahmed Lemu, former Grand Khadi of Niger state, with retired supreme court judge Samson Uwaifo as vice chairman. The report was submitted to the president on 10 October, alerting the nation to the existence of politicians' private armies, widespread unemployment and a security situation that might escalate into unprecedented social unrest. Earlier, on 29 June, the committee on security in the north-east was set up, which in some way officially acknowledged the reality of a deep North-South divide. Its findings were still pending at year's end.

Jonathan was sworn in on 29 May. At the senate's inaugural session on 6 June, PDP-senator David Mark, from Benue state, once again emerged as senate president, while Ike Ekweremadu (PDP), from Enugu state, was re-elected as his deputy. On the same day, Waziri Aminu Tambuwal (PDP) was elected speaker of the house of representatives and Chukwuemeka Nkem Ihedioha (PDP), from Imo state, became deputy speaker. However, these appointments did not meet the party's primary zoning formula, and thus the distribution of power among the top three positions in the Nigerian political system was not as balanced between the six *geo-political zones* as it had been in the past, since it excluded the south-west and the north-east.

In successive steps during July, Jonathan formed his *new cabinet*, reappointing several ministers from his previous government.

Diezani Alison-Madueke kept her petroleum resources portfolio, while outgoing finance minister Olusegun Aganga took over the new ministry of trade and investment. In his place, Ngozi Okonjo-Iweala, a managing director of the World Bank, took over the finance ministry for the second time – she had served former president Olusegun Obasanjo in 2005, when Nigeria had settled huge foreign debts with the Paris Club. The career diplomat Olugbenga Ashiru became foreign minister, engineer Bart Nnaji was appointed minister of power, former acting PDP-chairman Bello Harilu Mohammed emerged as the new defence minister, and the well-known editor of 'The Guardian' (Lagos) newspaper, Reuben Abati, was named government spokesperson. Thirteen women were appointed in the new cabinet of some 40 ministers.

In October, the new president dissolved dozens of *federal parastatals* and agencies and assigned their responsibilities to new personnel. Key bodies such as the petroleum product pricing regulatory agency and the department for petroleum resources were assigned to Reginald Chika Stanley and Osten Oluyemisi Olurunsola respectively. In August, Jonah Otunla had already been appointed as the new accountant-general of the federation, and Dahiru Musdapher was named the chief justice, succeeding Aloysius Katsina-Alu, who had reached the mandatory retirement age of 70. In June, two appeals court judges advanced to the supreme court, among them Mary Peter-Odili, bringing the number of *female judges* to two. On 2 December, a total of 144 promoted generals from the three branches of the armed services were awarded their new ranks, and on 14 December, the police force followed suit to the benefit of more than 1,200 police officers of middle and upper ranks. Towards year's end, 25-year-old Blessing Liman became the first female fighter pilot.

Jonathan signed *several acts* into law, including an amended National Minimum Wage Act (22 March), an amended Pension Reform Act (7 April), the Nigeria Sovereign Investment Authority (Establishment) Act (26 May), which inter alia created the controversial Sovereign Wealth Fund, an amended 2011 budget (27 May), and the Freedom of Information Act (28 May). Soon after the president had been sworn in, he signed the Terrorism (Prevention) Act and an amended and more rigorous Money Laundering (Prohibition) Act, which came into force on 3 June. Prior to that, on 4 March, the president had signed the Constitution of the Federal Republic of Nigeria (Third Alteration) Act, 2010, which altered the constitutional provision for the establishment of the national industrial court.

In the previous year, the *constitutional amendments*, which included significant alterations to executive powers and the electoral law, had been a serious bone of contention. Backed by a federal high court, legal experts insisted that the constitutionally passed amendments be signed by the president, but the National Assembly rejected this argument and challenged it in court. Despite the fact that the appeals court's verdict on this controversial issue was still pending, the president signed the amended constitution into law on 10 January and gave his assent to two new amendments to the electoral act, thus avoiding unpredictable legal wrangling both before and after the general election.

The second half of the year saw a clear deterioration in the already *precarious security situation*, particularly in the North where it reached a nadir, mainly due to clashes between factions of the Islamic sect 'Jama'atu Ahlis Sunna Lid Da'awati Wal Jihad', better known as Boko Haram, and the security forces. In the first half of the year, politicians and Muslim clerics had been assassinated, as had members of the royal family in Borno state. These included ANPP gubernatorial candidate Modu Fannami Gubio and Goni Sheriff, brother of the then ANPP governor, who were killed on 28 January, Abba Anas Umar, younger brother of the Shehu of Borno, killed on 30 May, the cleric Ibrahim Birkuti, killed on 6 June, and several policemen and civilians. The violence culminated in a wave of bomb attacks, suicide bombings, assaults and several deadly raids on police stations, barracks, state security offices and banks in large parts of the northern region. At year's end, at least 500 people, including many northerners of Christian faith, had fallen victim to the assaults. Given the fact that many of these attacks took place in areas with limited means of communication, it was almost impossible to verify the number of assaults and casualties. Although alleged Boko Haram speakers claimed the group's responsibility for most of the attacks, there were plausible indications that sophisticated criminal networks from the South were also at work. Over the years, they have shifted their deadly activities, particularly bank robberies, northward, and exploited the serious sectarian crisis there.

The *bomb attack* on a police headquarters on 16 June, in which at least eight policemen lost their lives, along with the bombing of the UN headquarters in the capital Abuja on 26 August, which cost the lives of 24 civilians, half of them UN staff, marked a clear watershed. At this point, if not before, the federal government showed that it was largely incapable of understanding the multidimensional causes and ramifications of the violence, as well as the threat it posed to the political system as a whole. A modest attempt by former president Obasanjo to establish some form of dialogue with *Boko Haram* was immediately shattered. On 15 September, two days after his meeting with Babakuru Fugu, a brother-in-law of the executed leader Mohammed Yusuf, Fugu was killed. In the wake of these bombings and killings, the worst political and strategic blunder was the direct involvement of the military, which, instead of enforcing and coordinating intelligence for all the security agencies, itself became part of the problem. Moreover, the president hinted that backers and sympathisers of Boko Haram might even have penetrated the state machinery, thereby hampering any effective response. On two occasions alone, on 9 and 25 July, more than 50 suspected *Islamic militants* were shot dead in the course of large-scale military actions in Maiduguri. The forthright criticism by top members of the Islamic establishment, including the Sultan of Sokoto, of the military's brutal behaviour was tantamount to an official acknowledgement of its contentious role. Despite such criticism, the government did not learn from its mistakes. Worse still, it continued to ignore the fact that radical Islamist thinking had gained the hearts and minds of many in the Muslim north. Moreover, it reminded the public of the extra-judicial killing of the Boko Haram leaders in 2009. In this regard, and despite damning footage, five policemen, who had allegedly conducted the execution in cold blood and who were charged in court, were eventually released on bail on 19 July.

In many cases, Boko Haram chose to target civilians at popular drinking spots in north-eastern urban centres such as Maiduguri, where, on 26 June alone, two dozen were killed. Attackers created *carnage* amongst the citizens of Yobe state capital Damaturu on 5 November, killing about 150 people, including some 20 soldiers. Shortly after, the minister for youth development ordered that no new youth service corps members be posted to Borno and Yobe states, while those who had already been posted should be redeployed to other states. On 27 November, the divisional police headquarters, the First Bank and the council secretariat in Geidam, the home of the governor of Yobe state, were bombed and a number of churches and market stalls destroyed. Four policemen lost their lives during the assault. On Christmas Day, two bombs targeting churches killed 44 people. One was set off at St Theresa's Catholic Church in Madalla in Niger State, not far from Abuja, killing 43 people, and another at the Mountain of Fire and Miracle Church in Jos, Plateau state, killing one. In addition, four state security officers lost their lives in a suicide bomb blast in Damaturu.

Despite several arrests and charges being brought against alleged Boko Haram militants and the indictment of Borno state PDP-senator Mohammed Ali Ndume for having *links to the sect*, the federal and various state governments could not contain the violence. The senator, who was arrested along with one Sanda Umar Konduga on 21 November, was charged with terrorism, but pleaded not guilty. On 10 December, Ndume was granted bail on stringent conditions, while Konduga was sentenced to three years' imprisonment on 6 December. The latter admitted that he had been a spokesman for the group under the name of Usman al-Zawahiri, but maintained that he had been expelled on suspicion of being a government agent.

On New Year's Eve, an allegedly exasperated but hesitant president declared a *state of emergency* in 15 local government areas in four states – Borno, Niger, Plateau and Yobe – while on the same day an Islamic school in the city of Sapele in Delta state was attacked, causing the exodus of the small Muslim community of ethnic Hausa-Fulani, although no one was killed. Prior to that, on 11 December, a bomb had been set off in a mosque in the same city and shortly thereafter one injured person died. On 6 December, 20,000 Muslims had joined a peaceful demonstration in Kaduna staged by Ibrahim Zakzaky's Muslim Brethren to mark Ashura day. Towards the end of the year, on 21 December, two factions of the purist Izala movement reunited, having been split for about 20 years.

Against the background of party primaries and the forthcoming elections in the eastern part of the *Middle Belt*, particularly Plateau and Bauchi states – for years a centre of sectarian clashes – conflicts continued unabated, leaving a relatively large number of people dead. In January, attacks and counter attacks in and around the city of Jos by members of both faiths cost dozens of lives. Once again, some of the worst incidents occurred in Barkin Ladi local government area, close to the capital Jos. Over the course of the year, this area alone experienced at least eight deadly attacks, with more than 60 people killed, the worst assaults taking place in mid-August and on 24 November. During the latter, a local Christian councillor lost four children.

The police in neighbouring Bauchi, capital of the state of the same name, foiled a bomb attack in a church on 31 January, days after *sectarian youth violence* had caused the death of some 20 people. The town of Tafawa Balewa, home of Nigeria's first prime minister of the same name, became another epicentre of violence. There, on 26 January, trouble broke out between a Christian billiard table owner and a Muslim player in a dispute over money. Soon after, mosques and dozens of houses were set ablaze with at least four people killed and more than 4,000 displaced. On 6 May, a further 16 people were killed when several houses were set on fire in a revenge attack, and a further dozen people lost their lives when a bomb blast rocked a popular drinking place inside an army barracks on the city's periphery on 29 May.

The security forces were limited in their ability to quell the sectarian violence. The seizure of a truck with bomb-making devices on the Kaduna-Jos road on 11 March was one of their rare success stories. The military was increasingly blamed for taking sides and even for shooting innocent citizens. On 24 January, for example, villagers hurled stones and burned the tents of *military personnel* whom they blamed for killing five locals in Farin Lamba, not far from Jos, a few days earlier.

Over the course of the year, news of the serious crisis in the North somewhat overshadowed volatile incidents in the *Niger Delta*, as well as the unabated spread of organised crime throughout the country. On 11–12 May, militants believed to be loyal to self-proclaimed 'General' John Togo and his Niger Delta Liberation Force fought a gun battle with soldiers of the joint military force near the Ayakoromo community in Delta state. In another encounter on 17 November, nine soldiers and an unknown number of the gang were killed. In addition, piracy was on the rise, though not on the scale seen off the coast of Somalia. On 30 October, for example, pirates seized the Maltese oil tanker MT Halifax off the coast of Port Harcourt. The ship was released the following week after part of the cargo had been siphoned off, but no crew members were harmed. On 10 November, a former lieutenant commander, Lawrence Adesanya, who was thought to have abused his former position within the petroleum task force, was paraded alongside four other suspected pirates. They were accused of having hijacked on 7 October and 3 November two vessels carrying tonnes of premium motor spirit and gas oil.

On 21 October, however, a federal court in Delta state sentenced two Ghanaians and seven Nigerians to ten years for illegal oil trade and conspiracy. This was one of the rare occasions when oil thieves were arrested and convicted. *Kidnappings* remained common in the area, although the overall numbers decreased. On 12 May, a British and an Italian construction worker were taken hostage in Birnin Kebbi, and their fate was still unknown at year's end. On 9 June, five members of the national youth corps, deployed in Rivers state, were abducted outside Port Harcourt and their captors quickly demanded a ransom of Naira 100 m, which they later reduced to Naira 10 m. The hostages were eventually freed by police on 20 June, but it was not clear whether any ransom had been paid. Michael Obi, father of the famous Chelsea midfielder Mikel Obi, suffered a similar fate, being captured on 12 August in Plateau state and released ten days later. Two soldiers attached to the joint military force in Jos, along with six others, were arrested in connection with the kidnapping. Months later, two Catholic clerics, Sylvester Chukwura in Edo and Chijioke Amoke in Enugu state, were abducted on 3 October and 2 November respectively. The first was freed by security forces on 16 October and some of the kidnappers were arrested, while the second regained his freedom on 9 November. As in most cases, no information was available as to whether a ransom had been paid.

Despite ongoing criticism of the 2009 amnesty programme, the federal government continued its programme for the rehabilitation and reintegration of some 26,000 *ex-militants*. However, it eventually emerged that the government had put even more emphasis on sending youths abroad for various vocational training courses in Africa, Asia, the US and the Middle East, with some 2,000 benefiting from this costly exercise. Moreover, those who had successfully passed through the non-violence and reformatory training in the Obubra camp in Cross River state, were to be paid a transitional safety allowance of an unknown amount over and above the so-called monthly stipend of Naira 65,000. Prior to that, in May, the then minister for petroleum had announced that 12,000 teenagers were to be employed to protect oil and gas pipelines. On 25 May, almost 4,000 guns and several rocket-propelled grenades recovered from the militants were publicly destroyed.

Raids on banks across the country ran into dozens and, almost out of the blue, south-western Ogun state became a centre for *armed robberies*. A police officer and three civilians were killed in Ilaro, when four banks were robbed on 11 August. In one day, on 10 November, a gang of 20 robbed five banks on the Olabisi Onabanjo University campus in Ago Iwoye and made off with millions of naira. This was one of the rare cases where no one was killed. On 23 November, four banks were raided in the Sabo/Akarigbo area of Sagamu and almost a dozen people killed; on 13 December, the police paraded some 17 suspects, allegedly responsible for this crime. On 14 December, a gang blocked the busy Ota-Idiroko road for some two hours, robbing traders and passers-by of hundreds of thousands of naira. By pure chance, some armed air force personnel on their way to an exercise ran into the robbers and engaged them in a shoot-out, which forced the bandits to flee. Again in early December, in protest against the incessant attacks, almost all the banks in the state abandoned their services for a few days, bringing business to a virtual standstill. On 15 November, about 20 people died in the Sango-Ota area, when opposing factions of the National Union of Road Transport Workers clashed over the control of car parks in the state. This occurred in the aftermath of the gubernatorial election, in which the PDP lost the governorship to the ACN.

The deteriorating general security situation, exacerbated by long-standing corruption within the upper echelons of the police force, was matched by a worsening *human and civil rights record*. Nevertheless, the courts discharged several suspected criminals for lack of evidence, while governors commuted prison terms and death sentences. On 17 January, for example, a Lagos court acquitted Lucky Igbinovia and Effong Elemi Edu, who were standing trial for the 1995 murder of Alfred Rewane, a leading critic of the then military regime. The two had been in detention for 16 years. Five other accused died while awaiting trial. On 4 February, the supreme court overruled a court martial judgement that had convicted and demoted then rear-admiral Francis Agbiti in 2005 for alleged fraud and related matters. Among other things, the unanimous judgement stated that the entire proceedings were invalid, as the court martial was not properly constituted.

On 18 October, six suspects accused of involvement in the January crisis in Plateau state were acquitted and, on 13 October, an appeal court confirmed the verdict of a lower court, which the previous year had discharged retired Major Hamza Al-Mustapha, a notorious chief security officer of the late dictator Sani Abacha, and three others, who were accused of the attempted murder of the celebrated newspaper publisher Alex Ibru. However, Al-Mustapha and one Lateef Shofolahan were remanded in custody pending another trial related to the much publicised murder of Mrs Kudirat Abiola in 1996. The judge eventually moved the date for the verdict of this controversial case to early 2012. To mark the 51st anniversary of Independence, the Ondo state governor commuted five death sentences to life imprisonment and empowered the prison authority to discharge six prisoners who had served part of their sentence. On 24 November, a high court judge in Lagos awarded more than $ 155,000 compensation to the ethnic Yoruba comedian Babatunde Omidina, alias Baba Suwe, for the flagrant abuse and infringement of his fundamental human rights by the national drug law enforcement agency. On 12 October, he had been detained on suspicion of drug-trafficking, but after more than three weeks in custody and some 20 bowel movements, no drugs were excreted and on 4 November the actor was released on bail. The agency appealed the ruling.

On 29 November, the senate introduced a rigorous bill *banning same sex marriage*, a bill backed by leading clerics, both Muslim and Christian. By year's end it had not yet passed into law. As for the internationalisation of jurisprudence, on 18 January, the ECOWAS court of justice in Abuja dismissed any objections by the federal government and the oil companies, asserting its jurisdiction over a case brought by a registered NGO involving both violation of human rights and oil pollution in the Niger Delta. Thus, the court concurred with its vice president, Benfeito Mosso Ramos, who had maintained in December the previous year that disregarding the court's verdict was tantamount to a violation of the ECOWAS treaty.

The *anti-corruption campaign* produced few positive results. Most charges by the Economic and Financial Crime Commission (EFCC) against politicians, such as the outgoing speaker Dimeji Bankole and deputy speaker Usman Bayero Nafada, and several bankers, were either dismissed outright in court or the accused were granted bail. In a rare case, on 2 March, a federal high court granted the EFCC an asset forfeiture order to seize properties of former Edo state governor Lucky Igbinedion over an alleged Naira 3.2 bn fraud case. He had already been convicted and fined in 2008, but the EFCC had appealed that verdict. After fresh evidence of embezzlement and money laundering, Igbinedion was declared wanted, but the case was still pending at year's end and showed that the EFCC's record was at best mixed. The subsequent sacking of the chairman, Farida Waziri, did not come as a surprise and, on 23 November, Ibrahim Lamorde, director of operations, was appointed acting chairman in her place. Much earlier, on 9 February, the senate had rejected the president's nomination for the Independent Corrupt Practices and other Related Offences Commission, maintaining that the nominee was too old. Soon after his inauguration as president, Jonathan nominated Francis Ugochukwu Elechi, which drew scorn from civil society groups. On 29 November, at the eleventh hour, Jonathan suspended the swearing-in after receiving disturbing calls and reports, and eventually appointed board member Ekpo Una Owo Nta as acting chairman.

On 20 November, the 66-year-old founder, chairman and publisher of 'The Guardian' (Lagos) newspaper, Alex Ibru, passed away. A few days later, on 26 November, 78-year-old Chukwuemeka Odumegwu Ojukwu, the leader of the breakaway state of *Biafra*, died after a protracted illness.

Foreign Affairs

Good relations with the *us*, Nigeria's most important crude oil and liquefied gas customer, were to some extent shaped by the Boko Haram complex. On 29 September, Secretary of State Hillary Clinton, at a joint press conference with her Nigerian counterpart, Olugbenga Ashiru, in Washington, assured Nigeria that the us would stand by the nation as it faced serious security issues. At the start of the year, the first FBI agents were already deployed to Nigeria to help investigate previous bombings. Other agents arrived after the deadly attack on the police headquarters in June and, soon after, the then inspector-general of police Hafiz Ringim went to the us for a five-day working visit. In addition, in November, Nigerian soldiers received training in counter terrorism tactics in the us, at a time when experts warned a congressional hearing on 30 November that Boko Haram posed an emerging threat to us interests and the us homeland. During a four-day visit in mid-August, the head of us Africa Command, General Carter Ham, had set the agenda when he made a broad reference to a potential alliance between al-Qaida in the Maghreb and Boko Haram, al-Shabaab and other alleged militant groups, fuelling rumours of a worsening security situation and the threat of international terrorism in West Africa. On 13 May, at a handover ceremony in California, the Nigerian navy took over a us coast-guard ship, donated by the us government, to patrol the Niger Delta region. For its part, Nigeria paid some $ 8 m for the refurbishment of the vessel. In June, both sides signed an in-flight security agreement, involving the deployment of security officers on international flights.

Earlier, on 17 February, USAID had signed a $ 50 m partnership with Chevron's Niger Delta partnership initiative to try to help develop local businesses and boost community relations in the restive oil and gas producing area. This may have been in anticipation of a pending lawsuit against Shell, in which, on 17 October, the us supreme court eventually decided to consider the potential liabilities of corporations under the long-standing Alien Tort Claims Act. The Nigerian plaintiffs, relatives of the Ogonis who were hanged in 1995 after a show trial, charged Shell with complicity in torture, extra-judicial executions and crimes against humanity. On 11 October, the trial of Umar Farouk Abdulmutallab, accused of trying to blow up a US-bound flight on Christmas Day 2009, began with a guilty plea. Both *law suits* were still pending at year's end. On 13 October, 42-old Nigerian-born Bidemi Bello was sentenced to almost 12 years imprisonment by a US court on human trafficking charges. Her US citizenship was revoked and, besides being ordered to pay compensation, she was to be deported upon completion of her sentence. Nevertheless, Nigeria retained its good ranking in the eyes of the State Department because of its genuine efforts to combat human trafficking.

In a move aimed at strengthening political and economic ties, the newly elected Goodluck Jonathan was given a warm welcome in the White House on 8 June. Earlier, on 10 March, high profile US companies, led by the Assistant Secretary of Commerce Suresh Kumar, had paid a visit to Nigeria to explore *investments*, particularly in the ailing power sector. In August, a working group of the bi-national commission in Abuja reaffirmed its commitment to the implementation of power sector reform and, in December, a Nigerian trade mission, accompanied by US Ambassador Terence McCulley, attended a power trade show in Las Vegas. Last but not least, the US government institution, the Overseas Private Investment Corporation, approved $ 250 m to finance two US firms helping to revitalise Union Bank of Nigeria to enable it to reach the many people in Nigeria who do not have a bank account.

During a high-ranking meeting between Britain's Prime Minister David Cameron and the Nigerian president and key ministers from both sides in Lagos on 19 July, Cameron assured Jonathan of *British support* for Nigeria's efforts in restructuring its anti-terrorism security. During a visit to Nigeria in late June, Secretary of State for International Development Andrew Mitchell announced that

Britain was to spend £ 50 m on family planning and nutrition in the states most affected by malnutrition. However, Nigeria's relations with Britain were shaped more by legal issues, involving members of the large *Nigerian diaspora*. The prisoners' transfer deal, which would permit Britain to transfer Nigerian offenders to Nigerian prisons, was still high on the agenda. The corresponding Nigerian bill had not yet been become law at year's end, but in late October, it was reported that both governments had signed a so-called Prisoner Exchange Agreement.

On 18 March, Lucy Adeniji, was jailed in Britain for 11½ years, having been found guilty of *trafficking children* into the UK for domestic servitude. She had entered the UK on a false passport in the mid-1980s and had become a pastor of the evangelical church TLCC Ministries. On 7 July, 32-old Anthony Harris, who was alleged to have several aliases and believed to be a key player in a sophisticated network of West African human traffickers, was sentenced to 20 years. Although refused asylum after his arrival in 2003, he was later granted indefinite leave to remain. Two girls from southern Nigeria, controlled by Juju magic rituals, had been imprisoned in his home in Stratford and were about to be sent to Greece and Spain as prostitutes. On 20 May, four Nigerian women, who came to Britain during their childhood, were awarded £ 5,000 each after a court verdict stated that the Metropolitan Police Service had failed to investigate allegations of slavery. On 18 December, a stewardess of the Nigerian airline 'Arik Air', Chinwendu Uwakaonyenma Ogbonnaya, was arrested at Heathrow Airport on suspicion of smuggling cocaine into Britain.

The most prominent lawsuit concerned James Ibori. The former Delta state governor had sought refuge in Dubai, where he had been arrested at the request of Britain's Metropolitan Police for various *money laundering* offences the previous year, and on 15 April he was eventually extradited to Britain. The court case was still pending at year's end, but his UK lawyer, Bhadresh Gohil, had already been given a seven-year sentence in March.

The dynamics of increasing economic cooperation with *China* almost came to a standstill, particularly in the energy sector. Nigeria's state-run oil company, the Nigerian National Petroleum Corporation, and the oil states concerned had failed to fulfil their obligations concerning the already planned and badly needed construction of three oil refineries, thereby postponing the project indefinitely. In February, diplomats and politicians celebrated the 40th anniversary of diplomatic relations in a rather low-key way. However, on 19 December, the China Great Wall Industry Corporation successfully launched the Nigerian communications satellite NIGCOMSAT-1R into orbit.

The 'Arab Spring' in North Africa did not fail to have an impact on Nigeria, which in late August recognised *Libya*'s National Transitional Council as that country's legitimate government. Apart from the fact that a number of Nigerians had served as mercenaries in Kadhafi's army, several thousand civilians were living and working in Libya and Egypt. An unknown number of Nigerians died during the uprising and, in the course of the year, a few thousand were evacuated, with several managing to return home across the desert, among them an undisclosed number of mercenaries whose presence strengthened Boko Haram in the north-east. In the light of security threats in the region, the ECOWAS committee of chiefs of defence met in Abuja on 3–5 October. Earlier, on 11 March, Nigeria and *Cameroon* had agreed to jointly exploit any cross-border oil and gas reserves in the Bakassi peninsula. And in May, the West African Gas Pipeline Project Company WAPCo finally started its commercial activities, if only on a rather limited scale.

On 1 February, Jonathan travelled to *Turkey* on a two-day state visit, after attending the AU summit in Addis Ababa. He joined the second AU summit in Equatorial Guinea on 30 June to 1 July, and received German Chancellor Angela Merkel in mid-July. It was the first visit by a German head of government for 25 years. Soon after, on 21 July, the president paid a visit to Liberia, and in early October he went for a two-day working visit to *Rwanda* in anticipation of the December launching of direct flights run by RwandAir between Kigali and Lagos. On 9 August, Jonathan received his Niger counterpart, Mahamadou Issoufou. However, when President Jacob Zuma of *South Africa* attended the annual Shehu Musa Yar'Adua memorial lecture in Abuja on 10 December, he was only welcomed by the vice president. Jonathan addressed the UN General Assembly in New York on 21 September, joined the 21st Commonwealth summit in Australia at the end of October, and in late November opened an international investors' council meeting in Paris, coordinated by Baroness Lynda Chalker. Prior to that, on 12 November, French Foreign Minister Alain Juppé met his counterpart in Abuja, offering France's assistance in tackling terrorism. The president rounded off the year on 19 December by welcoming the new managing director of the IMF Christine Lagarde, who attended an economic forum in Lagos the following day.

On 17 January, Babatunde Osotimehin was sworn in as executive director of the UN Population Fund by Secretary-General Ban Ki-moon, who paid his first official visit to the country on 22–23 May. In December, a Nigerian, Chile Eboe-Osuji, was elected to serve on the bench of the ICC for the first time.

Socioeconomic Developments

In the course of the year, oil and gas prices remained high and Nigeria benefited strongly from its high quality crude, which was sold at \$ 95 a barrel at the start of the year and close to \$ 110 at year's end.

However, the *2011 budget*, totalling Naira 4.48 trillion (\$ 28 bn) based on a benchmark of \$ 75 per barrel and an exchange rate of Naira 150 to \$ 1, was not signed by Jonathan until 27 May, and only after a series of deliberations with lawmakers. Earlier, on 16 March, the National Assembly had covertly inflated the initially proposed budget of Naira 4.2 trillion to Naira 4.9 trillion, which had prompted the president to send it back. On 13 December, Jonathan presented his 2012 budget proposal of Naira 4.75 trillion, emphasising the need to create jobs, particularly for young people, and to address the rising domestic debt profile. Interestingly, the sensitive issue of fuel subsidies, which accounted for up to $ 7 bn annually, was omitted. In fact, not long before, the senate had revealed that some 100 companies were the real beneficiaries of the heavily subsidised fuel import contracts, and that the latter were not unrelated to corrupt practices.

Against the background of Boko Haram and increasing youth violence in large parts of the country, however, the government finally acknowledged the existence of a "ticking time bomb". Regarding *demographic development*, it was suggested that the population had doubled to more than 160 m over 20 years, with some 40% aged under 15, and at least 20 m young people were jobless, posing a genuine danger to the political and socioeconomic system. Local observers estimated that the number was far higher.

As in previous years, the central banks issued bonds and treasury bills with varying maturities almost monthly, this year worth more than $ 12 bn. In addition, on 21 January, Nigeria issued a $ 500 m debut Eurobond, which was heavily oversubscribed. Towards the end of the year, the *debt management* office announced that external debt stood at an acceptable $ 5.6 bn, while Nigeria's domestic debt amounted to more than $ 34 bn, a steep increase of some 20% within a year.

While the promised wide-ranging reforms to the oil and gas industry were put on hold, to be considered by the new National Assembly the following year, the government, together with the central bank, continued to restructure and stabilise the *banking sector*. Thus, the court of appeal upheld the verdict of a lower court, which had ruled that the governor of the central bank had the power to hire and fire directors of any bank found to be in a serious financial predicament. In addition, in late November, the bank declared 82 of the 104 licensed finance houses to be unhealthy and undercapitalised. These institutions had been assigned the task of offering financial services to small and medium-sized enterprises. On 20 June, the central bank granted the first Islamic banking licence to Jaiz Bank International, run by well-known bankers and businessmen such as Umaru Abdul Mutallab, Falau Bello and Aminu Alhassan Dantata. Soon after, on 4 July, the Nigerian branch of South African Standard Bank was given approval to set up an Islamic banking division.

Nigeria's phenomenal growth in the *telecommunications sector* continued apace as the number of mobile phones in use rocketed to more than 80 m. In Africa's biggest and fastest growing telecoms market, demand was still outstripping supply. In the light of these developments, the UAE-based company, Etisalat, signed agreements on 10 March for a $ 650 m syndicated loan with local banks. The following day, the leading provider, MTN Nigeria, an arm of the South African MTN Group, announced that it was to spend $ 1 bn in the following year. And on 7 June, the indigenous company Globacom signed another long-term contract with Shell, to provide a high-speed broadband link, connecting Shell's operational hubs in Lagos and the Niger Delta. According to the science and technology ministry, Nigeria spends some $ 450 m annually on importing foreign bandwidth and $ 100 m on services, so the long-awaited launch of the communication satellite NIGCOMSAT-1R in December was a real boost for Nigeria's ICT. Earlier, on 17 August, two Nigerian earth observation satellites had already been successfully sent into orbit in Russia.

The spread of *HIV/AIDS* continued unabated and it was reported that the number of infections had passed the 7 m mark. Compared with previous years, progress in the fight to eradicate *polio* suffered a minor setback, indicated by the fact that 60 cases were reported towards year's end. The figure of more than 3,000 deaths and some 18,000 injured in over 2,200 road *traffic accidents* proved Nigeria's poor road safety record once again. In this respect, it was hardly surprising that, according to the Federal Road Safety Commission, some 60% of driving licences in Delta state were fake, indicating a serious and widespread problem.

The federal government continued to further the commercialisation of *education* when, on 2 March, it approved licences for four new private universities in Kwara, Edo and Osun state and the Federal Capital Territory. The overall number of universities thus increased to 118, comprising 36 federal, 37 state and 45 private universities.

On 3 April, the German, Uli Beier, passed away in Australia, aged 89. He had arrived in Nigeria in 1950 as a lecturer at the University of Ibadan, Nigeria's only university at the time. In the decades to come, Beier recognised the creative spirit and verve of *Nigerian literature* and arts, particularly in the Yoruba-speaking area, and enthusiastically represented their interests in other parts of the world. On 2 May, the US-based 2009 winner of the 'Caine Prize for African Writing', E.C. Osondu, was announced as one of the winners of the 'Pushcart Prize' for his short story "Janjaweed Wife".

While the U-20 soccer team won the sixth Africa youth championship final against Cameroon on 1 May, the Nigerian 'Super Eagles' failed for the first time in 25 years to qualify for the 2012 *African Cup of Nations*, after the last game in Abuja, on 8 October against Guinea, ended in a 2–2 draw, handing Guinea the ticket to the finals.

Nigeria in 2012

The most critical issue during the year was the deterioration of the precarious security situation, particularly in the urban areas of Maiduguri (Borno state), Potiskum and Damaturu (Yobe state), and Kano and Kaduna (capitals of the states of the same name). Clashes between factions of the Islamic sect 'Jama'atu Ahlis Sunna Lid Da'awati Wal Jihad', better known as Boko Haram, and security forces, particularly military units of the 'Joint Task Force' (JTF), took place almost every day, with dozens of deaths on both sides. (Boko Haram is generally translated as 'Western education is forbidden'. In fact, the original meaning is 'deceit, or fraud (*boko*), is forbidden'; the meaning 'Western education' accrued later.) The structural weakness of the Nigerian police forced the military to shoulder most of the burden of dealing with the insurgents and criminals. Several hundred people, including innocent persons and security personnel, as well as alleged members and sympathisers of the sect, fell victim to bomb attacks, suicide bombings, counterattacks, indiscriminate killings and deadly raids on barracks, police stations, churches, mosques, schools, hide-outs, villages, outdoor refreshment stops and prisons. At year's end, some 1,000 people had lost their lives. Boko Haram claimed responsibility for most of the attacks, although it had allegedly split into various splinter groups such as the more radical Jama'atu Ansarul Muslimina Fi Biladis Sudan (meaning 'Vanguards for the protection of Muslims in Black Africa'), better known as Ansaru. Sophisticated criminal gangs from all parts of the country were also at work, using the same name. Those arrested included a significant number of security personnel actively involved in the movement. Such complications defeated any attempt to draw a clear line between sectarian clashes and organised crime in the poverty-stricken far North.

© KONINKLIJKE BRILL NV, LEIDEN, 2017 | DOI 10.1163/9789004347410_010

Domestic Politics

Despite the state of emergency imposed in some areas of *Borno state*, where Boko Haram was founded, two students of the University of Maiduguri were killed on 7 January in their Mairi ward residence, and a scholar of the 'Goni College of Islamic and Legal Studies' was assassinated on 25 March on the outskirts of Maiduguri. Soon afterwards, on 3 April, gunmen attacked the city's 'Monday Market', robbing five traders of the day's takings and gunning down 12 people. On 9 April, six men, including a police inspector, the former chairman of Dikwa local government council, Babagana Karim, and three gunmen became victims of a clash between a gang of about 30, and the JTF. On 18 September, the Borno state attorney general, Zanna Malam Gana, was shot in his home town of Bama. The JTF was also involved in *clashes*, which drew heavy criticism: On two occasions alone, on 15 October and 1 November, the JTF killed dozens of alleged Boko Haram members but was heavily criticised by local observers and AI, which accused the security forces of human rights abuses, even against uninvolved civilians. Nevertheless, the often heavy-handed and at times brutal behaviour of the military had its effect on the Islamists and clearly unnerved Boko Haram. This development fuelled the use of brutality on both sides, so that more and more distinguished locals were targeted. One such was veteran soldier Muhammadu Shuwa, a retired major general and top commander during the civil war; he was killed on 2 November. On 12 November, Alhaji Babagana Kola, a university don, and Malam Yerima, a director in the Ministry of Lands and Survey, were gunned down. Two days later, Malam Ali Mohammed Sheriff, a top civil servant in the Ministry of Water Resources, suffered the same fate, and the Revd Ilesha Kabura of Eklesiya Yanwa Nigeria Church met his death on 18 November.

One of the cruellest incidents in Borno state involved 20 young women wearing mini-skirts and trousers who were *butchered* in the state capital on 23 November. On 1 December, late at night, ten

Christians, living in the remote village of Chibok had their throats cut and, on 28 December, in the village of Musari on the outskirts of Maiduguri, 15 villagers were killed in the same way, bringing the number of dead to more than 220 in Borno state alone, including foreign workers from China, India and Ghana.

Neighbouring *Yobe state* fared no better. On 10 January, eight people, including four policemen, were shot in a bar in Potiskum, the state's largest city and its commercial hub, and the next day, gunmen on motorcycles attacked a south-east bound bus, killing four passengers. On 6 March, the comptroller of customs in charge of Borno and Yobe states, Alhaji Adamu Ahmadu, also met his death in Potiskum. On 10 December, another gun battle in the city cost 14 lives, including that of a divisional police officer, and gunmen attacked the Church of Christ in Nigeria on Christmas Day in the nearby village of Piri, killing the pastor, Yohana Sini, and five worshippers. Shortly before New Year's Eve, on 29 December, the JTF killed four suspected Boko Haram members and arrested some 50 in the city's Yindiski area.

In the state capital Damaturu, nine soldiers died and several others sustained injuries on 5 August, when a suicide bomber drove a car loaded with explosives into two military patrol vehicles. On 24 September, the city became a *veritable battlefield* when military forces killed 35 alleged Boko Haram members during an overnight gun battle. In another raid on a hide-out in the town on 7 October, some 30 suspected members were killed in a shoot-out and several others arrested, among them the notorious one-eyed Bakaka, a close associate of the sect's self-proclaimed leader, Abubakar Shekau, who had assumed the leadership after the extra-judicial killing of Mohammed Yusuf in 2009. A retired comptroller of customs, Ajiya Waziri Golili, and his son were gunned down in their house on 20 October by a gang of ten, and the Buni/Yadi divisional police station in Gujba local government area was targeted on 9 November; three officers were shot and the attackers made off with a large haul of arms and ammunition. Some 100 people lost their lives in the state.

The most populous northern state, Kano, became a new focal point of the rapidly *spreading violence* in the northern region. According to official figures, 186 people were killed when, on 20 January, bomb attacks and some 50 gunmen disguised as military and police wrought havoc in the city. They targeted police stations and police command posts, offices of the sss (State Security Service) and other government agencies such as the immigration headquarters. Three days later, the police discovered cars and vans filled with explosives. Shortly thereafter, on 26 January, the German engineer Edgar Fritz Raupach, an employee of the Julius Berger Nigeria construction firm, was taken hostage. Later in March, a video message was released, demanding the release of a Turkish-born woman, Filiz Gelowicz, imprisoned in Germany the previous year for helping terrorists. She was the wife of a German Muslim convert and member of the 'Sauerland group', whose members were sentenced to prison terms in 2010 for plotting to attack us facilities in Germany. At the end of April, she was released early for good behaviour. Nevertheless, the hostage was eventually killed by his captors when security forces raided their hide-out in Kano on 31 May. None of the hostage takers survived the shoot-out.

In the days and weeks that followed, attacks on police stations continued unabated. *Another ugly incident* took place on 29 April, when gunmen equipped with 'improvised explosive devices' (IEDs) and rifles attacked Christian worshippers at the university theatre of the old Bayero University campus, which was regularly used for services on Sundays. At least 19 were killed and many more wounded. On 16 September in Hotoro, a national security and civil defence officer, his wife, daughter and brother were virtually executed in their house by assassins who had arrived on a motorcycle. The following day, security sources declared that they had killed the Boko Haram spokesman, Anwal Kontagora, alias Abu Qaqa. The authorities had already claimed to have arrested him in March, but the detainee turned out to be another member of the sect. This case highlighted the fact that establishing the identity of arrested leaders of Boko

Haram was problematic. Only two days later, the JTF intercepted and arrested the sect's accountant, travelling on a commuter bus on his way to Zaria, carrying 4.5 m naira (NGN) in cash. Prior to that, on 5 September, gunmen on motorcycles destroyed mobile phone masts. This action paralled *coordinated attacks* on at least 24 masts in other states in the northern region.

As in Borno state, *distinguished Kano residents* were not spared by the Islamists. State house members Ibrahim Abba Garko of the People's Democratic Party (PDP) and Daladi Isa Kademi of the All Nigeria People's Party were killed on 17 November and 14 December, respectively. Eventually, two suspects were arrested and allegedly confessed to having been paid NGN 40,000 each to carry out the plots. At year's end, at least 240 people had fallen victim to the many assaults, and 68 IEDs had been discovered and detonated by the police.

Kaduna state also experienced a new level of *sectarian violence* when, on Sunday 25 November, suicide bombers drove two vehicles full of IEDs into the famous military college in Jaji, close to the state capital, targeting the St Andrew Military Protestant Church, located within faculty premises. The blast killed at least 15 people and wounded many more, aggravating what was already a delicate situation. Already on Easter Sunday, 8 April, two car bombs had killed some two dozen Christian worshippers and motorcyclists. The latter are popularly known as 'Okada' or 'Achaba' riders, and offer a cheap alternative to taxis. However, these organised motorcyclists claimed that more than 100 of their members had been killed. On 26 April, two offices of the leading Nigerian newspaper 'This Day', in Kaduna and the Federal Capital Territory Abuja, were targeted. Six staff members died in the blasts and the Abuja office was completely destroyed. On 28 October, a bomb explosion at the St Rita Catholic Church in Malali, part of the Kaduna metropolitan area, claimed the lives of some 15 people, injuring at least 100 and bringing the death toll in the state to more than 60.

Not one of the *12 northern states* where Sharia law has been adopted, was spared, as Boko Haram extended its reach into all the other northern states. Even Sokoto state, with its capital of the same name, home of the sultan and considered a safe haven, was hit when two police stations in the state capital were attacked by suicide bombers on 30 July. The two suspected bombers, a policeman and a woman died. And on 1 September, the Muslim cleric Limam Danda Birkitawa was shot dead in his village in Dange-Shuni local government area.

In Birnin Kebbi, capital of neighbouring Kebbi state, a rescue operation was undertaken on 8 March to free British and Italian construction workers, Chris McManus and Franco Lamolinara, who had been abducted in May the previous year. Some of their guards had already been arrested and the rest were gunned down during the operation, but not before they had killed their hostages. Since British security forces were involved, the action received international attention. On 20 December, a group of about 30 attacked a heavily guarded compound in Rimi, close to the city of Katsina in the state of the same name, killing two security guards and *kidnapping* the French engineer Francis Colump, who was working for a French company on a wind power project. No information was available at year's end as to his whereabouts and fate. On 28 December, the divisional police station, the prison and the customs area office in Maiha local government in Adamawa state were attacked. Some 20 people lost their lives, and the gunmen made off with weapons and ammunition and freed several inmates. These are only some of the many acts of violence that were committed.

A modest attempt by the federal government to initiate dialogue with factions of Boko Haram, a proposal made by the Shehu of Borno and the Usman Galtimari committee earlier in the year, had little impact and was shelved, although the government acknowledged in August that it was still talking with some sect members through "back room channels". However, against this background of spiralling violence, it took another three months and many more attacks and victims before a new *strategy on counter-terrorism* was revealed at a conference in Abuja in early November. Apart from creating the post of coordinator in the office of the national security adviser, charged with the difficult task of dealing with the various and often divided security agencies, a list of the 19 most wanted members of Boko Haram was published on 23 November and generous rewards offered for information leading to their arrest. However, the creation of the new post prompted controversy in political and security circles, particularly concerning its affiliation with the national security adviser's office; it was still vacant at year's end.

The precarious security situation eventually took its toll on the *administration's key positions*. Early in the year, on 25 January, President Goodluck Jonathan sacked the controversial inspector general of police, Hafiz Ringim, and his six deputies and appointed the then assistant inspector general, Mohammed Dahiru Abubakar. The reason for sacking Ringim, only months before his retirement, was the escape of Kabiru Umar, also known as Kabiru Sokoto, from police custody a month earlier; Umar was one of the chief suspects in a bomb attack carried out on Christmas Day 2011. The consequences of Abubakar's leap-frog promotion were far-reaching, triggering further promotions, retirements and redeployment of police units. In March, the Economic and Financial Crimes Commission (EFCC), appointed in November 2011 under the chairmanship of Ibrahim Lamorde, also underwent a major reorganisation; this move sought to hasten the cleansing process and to reverse the widely perceived integrity deficit of the Commission. On 22 June, Sambo Dasuki, a retired colonel, was appointed national security adviser, replacing the unfortunate retired General Andrew Owoye Azazi. Minister of Defence Bello Haliru Mohammed was also removed, and no successor had been appointed by year's end.

The *military* also underwent a shake-up, when, on 4 October, three new service chiefs emerged, following the retirement of Air Marshal Oluseyi Petinrin and Air Marshal Mohammed Dikko Umar, chief of defence staff and of air staff, respectively. Jonathan replaced them with the chief of naval staff, Vice Admiral Ola Sa'ad Ibrahim, who took over defence, and Air Vice Marshal Alex S. Badeh, who was given the air staff portfolio. Lieutenant General Onyeabo Azubuike

Ihejirika retained his position, however, while Rear Admiral D.J. Ezeoba succeeded the former chief of naval staff. The air force had already redeployed six of its air vice marshals in March and, in November, 32 group captains were promoted to the next rank of air commodore. The army and navy followed suit in December, promoting 226 senior officers to the rank of colonel (91), brigadier (37), major general (22), commander (20), captain (33), commodore (40) and rear admiral (19). In response to the Boko Haram uprising, 2,000 soldiers were trained by counter-terrorism experts in Jaji in March, and several courses for commissioned and non-commissioned officers were run at the same venue in December, exposing them to the concept of asymmetric warfare and methods of combating insurrection.

However, the reorganisation of the security agencies made little or no difference to the lives of the vast majority of Nigerian citizens. In the southern region, with its commercial hubs of Lagos and Port Harcourt, the security situation was shaped not by Boko Haram but by organised crime. There were also sporadic clashes between remnants of *Niger Delta militias* and the JTF, which acknowledged having lost nine men in the oil producing area over the course of the year. However, the JTF also claimed to have arrested more than 1,900 suspects, destroyed more than 4,000 illegal refineries (small and very simple structures, located in hide-outs in the swamps), and impounded vessels, barges and even trucks. And in early June, the first Nigerian-made warship was launched, almost five years after work on it started. On 1 March, the commander of the JTF unit in Brass, Lieutenant Colonel Abubakar Malik, and three of his soldiers were attacked by militants in five speedboats and eventually killed. On the same day, a faction of the Movement for the Emancipation of the Niger Delta blew up a police checkpoint in Bayelsa state; four people lost their lives. On 15 October, pirates kidnapped seven men, all except one Russian citizens, on their way to an oil platform. They were released on 1 November. Prior to that, in early September, the federal government had agreed to start the third phase of an amnesty programme involving more than 3,600 ex-militants, and bringing the total number of those benefitting from the programme to 30,000.

Once again, *crime was widespread*, with kidnappings, bank raids and killings still prevalent. However, the security forces killed and arrested a significant number of gang members, particularly in southern parts of the country. In Lagos state alone, some 140 robbers were killed and more than 560 arrested, while 30 or so policemen lost their lives in the course of duty. On 26 January, a military unit on routine patrol in Ebonyi state intercepted a group of armed robbers after a failed bank robbery in Ikom in neighbouring Cross River state, in which eight civilians and one policeman had died. Nine robbers and one soldier eventually lost their lives during the ensuing gun battle. Although six robbers managed to escape, weapons, ammunition and two vehicles were recovered. In Sapele in Delta state on 18 March, gunmen attacked a beer parlour, mindlessly shooting seven guests. No reason was given for the bloodbath, but it was reported that the killers claimed to be unemployed and starving, while their victims were enjoying themselves. On 31 March, another ugly incident took place on the Ore-Sagamu expressway in Ogbere in Ogun state, when a gang robbed a bus and raped some 40 female students. The police were able to arrest the suspects shortly afterwards, including the bus driver. In late July, Cynthia Osokogu, a post-graduate student of Nasarawa university and daughter of a retired major general, was lured into a trap by male students in Lagos via 'Facebook'; she was raped and killed. The culprits were traced weeks later when her stolen mobile phone was located.

The actions of Boko Haram did not diminish the activities of *organised criminal gangs* in the north. Some of the ugliest incidents took place in Zamfara, Adamawa and Kaduna states. On 27 January, about 100 hooligans barricaded a main road in Zamfara and robbed a convoy of traders on their way to the Batsari market in neighbouring Katsina state. Pandemonium broke out and 15 traders were killed. In Adamawa, on the night of Independence Day (1 October), gunmen shot dead at least 26 students in their college residence at the Federal Polytechnic in Mubi. While alleged Boko Haram members denied any involvement, there were indications that the killings might have been motivated by a serious feud inside the college. In what seemed to be an act of reprisal, 24 villagers in Dogon-Dawa in Birnin Gwari local government area in Kaduna state were gunned down by bandits on 14 October. Shortly before, a vigilante group had captured four people in a village called Kuyello and taken them for questioning; those captured were believed to be members of a gang notorious for terrorising the area.

Kidnapping was still a common and lucrative activity, particularly in the south. As in previous years, kidnappers mostly targeted well-known local Nigerians, such as the wife of Senator George Sekibo, abducted in Port Harcourt on 22 March and rescued unharmed four days later. Others were Mrs Ngozi Chukwuebulim, a medical doctor in Warri, Delta state, who was kidnapped on 1 April and released three days later; Nwika Gbinu, a Catholic priest from Onne in the Eleme local government area of Rivers state, who regained his freedom on 1 May after a week in captivity; Hope Eghagha, Delta state commissioner for higher education, who was captured in an attack on 30 September, during which his police bodyguard was killed. He was set free two weeks later. The most spectacular kidnapping was that of the finance minister's 83-year-old mother, Kamene Okonjo, a retired professor of sociology, who was abducted from her husband's palace in Aniocha local government area in Delta state (9 December). The captors demanded NGN 200 m for her release, and, on 14 December, she was eventually freed some 30 km away. Security sources maintained that no ransom had been paid but it emerged that the captors had demanded the minister's resignation in connection with a controversial fuel subsidy scam. In contrast, when four South Korean nationals and various Nigerians working for Hyundai were kidnapped on 17 December, a ransom of $ 190,000 was paid before they were released a few days later, much to the consternation of the police. This was one of the rare cases in which such a deal became public.

The *Middle Belt*, particularly Plateau, Benue and Taraba states, was another focal point of *sectarian clashes*, which claimed many victims. In Gwer local government area in Benue state on 6 March, ethnic Fulani herdsmen raided Tiv villages, killing some two dozen inhabitants. On 29 October, at least five were killed in a predawn attack in a village in Barkin Ladi local government area in Plateau state. And in Taraba state, on 19–20 November, the death toll rose to ten and the number of injured to some 200 after violence broke out between Muslims and Christians in Ibi local government area over a temporary street closure for a religious service. Even the capital, Abuja, was not spared, when, on 29–30 December, Fulani herdsmen and local Gwari people clashed over farm boundaries in Garko in the Gwagwalada area, leaving some dead and more than 1,500 displaced in various communities.

In addition to appointing new personnel to top positions in the security agencies, President Jonathan filled several more important vacancies. On 16 July, a female justice of the Supreme Court, Aloma Mariam Mukhtar, succeeded Dahiru Musdapher as chief justice of Nigeria; Musdapher had reached the mandatory retirement age of 70. An overdue shake-up affecting most of the senior staff in the aviation sector, with its poor air safety record, took place in early October, and a re-organisation of the Nigerian National Petroleum Corporation followed towards the end of that month. On New Year's Eve, the president approved yet more boards of directors of federal agencies, offering highly paid positions by the dozen.

Nigeria's new and first female chief justice soon stirred up a hornet's nest, however, with steps that had controversial legal and constitutional ramifications. On 5 November, she declined to administer the oath of office to Abia state nominee Mrs Ifeoma Jombo-Ofo, who, together with 11 other justices, had been elevated to the Court of Appeal, the second highest court in the land. The chief justice's refusal was based on the fact that the candidate was originally from Anambra state, but, upon marriage, had transferred her service to her husband's state, Abia, so that her nomination was invalid. In fact, this issue touched on the sensitive and unresolved question of citizenship and '*indigeneship*', which continued to work to the disadvantage of non-indigenes in any state and to affect vacancies in public institutions and government at state and national level. The Federal Character Commission Act, established in 1996 and included in the 1999 constitution, had introduced an allocation system by which, it was hoped, a sense of balance might be achieved in Nigeria's power structure; however, the system was misused, often leading to communal tension. After strong political and legal pressure from the senate and the national judicial council, the chief justice rescinded her decision and Ifeoma Jombo-Ofo was sworn in on 22 November, but the real issue remained shelved.

The legal and constitutional controversy concerning *five PDP governors*, who, after the annulment of their election in 2007, were elected in a re-run the following year and whose tenure therefore expired in 2012, or in one case in late 2011, dragged on behind the scenes, although the verdict of the Supreme Court, passed on 27 January, seemed to have removed these governors from office. The court emphasised the fact that tenure should not exceed the four-year term prescribed by the constitution and argued that tenure started from the day of taking the first oath of office and should have expired in May 2011. However, with the exception of Kogi state, where the PDP candidate had already been re-elected in December 2011, the sitting governors of Adamawa, Cross River and Sokoto states won their elections in February and remained in power after all. These election victories were eventually confirmed by the same court, despite its earlier ruling. In Jonathan's home state, Bayelsa, PDP's Henry Seriake Dickson emerged as the new elected governor, after the incumbent Timipre Sylva had been controversially disqualified from the primaries. In July, despite wide public criticism, the new governor appointed the president's wife, Patience Jonathan, as a permanent secretary. Interestingly, in almost all cases, the Supreme Court strictly applied the amended deadlines for written submissions: 21 days for petitions, 180 days for tribunal judgments and 60 days for appealable verdicts. Thus the court avoided to some extent dealing with possibly overwhelming legal wrangling regarding content but, by insisting on the deadlines, overruled even appeal court verdicts.

In Edo and Ondo states, statutory *gubernatorial elections* took place on 14 July and 20 October, respectively, and were won by the incumbents, Adams Oshiomhole of the Action Congress of Nigeria and Olusegun Mimiko of the Labour Party. They had successfully contested the election results of 2007 and had eventually been installed as duly elected. In the north-western state of Kebbi, however, the elected governor, Usman Dakingari, was sacked by the Supreme Court on 24 February but won the re-run on 31 March with ease. All the other petitions concerning the gubernatorial elections in April 2011 were finally dismissed. On 13 December, however, in a surprise move the Electoral Commission deregistered 28 parties and indicated that more could be targeted.

The *anti-corruption campaign* did not yield any positive results, despite the EFCC's new leadership and restructuring. In March, Chairman Ibrahim Lamorde even admitted to being shocked, having realised that those charged with fulfilling the Commission's mandate were themselves caught up in widespread corruption. Moreover, in cases such as that brought against the former bank manager Erastus Akingbola, charged with serious fraud, the Commission and the attorney-general were berated by the Lagos federal high court in early April for providing insufficient evidence and for the prosecution team's general incompetence. As a result, the case was dismissed.

The report by the petroleum revenue special task force, set up in February in the wake of fuel subsidy protests and chaired by the former head of the EFCC, Nuhu Ribadu, was an example of how excessive corruption was handled. At the end of October, the leaked report unearthed ample evidence of large-scale fraud in the petroleum industry, including massive fraud connected to the lucrative import of highly subsidised fuel. Soon afterwards, however, an open disagreement between the chairman and his deputy, Steve

Orosanye, on how to compile the committee's report became so embarrassing that the office of the president eventually rejected the report on 8 November on the grounds that its recommendations were not workable. In its place, barely a week later, the president established three committees to draft 'White Papers' on the petroleum report and two other reports – on the national refineries and on the governance and controls special task force. Moreover, on 3 December, the federal government pardoned more than 80 stockbrokers, who, like business tycoons such as Femi Otedola and Aliko Dangote, amongst others, were largely responsible for the capital market failure in 2009.

There were, nevertheless, some successes. At least half a dozen Nigerians were intercepted with huge amounts of undeclared dollars, ranging from some $ 130,000 to $ 7 m, at the airports in Abuja, Kano and Lagos. They were arrested and charged, since only $ 10,000 was permitted to be taken out of the country without prior declaration.

The worsening human and civil rights record was to a large extent determined by the precarious security situation. Nevertheless, more governors used their executive powers to commute *death sentences* to life imprisonment and they even ordered the release of elderly and some long-term prisoners. Ogun state started in late January by commuting two death sentences and releasing seven prisoners. Cross River state acted similarly in September, followed by Lagos state, where some 280 were released in two batches in September and December. In October, Kano freed 58 inmates. A closer look, however, revealed that some 70% the 50,000 inmates across the country were awaiting trial in *overcrowded prisons*. On 30 January, in Nigeria's longest-running criminal case, the Lagos federal high court sentenced two men to death by hanging: Hamza Al-Mustapha, a notorious former chief security officer of military dictator Sani Abacha, and Lateef Shofolahan, protocol officer in Chief Moshood Abiola's presidential campaign in the early months of 1993. That election was annulled by the military regime of Ibrahim Babangida, who was succeeded by Abacha. The verdict, handed down for the 1996 murder of Kudirat Abiola, then senior wife of her detained husband who died in custody in 1998, ended the trial, which had begun in 1999. On 26 November, Attorney General Muhammed Bello Adoke inaugurated the governing council of the National Human Rights Commission.

On 4 November, the Biafran Zionist Movement under its self-proclaimed president of Biafra, Benjamin Onwuka, a faction of the Movement for the Actualisation of the Sovereign State of *Biafra* (MASSOB), raised the Biafran flag, marched through Enugu and declared Biafra's independence. Onwuka was arrested by the police, together with dozens of MASSOB members.

A walkout by members of the OIC, of which Nigeria is a member, from a UN panel of the Human Rights Council in Geneva on 6 March, once again highlighted the controversial issue of *same sex-marriage*. A rigorous bill banning it was passed by both houses of the Nigerian parliament, strongly supported by leaders of both the Muslim and Christian faiths but, somewhat surprisingly, the president had not signed it into law before year's end, which indicated that the bill had been quietly put to rest.

Foreign Affairs

Relations with the *United States*, the most important customer for Nigeria's crude oil and liquefied gas and its main supplier of wheat, were to a large extent shaped by the Boko Haram situation. On 16 February, Umar Faruk Abdulmutallab was sentenced to life imprisonment for his failed attempt to blow up a US-bound flight in late 2009. The then Nigerian security adviser, Andrew Azazi, had just published an article in the 'Washington Times' on combating terrorist threats in Nigeria and had urged the US to offer Nigeria its support. He referred to a high-level meeting in Abuja on 23 January under US-Nigeria Binational Commission, which was attended by Deputy Assistant Secretary of State William Fitzgerald and US military and intelligence officials. In early March, the State Department acknowledged that the FBI was assisting Nigerian security services in tackling Boko Haram and, to a lesser extent, the Niger Delta's militias. This was in line with the US commitment to Nigeria, confirmed in Abuja on 5 March by Under Secretary of State for Political Affairs Wendy Sherman, who was then on a five-nation Africa tour. Furthermore, the US even considered setting up a consulate in Kano. On 9 August, US Secretary of State Hillary Clinton stopped over in Abuja at the end of her Africa tour. In early September, a US navy ship undertook a week of joint training with the Nigerian navy, and, on 11 December, President Jonathan received the head of the US Africa Command, General Carter Ham. The previous month saw Assistant Secretary of State for Democracy, Human Rights and Labour Michael Posner visiting Nigeria.

On 11 April, the US and Nigerian vice presidents, Joe Biden and Namadi Sambo, met at the White House, and the Nigerian guest and his high-ranking delegation then attended the US Exim Bank annual conference. The Overseas Private Investment Corporation, a US government institution, approved a $ 250 m loan to fund a nitrogen fertiliser facility. At the end of the year, the US Supreme Court's decision on a law suit against Shell, initiated by relatives of the Ogonis, who were hanged in 1995 after a show-trial, was still pending.

Nigeria's relations with *Britain* were shaped once again by various legal issues. At the end of July, London's High Court, after hearing a $ 1 bn fraud case, handed down a judgement in favour of the Nigerian Excess Bank against Erastus Akingbola, a former executive of the Nigerian Intercontinental Bank, one of the banks bailed out during the Nigerian financial crisis of 2009. Also, on 17 April, the former Nigerian governor, James Ibori, who had been indicted for various money laundering offences in 2011, was sentenced to 13 years' imprisonment. This verdict ended an extraordinary legal battle between the former strongman of Delta state politics and the joint powers of the EFCC and the British legal system. Ibori, who rose from being a petty thief in London to become a powerful governor in Nigeria, was to spend only four-and-a-half years in prison in return for his decision to plead guilty, but nevertheless brought an appeal against the verdict in September, alleging a plea bargain with the prosecution for an even shorter prison term. The appeal was still pending at year's end.

In September, a British judge imposed a confiscation order on a Nigerian couple to pay almost £ 1.2 m under the Proceeds of Crime Act or be jailed for six years. The couple, Ovo Mayomi and his wife, Juliet Ubiribo, had already been convicted of fraud in 2010 for using an identity and immigration scam to claim welfare benefits amounting to some £ 43,000. Eventually, investigators discovered that they were living in a large house in Lagos, driving luxury cars and running several businesses. In another case in late October, Canterbury Crown Court jailed Osezua Osolase for 20 years after finding him guilty of human trafficking and rape. Entirely aware that he was carrying the HIV virus, he used 'juju' rituals to make girls submit to him as sex slaves. The *prisoners' transfer deal*, to be applied to Nigerians involved in fraud and other crimes in the UK, made headway in the Nigerian National Assembly in December and the bill was awaiting the president's assent.

DFID was forthrightly criticised by the Independent Commission for Aid Impact, whose report, published in November, claimed that, despite £ 102 m having been spent on basic education in ten Nigerian states, with a focus on the north, there was so far no evidence of any improvement. Even so, DFID had earmarked another £ 126 m for the next period until 2019. The British government vowed to review the report's recommendation and to respond in due course. Prior to that, in April, the BBC's 'Newsnight' programme and the 'Financial Times' had reported that DFID's private enterprise arm, the CDC group, had been accused of allowing huge amounts of money to be invested in Nigerian money laundering fronts linked to James Ibori that had been investigated by Nigerian officials.

On 8 March, 120 Nigerians were deported from Britain for various *immigration offences*. Shortly thereafter, David Armond, international director of the UK's Serious Organised Crime Agency held a meeting in Nigeria with Femi Ajayi, director general of the National Drug Law Enforcement Agency, to develop new strategies against the *drug cartels* by investigating their finances and assets.

Cooperation with *China*, which had almost come to a standstill the previous year, produced some headlines when, in January, the minister of youth development acknowledged that a number of Nigerians had been detained in China for various drug-related offences, although the number given seemed to have been exaggerated. Nevertheless, on 12 September in Bejing, the Nigerian finance minister signed an agreement on a $ 500 m loan from the China Exim Bank for a light rail project in Abuja. Eventually, in December, the long-awaited launch of the totally overhauled Lagos to Kano railway line, financed to a large extent by Chinese capital and built with Chinese know-how, came into service.

In January, six Nigerians were arrested in India, accused of defrauding hundreds of people through *cybercrime*. In October, two Nigerian nationals suspected of belonging to a *drug smuggling ring* were taken into custody in Thailand's capital Bangkok, after being found in possession of illegal drugs with a black-market value of more than $ 30,000.

Relations with *Saudi Arabia* were temporarily strained when, on 26 September, the Saudi authorities deported 150 female Nigerian pilgrims and held another 1,000 at Jeddah airport, because they had arrived for the hajj unaccompanied by men. Shortly thereafter, Saudi immigration officials denied Nigeria's ambassador access to these women and began deporting them. The diplomatic row dragged on when the speaker of the House of Representatives, Aminu Tambuwal, who was to mediate, was obliged to call off his trip to Saudi Arabia and was only received there on 8 October. Barely a week after the row began, Nigeria resumed flights to Saudi Arabia, which had been suspended, and the Saudi government eventually agreed to re-admit the deported female pilgrims on condition that they were accompanied by appropriate males.

President Jonathan attended the 18th AU summit in Addis Ababa in January, but conspicuously absented himself from the summit there in July. He joined the extraordinary ECOWAS summit in Abidjan on 26 April, which discussed the situation in Mali and Guinea-Bissau. On 10 September, he flew to Malawi and Botswana for a three-day visit and received Côte d'Ivoire President Allassane Ouattara and his Benin counterpart, Boni Yayi, in Abuja for a meeting behind closed doors on 14 September. On 18 October, he met Niger's head of state Mahamadou Issoufou in Niamey (Niger), proceeding then directly to the *Mali* capital, Bamako, where he held talks with the coup leader, Captain Amadou Ayo Sanogo. Another extraordinary ECOWAS meeting of heads of state and government took place in Abuja on 11 November and, not surprisingly, Nigeria decided to send a contingent of 600–700 soldiers to Mali as part of a planned international peacekeeping mission. A possible conflict arose when, in mid-December, the ECOWAS court of justice found the federal government legally responsible for alleged violations of human rights and related oil pollution in the Niger Delta. The government was also given responsibility for bringing the oil companies and the perpetrators to account.

On 21 October, *Gabon* expelled 215 Nigerians, most of them fishermen who had been living there for years. Deportations also played an important role in a diplomatic row with *South Africa* when, on 2 March, 125 Nigerians were expelled for alleged failure to provide genuine yellow fever vaccination documents. In a gesture that seemed to be based on the 'principle of reciprocity', the Nigerian immigration authorities denied 126 South Africans entry on three consecutive days shortly after, using the same reason. On 8 March, however, South Africa backed down and apologised for the "regrettable incident". South African businessmen in particular immediately realised the danger to their investments in the booming telecommunications sector and their department stores in Nigeria's principal cities.

Despite the fact that the demarcation of the maritime border with *Cameroon* was suspended indefinitely on 22 November, Nigeria and Cameroon surprised international observers when, in mid-December, both sides agreed to speed up decisions concerning demarcation in land-based areas of the Bakassi Pensinsula, which were yet to be identified.

On 26 March, President Jonathan joined the second international nuclear summit in Seoul (South Korea); he then participated in the first meeting of the bi-national commission in Germany on 19 April and held talks with German Chancellor Angela Merkel. On 19 June, he travelled with a large delegation to Rio de Janeiro (Brazil) for the UN Earth Summit and he also took part in Jamaica's celebrations of its 50th anniversary of independence in early August. On 25 September, he addressed the 67th UN General Assembly in New York, and took part in October in the International Telecommunication Union conference in Dubai, rounding off the year with the D-8 summit in Islamabad (Pakistan) in November.

Last but not least, on 24 October, the Vatican elevated the 68-year old Archbishop of Abuja, John Olorunfemi Onaiyekan, to the office of cardinal; he thus became the third living Nigerian cardinal.

Socioeconomic Developments

Oil prices remained high, well above the $ 100 per barrel mark, and production levels in the Niger Delta was kept fairly stable at about 2.4 m b/d. Foreign reserves rose to some $ 45 bn towards the end of the year. In April, reserves already stood at some $ 36 bn, a development that had prompted Mustafa Chike-Obi, chief executive officer of the 'Bad Bank', AMCON, to claim that the banking crisis was over. However, the 2012 budget, totalling NGN 4.877 trillion ($ 30.4 bn) based on a benchmark of $ 72 per barrel of crude oil and an exchange rate of NGN 160 to $ 1, was not signed by the president till 13 April. Not surprisingly security, including the military, took the lion's share: some NGN 920 bn. Prior to that, on 1 January, the government scrapped the fuel subsidy as part of sweeping economic reforms and more than doubled the pump price for petrol from NGN 65 to NGN 150 per litre. This decision was aimed at improving fiscal discipline and, probably more importantly, at curbing serious corrupt practices in the petroleum sector.

As in previous years, the increase in the *price of petrol* was hugely unpopular and triggered nationwide protests in almost all urban areas, supported by trade unions, Muslim and Christian religious leaders and civil society groups. Protesters shut down petrol stations and formed human barricades along main roads, prompting security forces to intervene. The protests turned violent and a small number of people were killed, with dozens wounded. Eventually, on 7 January, the president announced that the government would back down but then, in another broadcast on 16 January, he declared that the price was to be increased to NGN 97, rather than NGN 150, an increase of 15%. Because of increased oil prices, however, the cost of imported fuel per litre stood at NGN 167, which meant that every litre was subsidised to the tune of almost NGN 71. In this context, towards the end of the year, the government requested a supplementary budget of some NGN 162 bn to finance the *fuel subsidy*, which was eventually approved by parliament. On 20 December, the national assembly passed the 2013 budget totalling NGN 4.987 trillion ($ 31.6 bn) based on a benchmark oil price of $ 79 per barrel. The president's assent however, was still pending at year's end, probably delayed by the government's alleged insistence on a benchmark of $ 75.

As in previous years, the central bank regularly issued bonds and treasury bills worth several billion dollars. However, the debt profile increased slightly to some $ 45 bn made up of some $ 6.4 bn of foreign and a somewhat troubling $ 39 bn of internal debts. On 28 August, the finance minister announced that the controversial 'Sovereign Wealth Fund' would initially start with a sum of $ 1 bn, managed by local Nigerian finance experts such as the former deputy governor of the central bank, Mahey Rasheed, and Uche Orji from the diaspora. The fund faced objections from state governors, however, since its initial funding was to be taken from the excess crude account, which stood at more than $ 8 bn in October, and which, since it was shared by the three tiers of government, was an important source of state revenue. The controversy notwithstanding, the government aimed to merge the two funds in the near future and, on 20 December, it emerged that the fund would become active sometime in March 2013.

Mobile phone coverage continued to expand in one of the fastest growing markets on the continent. According to the Nigerian Communication Commission, mobile phone subscriptions passed the 100 m mark, and growth continued undiminished, thanks to the latest generation of iPhones and Tablets, which had no trouble reaching the huge and lucrative market. On the other hand, the 11-year effort to privatise the state-owned Nigerian Telecommunication Company was halted in March when the government realised that the company, with its huge debt portfolio, was simply unsalable. Nevertheless, with its SAT-3 submarine cable, exchange transmission stations and its substantial property assets, it was still of some value.

The *enduring power problems* took their toll, with hardly any real improvements. At the start of the year, the government liquidated the Power Holding Company of Nigeria, making way for 18 successor firms. Barely two months later, the National Council of Privatisation, chaired by Vice President Namadi Sambo, approved the sale of 60% of the shares in distribution companies to core investors. Interestingly, as well as the federal government, state governments were also allowed to bid, but participation was restricted in both cases to 49%. The fall in the power supply to some 2,000 MW prompted the president to sack three managers on 2 April, and, soon after, the government awarded a $ 24 m power transmission contract to the Canadian company, Manitoba Hydro, to overhaul the ailing electricity infrastructure. On 28 August, it was Barth Nnaji's turn to be sacked and his portfolio as minister of power remained vacant for the rest of the year. In late September, eight northern states were hit by a blackout lasting several days, but, somewhat surprisingly, the generally poor power situation improved slightly towards year's end when power generation increased to some 4,300 MW.

In October, the *privatisation* exercise in the power sector, promising new opportunities and immense profits, revealed new well-heeled players such as former chiefs of military juntas, Abdulsalami Abubakar and Ibrahim Babangida, the ex-governor of Lagos state, Bola Tinubu, and business tycoons such as Tony Elumelu and Emeka Offor, who were either bidding with their respective companies or backing others.

Nigeria's generally poor *air safety* record suffered yet another blow when, on 3 June, a plane on a domestic flight, operated by Dana Airlines, crashed while approaching Lagos airport. All 159 people on board and half a dozen people on the ground were killed. That trage-dy notwithstanding, the number one airline Arik Air secured a credit facility of some $ 2 bn in October to expand its fleet and destinations. On 5 December, it commenced services to Kinshasa (DRC), having started flights to Duala (Cameroon) in August and to Luanda (Angola) the previous year. On 15 December, a helicopter belonging to the navy crashed in Bayelsa state. All six persons on board lost their lives, including the governor of Kaduna state, Patrick Yakowa, and Andrew Azazi, the displaced national security adviser. Within 24 hours, Yakowa's deputy Ramalan Yero was sworn in as new governor. Earlier, on 14 March, a surveillance police helicopter suffered a fatal accident in Plateau state, killing all four men on board, including Haruna John, a newly promoted deputy inspector general of police. The governor of Taraba state, Danbaba Danfulani Suntai, and his aides were luckier when their plane, piloted by the governor himself, crashed near the Adamawa state capital, Yola, on 25 October; they escaped with their lives but were seriously injured. In this context, the Lagos 'Guardian', in its 29 October edition, quoted an aviation source claiming that Nigerians top the list of private jet owners in Africa – up to 200 in the year under review from 50 some four years earlier. Interestingly, most of the said jets carried foreign registration credentials.

The *road safety* situation showed no improvement. As before, the number of serious accidents with more than ten deaths was high. Two of the worst accidents happened in Kaduna and Ogun states on 28 March and 18 September, when at least 14 people were killed on the Kaduna-Abuja motorway and 30 near Abeokuta. However, the 480 accidents with almost 280 dead and 1,600 injured in a short period of 11 days around Christmas and New Year's Eve showed how poor road safety continued to be.

The second half of the year saw the worst *floods* since independence. From the Sahel in the north to the oil and gas producing areas in the south, some 3 m people were affected, with almost 400 dead and thousands injured.

In September, Chinua Achebe, one of Africa's most famous writers, published his long awaited memoir of the Biafran war 1967–70 under the title 'There was a Country'; the book gave rise to a controversial debate about Nigeria's darkest hour. Lateef Adegbite, an ethnic Yoruba Muslim and former long-serving secretary-general of the Nigerian Supreme Council for Islamic Affairs, died on 28 September. He was the co-founder and first president of the Muslim Student Society in the early 1950s, which was transformed in the 1970s into a radical group of ethnic Hausa-Fulani students within northern universities.

Nigeria in 2013

The precarious security situation in the northern regions deteriorated. Clashes between the security forces – particularly the army – and the Islamist sect Boko Haram and splinter groups such as Ansaru, took place almost every day, with hundreds of people killed. Over much of the year, sectarian violence with a noticeable ethnic undercurrent spread into states in the eastern and south-eastern Middle Belt. The sheer number of attacks, counter attacks and sectarian clashes rendered an adequate account of these events all but impossible. In contrast, the security situation in the southern parts of the country improved; this was due to the fact that several gangs involved in kidnapping, robbery and murder were captured or broken up. On the political front, the leadership of President Goodluck Jonathan was directly challenged by some state governors who were members of the ruling party, party members in the National Assembly, erstwhile party strongmen such as Olusegun Obasanjo and, last but not least, a potentially new political force that resulted from the merger of some smaller parties. These developments notwithstanding, Nigeria experienced another year of remarkable economic growth, financial stability and a building boom, particularly in the prosperous south, with the government finally breathing new life into the ailing power sector.

Domestic Politics

On 5 February, ten state governors met in Lagos to endorse a plan of the main opposition parties – the Action Congress of Nigeria, the Congress for Progressive Change, a faction of the All Progressives Grand Alliance (APGA) and the All Nigerian People's Party – to merge into a *new political party*, the All Progressives Congress (APC). Behind this move were well-known politicians such as Bola

© KONINKLIJKE BRILL NV, LEIDEN, 2017 | DOI 10.1163/9789004347410_011

Ahmed Tinubu, former governor of Lagos state, and Muhammadu Buhari, a former presidential candidate, defeated in three elections. An obvious threat to the ruling People's Democratic Party (PDP) in the 2015 elections, the creation of the new party prompted a power struggle within the PDP, with President Goodluck Jonathan and his inner circle facing a faction of powerful governors (all but one from the North) and partially backed by former president Olusegun Obasanjo. The fact that the president had quietly replaced key party figures appointed by his predecessors and unsuccessfully interfered in the leadership tussle within the 'Nigeria Governors' Forum' did not help his popularity. More important, however, was the deep-rooted desire, particularly within the northern power block, to prevent Jonathan from seeking re-election and, if at all possible, to ensure the success of a northern candidate in the presidential elections. At the end of January, it became obvious that the long-standing dispute between the federal government and the governors over the respective allocations of the lucrative Excess Crude Account and the Sovereign Wealth Fund could not be resolved out of court. The governors went to the Supreme Court, which, on 2 December, set a hearing for March 2014.

On 20 June, the PDP national executive committee retained septuagenarian Bamanga Tukur, the controversial party leader from Adamawa state, as the PDP's national chairman. Some weeks later, on 31 July, the newly founded APC was registered by the Independent National Electoral Commission (INEC) after the merger parties had their certificates of registration withdrawn, thus changing the composition of the National Assembly.

However, the APC failed its first test in the *disputed gubernatorial election* in Anambra state on 16 November. The election was poorly implemented by the state branch of the INEC and even partly cancelled. The APC candidate, Chris Ngige, polled badly; a close runner-up to the PDP candidate, he was far behind Willie Obiano of the APGA. Obiano was duly declared elected after additional by-elections in 210 polling units on 1 December, succeeding his party's twice-elected governor Peter Obi. The supplementary elections were boycotted by the APC and PDP, and the APC announced on 8 December that it would challenge the result in court.

On 18 December, 37 PDP members in the House of Representatives defected to the APC, giving the APC a majority in the house, with 174 members. Prior to that, on 31 August, seven PDP governors and several senators and members of the House of Representatives had announced the *formation of a splinter group*, New PDP (nPDP), a move that seemed to further undermine the PDP's once dominant position. Following the failure of yet another conciliatory meeting with President Jonathan, who had removed nine ministers (most of them, thanks to the political quota system, nominated by dissenting governors or by his former 'godfather' Olusegun Obasanjo), the seven PDP governors held talks with the APC in late September. Among the ministers sacked on 11 September were Olugbenga Ashiru (foreign affairs), Ms Ruqquayatu Rufa'i (education), Ms Amal Pepple (land and urban development) and Shamsudeen Usman (national planning). On 27 November, five PDP governors, Chibuike Amaechi (Rivers state), Ahmed Abdulfatah (Kwara state), Rabiu Musa Kwankwaso (Kano state), Murtala Nyako (Adamawa state) and Aliyu Wamakko (Sokoto state), together with 49 nPDP members of the House of Representatives, eventually defected to the APC, while only Mu'azu Babangida Aliyu (Niger state) and Sule Lamido (Jigawa state) reaffirmed their loyalty to the PDP.

The *power struggle* reached its climax on 2 December, when Obasanjo wrote the president an 18-page open letter entitled 'Before It Is Too late'. The letter was published shortly afterwards by the on-line platform 'Premium Times'. Such a direct attack was bound to be controversial but, according to the author, it was meant to draw the president's attention to a myriad of issues, which, if not addressed, could jeopardise Nigeria's survival. Jonathan finally replied on 20 December, denouncing Obasanjo's letter as a threat to national security. Towards year's end, the president fell out with the governor of the Central Bank, Sanusi Lamido Sanusi, when it transpired that the latter had allegedly leaked to Obasanjo a letter that had been written to the president, claiming that the state petroleum corporation had retained billions of dollars of oil proceeds that should have been remitted to the Central Bank. Moreover, towards year's end, the nPDP faction in the National Assembly showed no sign of backing down, thus keeping up political pressure on the PDP leadership and the president.

The *cabinet reshuffle* on 11 September saw almost all vacant post taken over by their respective minister of state, with, for instance, Ms Viola Onwuliri taking over the ministry of foreign affairs portfolio. Early in the year, on 4 February, the president had sworn in Chinedu Nebo as minister for the still ailing power sector, a post which had been vacant for over half a year, and Kabiru Tanimu Turaki as minister for special duties. The Ministry of Defence, also vacant for months, had been overseen by the then minister of state, Ms Erelu Olusola Obada. Since she was among those sacked 13 September, Labaran Maku was temporarily put in charge of defence alongside his responsibilities as minister of information. During August, September and October, Jonathan used his executive powers to appoint new board members and chairmen of the more than 40 state agencies and federal parastatals. As a constitutive part of the Nigerian political system, these short-term lucrative positions serve first and foremost to redistribute huge financial resources to a considerable number of the elite. One such appointment was that of Abisola Clark, a medical doctor turned businesswoman, who had just married the still influential octogenarian Ijaw leader, Chief Edwin Clark; she was appointed chairperson of the national ear centre in Kaduna. Earlier in the year, on 5 July, Justice Ms Kudirat Kekere-Ekun was elevated to the Supreme Court, which brought the number of female judges to four out of 17 currently on the bench.

The military promoted and redeployed their upper echelons more often than had previously been the case, an indication that all was not well in the military, particularly with respect to the ongoing insurgency in the Northeast and the widespread corruption throughout the security forces. According to local insiders, at least 80% of the annual budget of some $ 6 bn assigned to security had for years been pocketed by the upper ranks of the military and police, by top politicians dealing with security issues and by hundreds of self-proclaimed security advisers, such as retired officers, former politicians, businessmen and academics. Thus, it is not surprising that the insurgency in the North and Northwest had turned into a lucrative business, a situation whose significance was augmented by the fact that the political leadership had more or less put the destiny of the country into the hands of the security forces, particularly the military, which had not enjoyed such influence since the era of military rule. On 1 July, however, 18 soldiers including a lieutenant were court-martialled in Jos for alleged links to Boko Haram, and it was reported that more offenders were awaiting trial. In September, the media reported that the 18 had been sentenced to death, but government officials denied these reports and told reporters that the court-martial was on-going. The proceedings were not open to the public or the press.

At the start of the year, on 7 January, 14 officers were given the rank of one-star general; on 28 January, more than 300 officers as well as the strategically important *General Officers Commanding* (GOC) were redeployed. Major General Ahmed Tijani Jibrin took over the GOC 2 Mechanized Division based at Ibadan and Ebiobowei Awala of the same rank the GOC 3 Armoured Division in Jos. The latter, however, was replaced by Major General John Nwaoga at year's end. Major General Obi Umahi emerged as commander of the GOC 81 Amphibious Division, garrisoned in Lagos, and Major General Adebayo Olaniyi as new GOC 82 Airborne Division commander in Enugu. Furthermore, Brigadier Ibrahim Attahiru was appointed the new director of army public relations, and Major General Kenneth Minimah replaced Mohammed Isah as commander of the Infantry Corps and Centre, Jaji, in Kaduna state. Soon afterwards, on 19 March, Brigadier Chris Olukolade was named as new director of defence information, succeeding Colonel Mohammed Yerima, who had served in that capacity for quite some time.

On 1 July, a federal high court in the capital Abuja had nullified the appointment of all service chiefs. The court argued that the appointments had contravened the constitution because the president had failed to secure the senate's approval. However, this had been common practice ever since the redemocratisation of the political system at the end of the 1990s, and the verdict was ignored by the government and the military. A lawsuit against this practice had already been filed in 2008 by Festus Keyamo, a well-known lawyer and human rights activist. On 17 August, a *new army division*, tagged GOC 7 Infantry Division, to be garrisoned in Maiduguri with some 8,000 troops, was created against the backdrop of the Boko Haram insurgency in the Northeast. However, its first commander, Major General Obidah Ethan, was replaced unexpectedly soon, at the end of the year, by his colleague of the same rank, Junaid Bindawa. In September and at year's end, more than a dozen generals from the three arms of the military had to retire and another batch of top-ranking officers was redeployed. Another wave of promotions came at the end of November, when more than 300 high-ranking officers moved up a rank, followed by a further round of redeployment of no fewer than 30 generals on 27 December.

The *police forces* underwent similar changes. On 1 January, the promotion of more than 1,900 staff with the rank of constable or sergeant came into effect, obviously aimed at appeasing the middle ranks, who for years had suffered from poor equipment, housing and pay. A documentary on local Channels TV in mid-January, part of which was kept on the station's website, revealed the dilapidated condition of the foremost police institute, the police training college in Lagos, and confirmed the generally poor state of this security service. Nevertheless, in September and December, 47 senior officers, ranking from assistant commissioner to deputy inspector general, were given promotion. The redeployment of dozens of police commissioners and assistant inspector generals became a permanent feature, aimed at fighting the police's poor reputation for *corruption and brutality*. However, this did not prevent the police force losing dozens of staff on active duty over the course of the year.

In the course of the year, the already precarious security situation deteriorated further, particularly in the Northeast, where it reached another nadir. Half-hearted efforts by members of the northern establishment to initiate some form of dialogue with sections of the Islamist sect *Boko Haram* did not last long; this was due to the government's right of veto, the security services' own agenda and the lack of restraint on the part of the sect's leadership. Despite the state of emergency imposed by the president on 14 May in Borno and neighbouring Yobe and Adamawa states, extended for another six months in November, attacks and counter-attacks went on unabated. The formation in May–June of vigilante groups made up of youths and condoned by the military, the existence of safe havens, and the tacit approval of the Islamists by local politicians, added fuel to the flames. In the course of the year, more than 500 civilians (a conservative estimate), at least 450 suspected members of the sect and more than 50 members of the security forces lost their lives in Borno state alone. In addition, well over 1,000 people were held in military camps in inhumane conditions, which, according to a statement by AI on 14 October, had caused a number of deaths. In early December, the Nigerian Human Rights Commission (NHRC) was planning to investigate arbitrary detention centres, especially those used to incarcerate Boko Haram suspects.

One of the worst incidents took place on 19–21 April in the remote town of Baga near the Chad border, an assumed Boko Haram hide-out. Rocket-propelled grenades and heavy gunfire from a Multinational Joint Task Force, made up of Nigerian troops and reinforcements from neighbouring Niger and Chad, killed scores of people and destroyed large parts of the town. It was reported that close to 200 people fell victim to the attack, a figure vehemently disputed by the military, which put the number at 37. The NHRC, however, in an interim assessment at mid-year, found evidence of *atrocities* committed by both the security forces and Boko Haram. A report by HRW, published in May, maintained that its investigations showed 183 people had been killed; analysis of satellite images of Baga showed that more than 2,200 houses had been destroyed.

On 12 September, a confrontation took place at Kafiya Forest, which cost the lives of some *150 insurgents* and 16 soldiers with nine others missing. Immediately after the gun battle the military rejected claims that up to 100 security personnel had been killed. On 17 September, in another serious incident near Benisheik, in Kaga local government area, alleged members of Boko Haram killed more than 140 travellers on the Maiduguri-Damaturu road. In the early morning of 2 December, Islamist militants struck the *air force base* in Maiduguri, destroying five aircraft and killing two military personnel. Over 20 insurgents lost their lives, and the federal airports authority was forced to close the international airport. More was to come when, on 20 December, insurgents raided the barracks in the town of Bama in the local government area of the same name. The military repelled the attack, even using fighter jets, killing some 50 assailants. More than a dozen soldiers and an uncounted number of civilians living on the premises lost their lives during a *fierce battle* that lasted for hours. Soon afterwards, on 28 December, in a gun battle near the village of Alafa, not far from Bama, more than 50 suspected members of Boko Haram were killed during a military raid. Earlier in the year, however, during his two-day working visit to Borno and Yobe states on 7–8 March, President Jonathan had spent a night in Maduguri, which was seen in some quarters as an act of bravado.

Neighbouring Adamawa, Bauchi and Kano states were also seriously hit by the insurgents, though not on the scale seen in Borno and Yobe. At times, *foreigners* were *deliberately targeted*. Thus, three North Korean medical practitioners working in a state-run hospital in Potiskum in Yobe state, had their throats slit or were beheaded during the night of 9–10 February. Shortly after, on 17 February, a splinter group of Boko Haram called Jama'atu Ansarul Muslimina

Fi Biladis Sudan, better known as Ansaru, stormed a Lebanese road construction company in Jama'are local government area in Bauchi state, killing a security guard and kidnapping and eventually killing seven expatriate workers, a Briton, a Greek, an Italian and four Lebanese. Moreover, it was suggested that, on the same day, Ansaru was also responsible for the kidnap of a French family of seven in neighbouring Cameroon, very close to the Nigerian border, thereby substantiating suspicions concerning Boko Haram's wider regional agenda. On 19 April, the family, who had probably spent some time in captivity in Nigeria, were released unharmed in Cameroon. It was reported that a ransom of between $ 3 m and $ 27 m was paid, but the French government denied making any such payment. The French engineer Francis Colump, who had been taken hostage in December the previous year, was also fortunate to escape from his kidnappers' hide-out in Zaria on 17 November.

Kano city, capital of the state of the same name and one-time hub of the North, experienced several grisly incidents. On 19 January, gunmen opened fire on the convoy of the Emir, Alhaji Ado Bayero. The Emir survived the attack unharmed but four others died. Barely three weeks later, seven suspects were arrested, among them one Adamu Sani, who allegedly revealed that he had been recruited by two local Muslim clerics. In addition, on 18 March, a series of explosions rocked a car park in Sabon Gari, a Kano district traditionally frequented by immigrants and quite a number of Christians. More than 20 people died, scores were injured and several luxury buses went up in flames. At the end of March, men belonging to the Joint Military Task Force were shot at by gunmen during a routine patrol in Unguwa Uku, another city district. The immediate retaliation led to the death of 14 suspects. On 1 April, a police patrol vehicle was ambushed at Yan Kaba market and three policemen were gunned down. On 29 July, Sabon Gari, an urban quarter where bars and beer gardens can be found, was again hit by serial explosions, leading to *dozens of fatalities*.

A more isolated incident took place on 19 January in Kogi state, south of the Federal Capital Territory (FCT) Abuja. A Mali-bound military detachment was attacked, with two soldiers killed and five others seriously injured.

In addition to the almost daily attacks and counter-attacks, the *media campaign* between Boko Haram and the security services reached new heights during the second half of the year. In early June, the US government offered a bounty of $ 7 m for the self-proclaimed Boko Haram leader, Abubakar Shekau; this coincided with the government's decision to declare the sect a 'terrorist organisation'. On 19 August, military sources suggested that the sect's leader had been wounded in a military raid at Sambisa Forest on 30 June, and had died a few weeks later in a hide-out in nearby Cameroon. They also suggested that the second-in-command, Momodu Bama, alias Abu Saad, had been killed, too. Despite the fact that the military authorities dismissed as a fake a video showing Shekau alive, their claims were not verified. On 25 September, to the surprise of all, Shekau or his double again appeared in a video, dressed in military camouflage battledress, claiming to be alive and well. This encouraged increasing scepticism with regard to intelligence reports and the military's capacity to handle the crisis.

Despite the fact that hundreds of suspected terrorists had been detained and scores had been killed, only a small number were eventually charged and sentenced, among them four alleged members of Boko Haram who were sentenced on 9 July to *life imprisonment* for masterminding and carrying out a deadly attack on an INEC office in Suleja before polls in 2011, and for bombing a church in the same vicinity three months later. On 15 November, Mustapha Umar was given the same sentence for bombing the Kaduna office of the national daily newspaper 'This Day' in April of the previous year, a sentence that was also handed down to Kabiru Umar alias Kabiru Sokoto on 20 December for his role in terrorist activities, including the bombing of St Theresa's Catholic Church in Madalla, Niger state, in December 2011.

In the Middle Belt, particularly in Plateau, Benue, Nasarawa and Taraba states – for years a centre of *sectarian clashes* – conflicts continued unabated, leaving hundreds of people dead. One of the worst incidents took place in Nasarawa in early May, when the 'Ombatse Cult', made up of ethnic Eggons, killed more than 60 policemen and several members of the State Security Service (SSS). This brutal act eventually revealed a long-standing, deep-rooted and violent power struggle in several local communities, mainly involving Eggons, but also ethnic Idomas and Fulani herdsmen. In mid-September, for example, hundreds of soldiers had to be deployed to end *days of violence*, blamed on militias of the 'Ombatse Cult'. The other states mentioned fared no better.

In August, the Miyetti Allah Cattle Breeder Association disclosed that, over a five-year period, more than 10,000 herdsmen had been killed nationwide and some 12 m cattle rustled. These estimates could not be verified but they were an indication of the state of *rural insecurity*.

The continuing deep crisis in the Northeast and the aforementioned Middle Belt states somewhat overshadowed the *volatile Niger Delta* and the other parts of the economically booming South. Although lucrative piracy along the coast increased slightly, the security services exposed and arrested a number of notorious criminal gangs in the southern parts of the country. In January, a South African court found Henry Okah, an alleged militant leader of the Movement for the Emancipation of the Niger Delta (MEND), guilty of masterminding a car bombing during celebrations of the 50th anniversary of Nigeria's independence on 1 October 2010. He was given a 24-year prison sentence. A co-perpetrator, Edmund Ebiware, was sentenced to life imprisonment by a Nigerian court on 25 January.

The vast majority of those kidnapped off the *Nigerian coast* were released unharmed: three Italians regained their freedom on 8 January, after being held captive for more than two weeks; five Indians, who had spent more than a month in captivity, were set free on 26 January. Another group of expatriates from Russia, the Ukraine and India, kidnapped on 17 February, were released nine days later, and, on 18 June, a French national, who had been taken hostage off the coast of Togo a week earlier, was rescued by security forces in Bayelsa state. On 23 October, two US citizens, a captain and a chief engineer, were taken hostage by armed men who had entered their US-registered oil supply ship; they were freed on 12 November. On 5 February in Bayelsa state, during a gun battle involving men of the Joint Task Force and pirates, two soldiers, a retired naval officer and the pilot of a tugboat were killed. Another deadly attack took place in Delta state in early March, when militants attacked an oil barge, killing four soldiers, a former naval officer and two civilians. In another ambush on a vessel on 22 October, two soldiers lost their lives; the coxswain and three staff of a construction company were wounded. On 17 August, during a rescue operation on a hijacked vessel, the Nigerian navy killed a dozen pirates and captured four. This was one of the rare cases in which pirates were arrested. The list was in fact longer, the International Maritime Bureau claiming to have recorded more than 40 attacks in the area with some 132 crew taken hostage in the course of the year. Shortly before year's end, a spokesman claimed that what had been dubbed 'operation pulo shield' had killed 40 pirates and lost six active staff. On 23 December, Vice-Admiral Dele Ezeoba, the chief of naval staff, had informed the public that, in the course of the year, more than 1,500 illegal oil refineries, over 100 barges, some 1,400 large wooden boats and a huge quantity of equipment had been destroyed, with more than 1,600 suspects arrested.

Kidnappings and killings in the Niger Delta also continued. In early March, Chika Richard Nwabiarijie, a notorious gang leader from Rivers state, and members of his gang were arrested. They had kidnapped a hotel manager in Oguta in Imo state on 24 February, then collected a ransom and finally killed the hostage. On 21 March, Ms Olubunmi Oke, broadcaster with the Nigerian Television Authority in Ondo state and married to a banker, was kidnapped. Two days later, after the family had paid a NGN (naira) 1 m ransom, she was re-united with her loved ones. Probably the ugliest incident took place in Southern Ijaw local government area in Bayelsa state when, on 5 April, 12 policemen were gunned down by remnants of the ethnic Ijaw militia group, MEND. The brutality of this attack suggested that it was related to the conviction of Henry Okah. The policemen had been deployed to provide security at the burial of the mother of a repentant warlord, Kile Selky Torughedi, alias General Young Shall Grow. Jackson Fabouwei, alias General Jasper, alleged to have masterminded the killing, was arrested on 3 June after a manhunt. On 24 August, the senior advocate of Nigeria and human rights activist Mike Ozekhome was abducted by armed men and the four policemen guarding him were killed, but he was released by his kidnappers on 12 September. An Anglican archbishop, the Most Reverend Ignatius Kattey, the church's number two, and his wife Beatrice, were abducted in Eleme in Rivers state on 6 September. He regained his freedom a week later, the captors having already released his wife. Ms Bridget Osawaru, taken hostage on 10 December in Benin City, the capital of Edo state, was killed by her captors after they collected NGN 1.5 m. The scale of hostage taking and the killing of an abducted businessman, Emmanuel Obiyan, on 17 October finally prompted Edo state governor Adams Oshiomhole to sign an amended bill into law the following day, making kidnapping a capital offence. Neighbouring Ondo state had passed a similar law in 2010, almost unnoticed.

Persistent crime in almost all federal states cost the lives of countless policemen, bank officials, politicians, traditional rulers – in fact, people from all walks of life. The combined security services broke up several gangs, particularly in the South and Southwest. On 29 January, the SSS in Abuja paraded a gang of six that had carried out several kidnapping operations, allegedly led by the dismissed police officer Ndidi Cletus. The Nollywood actress Nkiru Sylvanus was one of the gang's victims, taken hostage in December of the previous year. She was released after payment of NGN 8 m. Soon afterwards, on 4 February, police in Oyo state paraded another gang that had acquired some notoriety after taking hostage the wife of former military governor Oluwole Rotimi in neighbouring Ogun state;

Rotimi paid a ransom of NGN 13 m for her release. In early August, the notorious gang leader Abiodun Ogunjobi, alias Gododogo, who had ruled the underworld of Lagos and the Southwest for some 14 years and had left many policemen and civilians dead, was finally apprehended. The dreaded gang leader Kelvin Ibruvwe Oniarah, who had carried out a number of kidnappings and killings in the greater Niger Delta area, was arrested on 25 September. Among other things, he was believed to have abducted Mike Ozekhome, the human rights activist, as well as a judge of the Edo state judiciary, Daniel Okungbowa, and to have killed the hostage Chudi Nwike, a former deputy governor of Anambra state.

Last but not least, Ondo state police announced that, in the course of the year, they had arrested 105 suspected robbers and 26 suspected kidnappers, while the authorities in Akwa Ibom state claimed to have arrested more than 1,400. Lagos and Ogun states claimed to have arrested almost 800 suspected armed robbers and 76 alleged kidnappers, numbers that had an impact on the security situation in the South as a whole.

The *anti-corruption campaign* slowed down, due in part to lack of funds. Mainly sponsored by donors such as the EU, the Economic and Financial Crime Commission (EFCC) admitted on 16 December that it was insolvent and unable to pay the lawyers handling its prosecution cases. Earlier in the year, on 4 July, the federal high court in Abuja discharged and acquitted a former minister of works, Hassan Lawal, and an erstwhile bank official, Adesanya Adewale, on charges of laundering several million naira. And, on 19 September, Ms Bridget Omotunde Sokan, executive secretary of the Universal Basic Education Commission, was acquitted by the court, along with six others, five years after being charged with defrauding her Commission to the tune of almost NGN 800 m. The EFCC suffered a further setback on 13 December when the Supreme Court overturned a guilty verdict reached in 2009, when Olabode George, then chairman of the board of directors of the Nigerian Port Authority, and five board members, had been sentenced to

30 months imprisonment for financial crimes, a sentence they had already served. On the same day, an Abuja high court discharged and acquitted the former minister of the FCT, Nasir el-Rufai, and two staff of the Abuja Geographic Information System, who had been charged with abuse of office and corruption. In October, the controversial purchase of two bullet-proof BMWs by Aviation Minister Stella Oduah on behalf of her ministry at an inflated price of $ 1.6 m instead of the market price of some $ 267,000 each, brought the ministry under public scrutiny. The cars were never delivered and some newspapers speculated that she had shared the purchase price with a Lagos car dealer. This allegation notwithstanding, she was still in office at year's end. Interestingly, in December, the German firm Bilfinger was fined $ 32 m by a US court for violating the Foreign Corrupt Practices Act, having bribed Nigerian government officials some ten years earlier. Bilfinger was closely connected with Nigeria's biggest construction company, Julius Berger.

Nevertheless, there were some minor successes, including the fact that, on 18 October, the international Financial Action Task Force removed Nigeria from the list of countries with significant deficiencies in their policies regarding money laundering and the financing of terrorism.

The precarious security situation in most parts of the country had grave effects on *human rights*. On 20 September, the military killed eight squatters in a building in the Apo area of Abuja, claiming that it was a Boko Haram hide-out. The claims could not be substantiated and, with the investigation continuing at year's end, the NHRC had started to attend the proceedings. Nevertheless, at least nine governors used their executive powers to free several hundred prison inmates, most of them common criminals. A number of them were awaiting trial, while others were granted amnesty or unconditionally pardoned.

Nigeria's longest-running court case was about to come to an end, when, on 12 July, the Court of Appeal quashed the death sentence and acquitted Hamza Al-Mustapha and Lateef Shofolahan. The court held that the prosecution had completely failed to prove a charge of conspiracy and murder. The accused had been sentenced by a Lagos high court in January 2012 for the murder of Ms Kudirat Abiola in 1996. Lagos state government, which had originally sought to appeal against the verdict, withdrew the application on 29 November and quietly withdrew its appeal to the Supreme Court.

Contrary to reports from the National Assembly in 2012, the controversial legislation banning *same sex-marriage* had been passed but not signed by the president and had allegedly been quietly set aside. On 10 December, almost unnoticed, a committee adopted a revised version which was passed on 17 December and awaited the president's assent sometime in early 2014.

Foreign Affairs

Foreign policy focused on cultivating good relations with the US, the most important customer for Nigeria's crude oil and liquefied gas and its main supplier of wheat. It increased cooperation with Britain and consolidated its relations with China, while expanding its activities in other Asian countries.

At the start of the year, President Jonathan attended the World Economic Forum in Switzerland where, on 23 January, he was interviewed by CNN's Christiane Amanpour on such crucial issues as combating Boko Haram, improving the ailing power sector and preventing oil theft. Most Nigerians watching the interview were embarrassed by the president's poor performance and weak arguments, but it had no particular impact on relations with the US. On 23 September, Jonathan paid a visit to the White House and, on 26 November, received the new US ambassador, James Entwistle. Earlier, on 15 August, under the umbrella of the US-Nigeria Binational Commission, Under Secretary of State for Political Affairs Wendy Sherman underlined security cooperation and the intention of the US to invest in Nigeria's institutions, people and businesses. To that end, on 29 August, USAID disclosed that it would invest $ 100 m in the education sector in five northern states. Earlier in the year, General Electric sealed a $ 1 bn deal with the Nigerian government to boost the ailing power sector, and, in April, the Maryland-based firm Grip2Grip opened an office in Lagos, its first foreign trade office in Africa, overseeing its business activities in four other African countries.

On 13 November, the US formally designated Boko Haram and Ansaru as foreign terrorist organisations and global terrorists. Canada followed suit at year's end.

On 17 April, the US Supreme Court, in a unanimous decision, rejected the complaint brought by the relatives of the Ogoni executed in 1995 after a show-trial in Port Harcourt. The plaintiffs had accused the Anglo-Dutch company *Shell* of complicity in human rights violations in the Niger Delta. The court held that the US justice system had no jurisdiction over the issue. However, concern was growing over the fate of the charitable trust (Kiisi) set up with $ 5 m of the $ 15.5 m out-of-court settlement between Shell and the relatives in 2009. Since then, no activities had been recorded and, after alleged problems amongst the trustees, the death of one and the resignation of another, the trust lay idle in a New York bank account.

After legal wrangling in Nigerian courts, Lawal Olanyi Babafemi, alias Ayatollah Mustapha, was extradited to the US on 28 August, where he had been indicted by a federal court in Brooklyn for providing material support to al-Qaeda in the Arabian Peninsula and recruiting prospective members to Yemen. He had lived in the US but had fled the country the previous year after the FBI put him under surveillance; he was eventually arrested in Nigeria.

Legal issues also shaped relationships with *Britain*. Several hundred Nigerians were serving various jail terms in UK prisons. For years, both governments had tried to reach agreement and, eventually, on 24 April, President Jonathan signed the *prisoners' transfer deal* into law, thereby paving the way for a legally binding treaty that would empower both countries to repatriate eligible prisoners without their consent.

On 12 June, the UK Supreme Court ruled in favour of Yasmin Prest, the English ex-wife of the Nigerian oil tycoon Michael Prest, in a divorce settlement and ordered him to transfer part of his properties in Nigeria and the Caribbean, worth several hundred million pounds, to his ex-wife. The extraordinary case was carefully watched by wealthy couples, particularly from outside Britain. The lower court had passed a contrary verdict.

There was a new twist in the James Ibori saga, when, on 17 December, Southwark Crown Court postponed the former Delta state governor's complicated confiscation of assets hearing to 2014. The accused had already served a sentence for money laundering. A week earlier, on 9 December, a former Goldman Sachs banker, Elias Preko, a Ghanaian national, was sentenced to four-and-a-half years in prison by the same court for laundering $ 5 m on Ibori's behalf.

On 19 December, the Old Bailey convicted Michael Adebolajo and Michael Adebowale, two young British nationals of Nigerian ancestry, of the murder of Lee Rigby, a British soldier out of uniform. Both were Muslim converts and, on 22 May, claiming they were acting in the name of Allah, they hacked the soldier to death with a meat cleaver in broad daylight in south London. Sentence was pending at year's end. Adebolajo was not an unknown quantity. He had appeared in court in Mombasa in 2010 and was deported from Kenya for having contacts with al-Shabaab. On his return to Britain, he had to some extent been under MI5 surveillance.

Early in the year, on 6–11 February, Nigeria's president paid a six-day visit to the UK and met Prime Minister David Cameron on 10 February. In November, Jonathan, accompanied by top-ranking politicians, attended a three-day meeting of Nigeria's Honorary International Investor's Council in London, coordinated by Baroness Lynda Chalker. At the same time, the Archbishop of Canterbury, Justin Welby, held talks in London with the Emir of Kano, Alhaji Ado Bayero. The British government had declared Boko Haram a terrorist organisation in July.

At the beginning of the year, Sino Arab Energy, SAE, a Chinese company in partnership with the local firm Osabo Refining and

Petrochemical Industry Limited, concluded plans to build a refinery in Cross River state valued at some $ 7.5 bn, despite the fact that all previous attempts to set up privately run refineries had failed. The new dynamics of economic *cooperation with China* was fostered by Jonathan's five-day state visit on 9–13 July, when several agreements were signed, covering the construction of power plants, defence cooperation and trade and investment. Trade between the two countries already exceeded $ 13 bn per annum. In the run-up to the state visit, the Nigerian ambassador to China, Aminu Bashir Wali acknowledged that 300 of some 400 Nigerians incarcerated in China were being held for drugs-related offences.

On 2 February, *Indonesia*'s President Susilo Bambang Yudhoyono met his counterpart in Abuja, where they discussed, *inter alia*, options relating to the exchange of prisoners as well as mutual legal assistance; finally, they signed a memo to combat drug abuse and trafficking in narcotics. The meeting was overshadowed by the fact that 14 Nigerians were awaiting execution and some 30 others were serving various jail terms in Indonesian prisons.

India was an important customer for Nigeria's crude oil and the volume of trade had risen to some $ 16 bn. In addition, there were some 100 Indian companies in Lagos alone. The growing economic cooperation notwithstanding, the killing of a Nigerian, Simeon Obodo, in Goa on 31 October, revealed the existence of a considerable Nigerian diaspora of as many as 40,000 in India, many of them living there illegally. The killing was said to be related to drug gang rivalry, and the police started cracking down on illegal immigrants, including Nigerians, and deporting them.

In October, Jonathan went on a three-day pilgrimage to *Israel*, being the first Nigerian president to do so. Interestingly, in April, the government had awarded the Israeli company Elbit Systems a contract worth some $ 40 m to monitor Internet communication in Nigeria.

Relationships between the AU and African countries were largely shaped by the *Mali crisis*. On 18 January, Jonathan attended an extraordinary meeting of ECOWAS and raised the contingent of Nigerian troops from close to 800 to 1,200. He joined the 20th AU meeting in Addis Ababa (Ethiopia) towards the end of the month, held talks in France with President François Hollande on 11 February, and, on 9 April, attended the signing of two agreements by ECOWAS and the EU worth € 76 m to support the African-led mission to Mali and the free movement of persons in the sub-region. To the consternation of the member countries of the UN stabilisation mission in Mali, Nigeria withdrew most of its troops in July, with the justification that they were needed to tackle the growing insurgency in Nigeria's Northeast.

On 9 April, Jonathan joined other African leaders in Nairobi for the inauguration of President Uhuru Kenyatta, whom he met again on 5–7 September on a three-day state visit to Kenya. On 16 April, he received South African President Jacob Zuma in Abuja. In mid-July, he had hosted the AU's special summit on HIV/AIDS, tuberculosis and malaria together with UN Secretary General Ban Ki-moon and Sudanese President Omar al-Bashir. Some hours after his arrival, al-Bashir quietly slipped out of the country and returned home to avoid possible arrest by the ICC. On 1 September, Jonathan welcomed his counterpart from neighbouring Benin, Boni Yayi. On 12 October, the president attended the AU's extraordinary session in Addis Ababa on Africa's relationship with the ICC and, on 9 November, Jonathan met Gambia's controversial president, Yahya Jammeh, in Banjul. In December, dozens of Nigerians were killed in the CAR capital, Bangui, in a wave of sectarian violence, triggering the flight of hundreds of Nigerians in the weeks that followed.

On 24 February, Jonathan received Brazil's President Dilma Rouseff; on 24 September he addressed the 68th UN General Assembly in New York and, on 5 November, at a meeting in Abuja, he assured the president of the ICC, Sang-Hyun Song, that Nigeria would not withdraw from the court's jurisdiction. He travelled to France in early December for a two-day summit on peace and security in Africa hosted by President Hollande, and attended the funeral of Nelson Mandela shortly thereafter. On 17 October, Nigeria was elected as a non-permanent member of the UNSC for the two-year period 2014–15 in recognition of its role in peacekeeping operations.

Socioeconomic Developments

Nigeria enjoyed high oil and gas prices the whole year round and benefited strongly from its high quality crude, which was sold at well above the $ 100 per barrel mark. Foreign reserves were kept stable at more than $ 43 bn throughout the year. External debt stood at $ 6.5 bn and domestic debt amounted to $ 41.5 bn. The external *debt stock* of the 36 federal states and the FCT stood at $ 2,384 bn, in which Lagos state led the debtors list with more than $ 600 m of debt, while Borno state had the lowest debt stock at $ 14 m. The 2013 budget, totalling NGN 4.987 trillion ($ 31.6 bn) was transmitted to the president on 15 January and he signed the appropriation act into law on 26 February, albeit reluctantly. By signing it at the eleventh hour, he forestalled the likely passing of the budget without his agreement by a two-thirds majority of both chambers of the National Assembly. Though he had identified some grey areas in the document, these were eventually dealt with by the passing of an amendment bill on 25 July, ending months of disagreement. The budget was based on an average oil price of $ 79 a barrel, against the president's original proposal of $ 75, and an assumed production level of 2.5 m b/d. This was a rather over-optimistic figure, given the welter of political and production problems in the Niger Delta, an average exchange rate of NGN 160 to $ 1 and *GDP growth* of 6.75%.

The frequent disputes over the *annual budget* even led to the cancelling of the president's 2014 budget speech just before it was due to be given on 19 November. The budget framework was aimed at reducing the budget by some 6% to NGN 4.6 trillion and set the oil bench mark price at $ 74 a barrel, well below the $ 77.5 eventually proposed by the National Assembly and eventually agreed upon by the executive. Finally, on 19 December, Ms Ngozi Okonjo-Iweala, co-ordinating minister for economy and finance, presented the federal budget for the 2014 fiscal year separately before the two chambers of the National Assembly.

On 21 February, ahead of the formal launch of the $ 1 bn *Sovereign Wealth Fund* (SWF) on 1 March, to be composed of the stabilisation, infrastructure and future generation funds and managed by the internationally known investment banker Uche Orji, the federal government appointed leading international financial services firm JP Morgan as the fund's custodian. On 19 September, the president inaugurated the SWF council with himself as chairman. Other members were the 36 state governors, the minister of the FCT, the attorney general and the top federal representatives dealing with fiscal matters. On 2 July, the Nigerian government issued a € 1 bn Eurobond, half in five-year and half in ten-year *bonds* with yields of 5.3% and 6.6%, respectively. The issue was four times oversubscribed. Barely two months later, on 27 August, the International Islamic Liquidity Management Cooperation (IILM), a Malaysian-based consortium of central banks including Nigeria's, issued a $ 490 m Sukuk, the Islamic equivalent of bonds. IILM was founded in 2010 to develop a cross-border market in Islamic financial instruments.

After a cautious start in 2012, the government made concrete efforts to halt further deterioration in the *power sector*. Long-standing wilful neglect had led to an annual import of generators worth some $ 160 m, which made Nigeria one of the leading importers worldwide. A new round of privatisation efforts took off in March and prospective investors started bidding for power assets. In early September, United Bank for Africa announced that, in the current year, it had already invested $ 700 m in power assets in Nigeria alone, claiming that a further $ 1.2 bn would be earmarked within the next three years. In addition to these investments, on 17 October, the Lagos state government inaugurated the 10.4 MW Alausa power project, run on natural gas and intended to supply power to the state secretariat in Alausa and its environs. It was set up as a public-private partnership and developed by the well-known local company Oando and Fidelity Bank. One way or another, the privatisation exercise was completed by the end of October, and the federal government had collected some $ 2.7 bn from successful bidders. Soon afterwards, core investors began to complain about the operational challenges facing them, but the federal government nevertheless went ahead in October with plans to establish a solar energy sector in nine northern states, to be implemented within five years by the Nigerian-German Energy Partnership, Renewable Energy and Efficient Energy Projects. This scheme was expected to have a capacity of 500 MW.

On 4 September, the Nigerian tycoon Aliko Dangote and his Dangote Group signed an agreement worth $ 9 bn with a consortium of local banks and foreign investors, to build a refinery and a petrochemical complex in the Southwest. The long-awaited privatisation of Nigeria's four *refineries*, allegedly directed by the president, was eventually announced by the Bureau of Public Enterprises on 24 December, but took a new twist at year's end. After it became known that the two trade unions involved in the oil and gas sector were threatening industrial action over the planned privatisation exercise, the government back-pedalled. Towards the end of the year, for the umpteenth time, the start of work on the Mambilla *hydroelectric power plant* in the mountainous area of Taraba state, close to the Cameroon border, was once again delayed.

The *road safety situation* went from bad to worse. According to the Federal Road Safety Commission, more than 1,900 lives were lost on Nigeria's trunk roads between January and June. During the festive period in December alone, 252 people died in traffic accidents. The worst accident happened at Ugbogui Village in Edo state, when, on 5 April, 70 people were burned to death following the collision of a luxury coach, a tanker and a van. In addition, the aviation sector suffered another setback on 3 October, when an aircraft carrying the body of the late governor of Ondo state, Olusegun Agagu, crashed on take-off at Lagos airport. Most of the 13 passengers died.

On 16 December, the Academic Staff Union of Universities suspended its five-month strike after the federal government backed down and disbursed NGN 200 m to revitalise the *university* infrastructure. The government also promised to progressively increase the education sector's budgetary allocation.

On 10 February, the Nigerian national football team, the Super Eagles, won the *Africa Cup of Nations* in South Africa, defeating Burkina Faso 1–0, 19 years after their previous win; they also qualified to compete in the FIFA World Cup in Brazil in 2014. In addition, on 8 November, the Nigerian under-17 team sealed its fourth World Cup title by beating Mexico 3-0. Last but not least, on 11 August at the International Association of Athletics Federations World Championships in Moscow (Russia), Blessing Okagbare won the silver medal in the women's long jump, becoming the first African woman to win a World Championship medal in this event.

On 21 March, the world-famous writer *Chinua Achebe*, passed away at the age of 83 in Boston in the US. Achebe, the most widely read African author on the continent, who was seriously disabled following a car accident in 1990, first gained international attention for his novel 'Things Fall Apart', published in 1958. He was buried on 23 May in Ogidi, his birthplace, now in Anambra state.

Nigeria in 2014

Throughout the year, Nigeria had to face up to enormous security and political challenges. Despite the fact that democratic institutions were quite stable, the president and his government dealt with the endless deterioration of the security situation in the North with brinkmanship. Clashes between security forces and factions of the Islamic sect Boko Haram took place almost daily with a high death rate on both sides. Almost unnoticed, Boko Haram had changed its name, and now called itself 'Jama'at ahl al-sunna li-l-da'wa wa-l-jihad 'ala minhaj al-salaf' (Community of the people of the Sunna who fight for the cause of Islam according to the method of Salaf). Several hundred people, including innocent persons and security personnel, as well as alleged members and sympathisers of the sect, died in bomb attacks, suicide bombings, indiscriminate killings, rape and deadly raids on barracks, police stations, mosques, churches, schools, hide-outs, villages, outdoor refreshment stops, markets and prisons. The sheer number of attacks, counter attacks and sectarian clashes makes an accurate account of these events all but impossible. At year's end, Boko Haram was ranked second of the top ten terrorist groups worldwide. Over 2,000 people had lost their lives, bringing the number to around 12,000 victims (a modest estimate) since the Islamist insurgency started in the aftermath of the killing of the Boko Haram leadership by security forces in 2009. In addition, Nigeria's human and civil rights record was mixed at best. These developments notwithstanding, Nigeria experienced another year of remarkable economic growth, particularly in the prosperous and booming South. This, together with financial stability, consolidated the Nigerian economy as one of the leading economies in Africa, although the plummeting oil price in the last quarter of the year heralded what would probably be painful structural socioeconomic adjustments. At the end of the year, however, all eyes were on the elections due in early 2015, particularly the battle for the

© KONINKLIJKE BRILL NV, LEIDEN, 2017 | DOI 10.1163/9789004347410_012

presidency between President Goodluck Jonathan and his challenger, Muhammadu Buhari, a repeat of the last election in 2011.

Domestic Politics

The *state of emergency* in Borno and neighbouring Adamawa and Yobe states was extended in May for a further six months. However, the already precarious security situation in the North-East continued to deteriorate and reached another low point. Almost every day, Boko Haram members, security personnel and civilians lost their lives in numerous attacks and subsequent counter-attacks. The most affected towns in Borno State were the capital, Maiduguri, as well as other towns such as Bama, Chibok, Damboa, Dikwa, Gwoza and Konduga, turning Borno State into a veritable battle-field. On 14 January, as people of the Muslim faith were celebrating the birth of the Prophet, a suicide bomber detonated a bomb in Maiduguri, killing more the 40 persons. The city's 'Monday Market' was hit by a car bomb on 1 July, which killed dozens, including a group of vigilantes, known as the civilian joint task force. Soon afterwards, towards the end of July, the city's famous Eid Durbar, a three-day festival marking the end of Ramadan, was cancelled for the third year running for security reasons. Earlier in the year, on 16 February, suspected Islamists, armed with sophisticated weapons, gunned down at least 90 people in the village of Izge near the Cameroonian border; three days later some 80 died in Bama, where properties worth several million naira were destroyed, including the palace of the Shehu of Bama. On 14 March, the notorious Giwa barracks in Maiduguri, which also served as an illegal prison camp, was attacked by hundreds of militants who were able to free many alleged Boko Haram members and sympathisers. Within hours, in a cruel act of revenge, the security forces re-arrested suspects by the dozen and, according to AI, executed more than 600, burying them in mass graves. These extra-judicial killings were seen as a tipping point, further fuelling the unprecedented brutality on both sides.

One of the cruellest incidents in Borno State was the abduction of more than 270 *female students in Chibok*, a town in the southern part of the state with a significant Christian population. The students, aged 16–18, were about to sit their final year exams. On 14 April, late at night, gunmen in a convoy of vehicles stormed the school hostel and abducted them. Some of them managed to escape when the truck they were in had a problem and slowed down. For more than two weeks, President Goodluck Jonathan and his government ignored the incident, an act of gross negligence. Hundreds of mainly women protesters marched through the Nigerian capital, Abuja, to press for the release of the abducted students and to put pressure on the government to act, including initiating some form of dialogue with factions of Boko Haram or at least an exchange with some of the sect's imprisoned members. Their campaign received international attention, particularly in Europe and the US, and exposed a helpless and rather embarrassed leadership. On 2 June, the police banned the ongoing rallies, calling them a security problem, but immediately back-pedalled when a court order in favour of the protesters was about to be issued.

The security forces did not perform much better than the government, despite their claims that they would stand up to the insurgency and the *terrorist threat*. Interestingly, the sect's self-proclaimed leader, Abubakar Shekau, who, according to the security forces, had died after a military raid at Sambisa Forest in June 2013, appeared in video messages. As with similar videos in 2013, the military authorities once again dismissed them as fakes, or insinuated that the videos showed Shekau's double, but their claims were not verified. On 24 August, he declared his claimed territory an 'Islamic Caliphate'. A second video showing the abducted schoolgirls was a further rebuke to the handling of the crisis by both the military and the government. More was to come when, in mid-October, the federal government announced that the schoolgirls were about to be released.

Soon, however, it became clear that there was no truce, and neither had negotiations with Boko Haram succeeded.

The *relentless killings* went on unabated and, on 5 May, at least 300 people including more than a dozen policemen were killed in Gamboru, a town on the Cameroonian border and headquarters of Ngala local government. On 30 May, the insurgents struck again, killing the Emir of Gwoza, Alhaji Idrissa Shehu Tinta, who was on his way to the burial of the Emir of Gombe. Shortly thereafter, on 1–2 June, villages in Gwoza local government such as Attagara, were raided and up to 200 people, mostly Christians, killed.

On several occasions, the insurgents overran strategically important villages and communities in areas such as Damboa, where they hoisted the sect's flag on 18 July. Gwoza, home to a police mobile training academy, was taken over in mid-August and more than two dozen of its police officers were reported missing. Soon afterwards, Boko Haram fighters attacked the barracks near Gamboru and seized parts of the border town for the second time, forcing almost 500 soldiers to flee to neighbouring Cameroon. On 1 September, the sect overran Bama town and hoisted its flag. Only on 5 September did the military leadership commence a 'special operation', including an aerial attack, which had some success in dislodging the insurgents from major towns including Bama, Damboa, Gamboru and Gwoza. In the strategic town of Konduga, east of Maiduguri, on 12 September, security forces killed more than 200 insurgents marching to capture the capital. Two weeks later, on 25 September, troops repelled another advance on Konduga and the town of Benesheik, some 70 km west of Maiduguri. During the weekend of 24–25 October, the *Multinational Joint Task Force* (MNJTF), made up of Nigerian troops and reinforcements from neighbouring Niger and Chad, based in Baga, re-captured the town of Abadam, close to the Nigerien border and Lake Chad, which had fallen under insurgent control the previous week. However, the MNJTF had little impact on the security situation in the area. On 12 November, insurgents invaded the headquarters of the 174th motorised battalion, deployed from its base in the South-West, forcing the remaining soldiers to withdraw. On 20 November, a group of fish traders on their way to Chad to buy fish were attacked and killed near the village of Doron Baga. Towards the end of November, the National Assembly refused President Jonathan's bid to have the state of emergency extended for another six-month period. On 13 December, Boko Haram attacked the village of Gamsuri, some 70 km south of Maiduguri, killing more than 30 and kidnapping more than 150 persons.

Yobe State fared no better. Late at night, on 25 February, the Federal Government College in Buni Yadi, the headquarters of Gujba local government area, south of the state capital Damaturu, was raided by suspected Islamists; 59 students, all boys, died in the raid. On 27 May, the town was targeted again and a security camp attacked; close to 50 security personnel and almost a dozen civilians fell victim to the insurgents, who arrived in several Hilux vans and on motorcycles. Earlier, on 5 April, neighbouring Buni Gari was targeted when gunmen opened fire on a mosque, killing some 20 worshippers and seriously injuring others. During the FIFA World Cup, on 17 June, a bomb blast rocked a centre in the state capital, where football spectators were watching a match; several spectators died in the blast and dozens were hurt. Potiskum, Yobe's largest city and its commercial hub, was seriously hit in a blast on 3 November, when a suicide bomb killed ten members of the Muslim Brethren, who call themselves 'Shiites', as they celebrated the Islamic new year (there are no recognised Shiites in Nigeria, but the group admires the model of the Iranian revolution). On 10 November, another suicide bomber, disguised in a school uniform, killed almost 50 students of the senior science secondary school. Damaturu was attacked again on 1–2 December; almost 40 police officers, a few soldiers, some 60 insurgents and more than 100 civilians died when the army, backed by air force helicopters, repelled the attackers.

Adamawa State, with a significant Christian population, became a veritable battlefield as a result of both the Boko Haram insurgency and, to some extent, a serious leadership crisis in the state;

Governor Murtala Nyako was impeached on 15 July. Two of the larger towns, Michika and Mubi, and the surrounding areas were for a short period in the hands of Boko Haram fighters. Only after several fierce battles, with hundreds dead on both sides, were the insurgents driven out in the final quarter of the year. One of these battles, in which vigilantes and local hunters joined the troops, took place in the towns of Gombi, Hong and Pella and lasted for four days (16–19 November); more than 400 insurgents were killed but the government remained very tight-lipped about the number of victims among the security forces. At the same time, in a night-time attack, local vigilante groups, popularly called 'Yan Tauri' (meaning in Hausa 'those who resist/are invulnerable [to wounds]'), drove most insurgents out of Mubi. By 5 December, the remnants were dislodged by military forces and the emir of the town, Abubakar Ahmadu, re-entered his palace on 12 December, after a two-month temporary exile. In neighbouring Gombe State, on 6 December, military forces repelled a strong attack on the town of Ashaka, where the main objective was a dynamite store. Ten soldiers fell to the attackers, who lost some 70 fighters. It was the second time within a month that the town had been targeted.

Kano city, capital of the state of the same name and one-time hub of the north, became another focus of the spread of violence, experiencing several grisly incidents. On 18 May, a car bomb explosion rocked the urban quarter of Sabon Gari ('New Town'), causing some 15 deaths. The quarter is made up of a mixture of indigenous ethnic Hausa-Fulani Muslims and migrants from other parts of the country, many of them Christians. The following month, on 23 June, an explosion struck the Kano School of Hygiene and at least eight students lost their lives. Towards the end of July, within the space of five days, three bomb attacks on a Catholic church (27 July), a petrol station and a kerosene queue at a storage facility of the National Nigerian Petroleum Corporation (NNPC) (28 July) left seven people dead and many more injured. The newly enthroned Emir Muhammad Sanusi II remained defiant and, despite the blasts, he performed the traditional evening 'Sallah Durbar' on 28 July. Despite the president's reluctance, the kingmakers and Governor Rabiu Kwankwaso, who had fallen out with Jonathan, enforced the enthronement of the former governor of the Central Bank to succeed Kano's longest sitting emir, Ado Bayero, who had passed away on 6 June.

In the weeks and months that followed, *deadly attacks* continued. On 17 September, a twin explosion at both the old and new campuses of the federal college of education caused the deaths of at least 15 students. Dozens sustained various injuries and both suicide bombers lost their lives. On 14 November, a petrol filling station in the Hotoro area was targeted, and six people, including three policemen, were killed. The ugliest incident, however, happened on 28 November, when, during Friday prayers, gunmen set off three bombs and opened fire on worshippers at the central mosque close to the emir's palace. At least 130 people died and many more were wounded. Once again, the emir, by cutting short his lesser hajj trip to Saudi Arabia the same day, and leading the evening prayer at the site of the bombed mosque the following day, set an example, standing up to the suspected Islamists.

Nor was the *Federal Capital Territory Abuja* spared by the Islamists. On 14 April, during morning rush hour, two blasts hit a crowded bus station in the suburb of Nyanya, claiming more than 70 lives and injuring scores more. Rather surprisingly, the following day, Jonathan flew to the city of Kano for a People's Democratic Party (PDP) jamboree. Less than three weeks later, on 2 May, another bomb explosion ripped through the same area, resulting in the deaths of at least 19 people; 60 more were injured. More than 20 people were killed and many more wounded on 25 June, when another blast hit the EMAB Plaza shopping centre in Wuse II, close to the city centre. The incident forced Jonathan to cut short his trip to the AU summit in Equatorial Guinea. This attack fuelled further speculation that corruption was widespread within security circles and that millions of dollars had been wasted on purchasing inoperative security devices such as video surveillance equipment.

Late in the year, a number of events embarrassed the government. On 5 September, a private jet chartered by the Nigerian intelligence apparatus, with $ 9.3 m on board for the purchase of weapons, was seized at Johannesburg airport; some three weeks later, a further $ 5.7 m was impounded. However, in late October, after several controversial discussions, the National Assembly finally granted the president's request for a $ 1 bn loan to intensify the fight against the Boko Haram insurgency.

The *Middle Belt*, particularly Plateau, Benue, Gombe, Nasarawa, Taraba and Kaduna states, was another focal point of sectarian and ethnic clashes that claimed many victims. One of the most devastating attacks occurred in the Plateau state capital Jos, which was seriously hit by twin blasts on 20 and 24 May, with more than 120 and half a dozen people killed, respectively. And in Kaduna State, on 23–25 June, several villages were raided by alleged Fulani herdsmen, leaving some 250 people dead. As in previous years, however, these states were the scene of serious political and socioeconomic conflicts concerning the fragile local political power and leadership structure, distribution of revenues, rights over fertile farmlands, housing and cattle rustling.

On 31 March, a *peace accord* was signed in Makurdi. It had been drafted by the presidential peace committee, a conflict resolution and peace building committee and the Fulani socio-cultural organisation 'Miyetti Allah Kautal Hore'. It was agreed that the Fulani could freely use the grazing areas but should do so in cooperation with the farmers. In addition, a joint committee, made up of Fulani herdsmen, ethnic Tiv and some Agatu (related to the ethnic Idoma), was to check criminal activities on both sides of the divide. In the end, the agreement had little impact on the volatile situation. This also applied to similar efforts in Taraba and Nasarawa, where on 5 April and 8 November, respectively, peace accords were signed or negotiated. In the Taraba state capital Jalingo, representatives of ethnic Tiv, Jukun, Hausa-Fulani and Fulani signed the accord presided over by the deputy inspector general of police Michael Zuokomor, representing the presidential peace committee. The negotiations in Nasarawa, however, were overshadowed by a cruel assault when, in a classic case of irony, gunmen ambushed and killed almost 40 participants returning from the peace summit convened by the traditional ruler of the Akriya chiefdom, Alhaji Usman Babba.

The precarious security situation eventually took its toll on *key positions in the military*. At the start of the year, on 16 January, three new service chiefs were appointed in a sweeping shake-up. Lieutenant General Onyeabo Azubuike Ihejirika, the army chief of staff, Vice Admiral Ola Sa'ad Ibrahim, chief of the defence staff, and Rear Admiral D.J. Ezeoba, the naval chief of staff, were replaced. The survivor of the purge in the military high command was the air force chief of staff, Air Vice Marshal Alex S. Badeh, who became the new chief of the defence staff. His portfolio was taken over by Air-Vice Marshal Adesola Nunayon Amosu. Major General Tobiah Jacob Minimah became the new army chief of staff and Rear Admiral Usman Jibrin the new naval chief of staff, being subsequently promoted to admiral. The appointments were confirmed by the senate on 30 January, in line with a 2013 decision of the Abuja Federal High Court that such confirmation was mandatory under the Constitution.

Soon afterwards, on 12 February, 107 senior officers, including six newly-appointed *General Officers Commanding* (GOC), were redeployed. Major General K.C. Osuji took over the GOC 1 Division based in Kaduna, Major General Emanuel Abejirin the GOC 2 Mechanized Division in Ibadan and Major General John Zaruwa the GOC 3 Armoured Division in Jos. Major General T.I. Dibi emerged as commander of the GOC 81 Amphibious Division, garrisoned in Lagos, and Major General S. Yusuf as the new GOC 82 Airborne Division commander in Enugu. The GOC 7 Infantry Division, garrisoned in Maiduguri and created the previous year against the backdrop of the Boko Haram insurgency in the North-East, had been led by four commanders within just nine months, which suggested internal wrangling and serious structural problems within the military as a whole. The latest appointment was made on 16 May, when Brigadier M.Y. Ibrahim emerged as acting commander, succeeding his controversial predecessor Major General Abubakar Mohammed. In mid-August, the air force experienced a shake-up in its high command with the appointment of new Air Force Officers Commanding and, on 24 November, 16 officers were promoted to the rank of air vice marshal and 35 others to air commodore. On 9 December, the navy followed suit and carried out a far-reaching redeployment of senior officers.

All was not well at the top of the military hierarchy. 14 May was seen as the beginning of a chain of mishaps within the military and its fight against the Islamist insurgents. On that day, aggrieved soldiers who had been ambushed in a deadly attack the previous night on their way from the Chibok area to Maiduguri staged a *mutiny in Maimalari cantonment* against the then commander of the 7 Infantry Division, Abubakar Mohammed. They were said to have pleaded for their return to be delayed until dawn because moving at night was a risk, which proved to be true. Abubakar Mohammed was almost immediately relieved of his command and 12 mutineers were court-martialled and sentenced on 15 September to death by firing squad. Abubakar Mohammed was quietly retired in August. On 17 December, a court martial imposed the death sentence on another batch of 54 soldiers who had allegedly refused to obey orders on 4 August. In the Nigerian legal system, any sentence handed down by a court martial can be challenged in the two highest secular courts of the land.

Shortly after, it was revealed that another batch of 15 soldiers had been given prison sentences of four years for their refusal to go to the front line in northern Adamawa. These verdicts heralded a massive investigation of the rank and file and of both non-commissioned and commissioned officers for alleged offences such as 'cowardice' and 'disobeyed deployment directives'. In the weeks that followed, a few hundred were arrested, *court-martialled* behind close doors and sentenced, with the aim of countering the indiscipline that was allegedly spreading within the armed forces. These efforts notwithstanding, this purge also served as a cover-up for widespread corruption within the upper ranks, which, to a large extent, had long denied the combatants the necessary equipment, maintenance and training to successfully fight the insurgency.

The *police forces* also underwent major changes. On 1 August, Suleiman Abba emerged as the new inspector general of police. He succeeded Mohammed Abubakar, who took statutory retirement after 35 years of service. Prior to that, on 26 February, the police service commission promoted more than 5,100 policemen to the rank of assistant superintendent. On 20 August, 19 commissioners of police rose to the rank of assistant inspector general and eight to the rank of deputy inspector general following a redeployment of 36 senior officers.

At the start of the year, the *embattled president* tried to regain the initiative to show that he and his government were still in charge. The controversial chairman of the ruling PDP, septuagenarian Bamanga Tukur, held partly responsible for the party's internal wrangling, was forced to resign in mid-January. On 20 January, the respected former Bauchi state governor, Adamu Mu'azu, emerged as the new party chairman. On 11 February, Goodluck Jonathan sacked his chief of staff, Mike Oghiadomhe, and appointed retired Brigadier Jones Oladehinde Arogbofa. In the days that followed, more ministers suffered the same fate, including Ms Stella Oduah (aviation), Godsday Orubebe (Niger Delta), retired Navy captain Caleb Olubolade (police affairs) and the governor of the Central Bank, Sanusi Lamido Sanusi.

Unexpectedly, the septuagenarian Aliyu Mohammed Gusau, a retired lieutenant general, became minister of defence. He had served as *national security adviser* to the former president, Olusegun Obasanjo, as well as to Jonathan. Soon afterwards, on 5 March, a career diplomat, Aminu Bashir Wali, was made minister of foreign affairs. On 3 June, Godwin Emefiele took over the Central Bank's top position and, in the weeks that followed, the education, aviation and national planning portfolios were given to Ibrahim Shekarau, Osita Benjamin Chidoka and Abubakar Sulaiman, respectively. Abdul Jelili Adesiyan was appointed to oversee the Ministry for Police Affairs, Steve Oru became minister for the affairs of the Niger Delta and, on 13 August, Danladi Kifasi became the new head of the federal civil service, following Abubakar Goni Aji's retirement after 35 years of service.

On 17 April, Ms Zainab Bulkachuwa became the first female president of the Court of Appeal. On 20 November, Mahmud Mohammed became Nigeria's chief justice, succeeding Ms Aloma Mariam Mukhtar, who had reached the mandatory retirement age of 70.

With regard to the planned 2015 elections, the *Independent National Electoral Commission* (INEC) released the election time-table on 24 January, with presidential and national assembly elections due to be held on 14 February 2015, and governorship and state elections scheduled for 28 February 2015. At year's end, some 68 m voters were registered. By December, however, the INEC had failed to issue all the permanent voter cards as planned, and was forced to extend the deadline for them to be collected until shortly before the elections. The question of IDP suffrage remained unresolved at year's end, since the law stipulated that voters had to cast ballots in their home constituencies.

On 21 June and 9 August, *gubernatorial elections* took place in Ekiti State and Osun State, respectively, In Ekiti, the PDP candidate, Ayodele Fayose, who had been governor during the second legislative period (2003–7) and impeached in 2006, defeated the incumbent governor Kayode Fayemi of the All Progressives Congress (APC). While many observers considered the election to have been largely free and fair, the PDP had, in fact, frequently used federal and security machinery to intimidate their political opponent in the run-up to the election. In Osun however, the sitting APC governor Rauf Aregbesola was returned, confirming the APC's hold on the ethnic Yoruba dominated southwest.

In the meantime, it became clear around mid-year that all the attacks and challenges from within and without the ruling party to prevent Jonathan from seeking re-election were failing to materialise. On 11 December, at the PDP convention in Abuja, Jonathan emerged as the sole candidate keeping Vice President Namadi Sambo as his running mate. Earlier, on 15 July, Murtala Nyako, governor of Adamawa State, had been impeached by the state assembly, largely orchestrated by the federal government, and the speaker Umaru Fintiri had been sworn in as acting governor. Nyako was one of five PDP governors who had defected to the APC in 2013, which the presidency feared might have a decisive impact on the presidential election. Although it was said that the deputy governor, Bala James Ngilari, had resigned, the Abuja Federal High Court, shortly before the gubernatorial election scheduled for 11 October, declared the parliament's action invalid and Ngilari the legal governor, a verdict decision accepted by all.

At the same time, under its new chairman, John Odigie Oyegun, an old-hand politician from Edo State in the South-South geopolitical zone, the APC was still struggling to establish a platform acceptable to all. Finally, on 11 December, at a convention in Lagos, the party endorsed the candidature of retired Major General Muhammadu Buhari, a former military dictator and three-times unsuccessful presidential candidate. On 17 December, and after intense discussion within the APC's top hierarchy, Yemi Osinbajo, a former Lagos state attorney general and commissioner for justice, was named as his running mate. This sealed a strong alliance between the North-West and South-West, which Nigeria had last seen on the eve of the civil war. Earlier in the year, on 23 July, Buhari had escaped unhurt when his convoy was attacked in Kaduna by a car bomb, but his chances of becoming the APC's presidential candidate were still vague at that time.

Nigeria's *human and civil rights record* during the year was mediocre at best. To a large extent this was due to the precarious security situation in the North, which had made more than 3 m people homeless, although the government claimed that Nigeria only had about 1 m IDPs. On 10 January, a presidential directive forced the defence headquarters to release more than 165 suspects apprehended in the course of the anti-terror campaign in the North-East and more suspected terrorists were released during the year, including a group of 42 detainees on 6 November. These actions, however, contrasted with the severe criticism of government policy, illustrated, for example, in the AI report "Welcome to hell fire: Torture and other ill-treatment in Nigeria", published on 18 September, which focused on illegal detention centres and the brutal behaviour of the security forces. The governing council of the National Human Rights Commission had previously, on 15 June, labelled Boko Haram's activities as war crimes and crimes against humanity and had expressed concern over detention centres run by unauthorised persons.

A serious incident occurred in the ancient city of Zaria, when soldiers opened fire on 25 July during a 'Qud's Day' procession that had caused serious congestion on a major road. Three sons of Shaykh Ibrahim Zakzaky, founder of the *Muslim Brethren*, a sect that calls itself Shiite, and more than 30 other members of the group lost their lives.

The precarious security situation in the North also had serious consequences for the *private media*. On 6 June, security agencies, particularly the military, laid siege to the offices of leading newspapers such as 'Daily Trust', 'Leadership', 'Nation', 'Punch' and 'Vanguard', closing their distribution depots in the major cities. The government justified the clampdown by citing intelligence reports that indicated the movement of materials with serious security implications. The government's arguments were not substantiated and after around five days all the newspapers returned to the newsstands.

The movie "Half of a Yellow Sun", an adaptation of Chimamanda Ngozi Adichie's famous novel about the Biafran War, filmed by the Nigerian-born British director Biyi Bandele, was set to open in Nigerian cinemas in late April, having premiered on 8 April in London. Following a directive of the State Security Service (or

Department of State Services), the *Nigerian film and censors board* initially refused its release on security grounds. After heated debates and severe criticism, the board backed down on 4 July, realising that the movie was listed for online viewing in the US.

On 7 January, Jonathan signed into law the controversial legislation banning same sex-marriage, despite strong criticism from Western counties and the UNCHR.

Organised crime persisted and kidnappings, piracy, bank raids and killings frequently took place, although Lagos state governor Babatunde Fashola declared on 10 September that Lagos city, Nigeria's economic hub, had not seen a successful armed bank robbery in the past six years.

The security forces killed and arrested a significant number of gang members, particularly in the southern parts of the country where the economy was booming. In April alone, *police forces broke up seven gangs* in Anambra, Delta, Lagos, Ogun, and Rivers states. Among those arrested were the kidnappers of Anglican Archbishop Ignatius Kattey and his wife, who had been abducted in September 2013 and released after payment of a NGN (naira) 10 m ransom. A further success was the capture of a gang that had kidnapped the owner of a private school and a chief executive officer of a micro bank, Ms Edith Aliyu, on 29 June. Although a NGN 2 m ransom was paid, she was still killed. The gang was paraded in Abuja on 23 July. In most cases, kidnap victims were released when a ransom was paid. Generally speaking, the amounts involved were eventually revealed, as in the case of human rights activist Mike Ozekhome, who been abducted in 2013 and had paid NGN 40 m to regain his freedom. Wealthy churches were increasingly targeted after it became clear that quite a number of them were making billions of naira every year. One such was the Assemblies of God Church, which suffered an assault on its senior staff in Abakaliki in early December.

Piracy along the coast was on the increase and, according to the International Maritime Bureau, Nigerian pirates accounted for 31 of 51 attacks in the West African region.

As in the previous years, the government's *anti-corruption campaign* did not yield too many results, due in part to the Economic and Financial Crimes Commission's incompetence in providing sufficient evidence, or to controversial government decisions such as the presidential pardon granted to Diepreye Alamieyeseigha, former governor of Bayelsa State. Overburdened courts and lack of administrative capacity also stood in the way of an effective anti-corruption policy. For example, on 17 January, the Supreme Court confirmed a judgment of the Appeal Court, which said that Mohammed Abacha, son of the late dictator Sani Abacha, had to face trial in a lower court for retaining properties allegedly stolen by his father while in office. The court held that the father's immunity in office did not extend to his son, as was claimed. On 18 June, however, to expedite the proceedings, which had been going on for several years, the government withdrew the suit in favour of a compromise settlement. In return, Abacha and his family withdrew their case at the European Court of Human Rights for alleged infringements of their right to a fair trial and the peaceful enjoyment of their property. This case had delayed the return of the funds for several years. The deal enabled the Abacha family to retain quite a portion of their wealth but, immediately after the agreement, the Principality of Lichtenstein transferred $ 227 m to the Nigerian government.

Towards the end of the year, the Fiscal Responsibility Commission released a report on massive *fraud within ministries*, departments and agencies, pointing out that the NNPC and the capital market regulator, Securities and Exchange Commission, led the field. This report and the already widely believed allegations about stolen funds worth several billion dollars within the NNPC only increased the public's increasing mistrust of the president and his government.

Foreign Affairs

Over the course of the year, Nigeria's domestic security crisis shaped its foreign policy. Relations with the US cooled significantly because of disagreement on how to tackle Boko Haram and in the wake of serious cuts by the US of oil and gas imports. At the start of the year, on 18 January, Nigerian soldiers received training in counter-insurgency tactics, organised by special units from both sides. General James Lindner, commander of Special Operation Command Africa, was one of the key resource persons. On 18 February, during the two-day meeting of the US-Nigeria Binational Commission in Abuja, US Assistant Secretary for African Affairs Linda Thomas-Greenfield was still expressing confidence in Nigeria's ability to defeat Islamist insurgents. At the second meeting on 4 September, however, her remark that the reputation of the Nigerian military was at stake indicated an undercurrent of tension between Nigeria and the US.

Against the background of increasing *piracy and oil theft*, a joint multinational maritime security exercise tagged 'Operation Obangame' took place on 19 April. Apart from the US and Brazil, 20 African and European countries participated in the off-shore exercise.

In June, the US government announced the speedy installation of a 24-hour satellite television channel in Kano as part of its campaign against Boko Haram, although the project had not been implemented at end of the year. Meanwhile, on 10 June, the US, the UK, France, Nigeria and its neighbouring countries set up an *external intelligence response unit on terrorism*. This was in line with a US pledge to spend $ 110 m annually over a period of three to five years to support peacekeeping forces that could be rapidly deployed to deal with terrorist threats and other crises. This commitment was to some extent negated, however, by the fact that, in late June, Nigeria had only received non-lethal transportation, communication and force protection equipment. In September, it was even revealed that any effort by the Nigerian military to purchase US-made Chinook helicopters from Israel would be blocked by the US. This freeze was triggered, according to the then ambassador, James Entwistle, by severe human rights abuses committed by Nigerian troops in the North. His remarks, made on 9 October, during a visit to the American

University of Nigeria, located in the Adamawa state capital Yola, did not go down well with the Nigerian government and its Washington representative, Ambassador Adebowale Ibidapo Adefuye, sharply criticised the US administration's attitude when he appeared before the Council on Foreign Relations on 10 November. Furthermore, on 1 December, the US cancelled a planned joint training programme.

Against the background of these disagreements on security and the expansion of fracking in the US, Nigeria did not export a single barrel of crude oil to the US after July – the first time this had happened since records began in the early 1990s. The US had previously been one of Nigeria's most important trading partners, importing about half of its total crude exports of some 2.2 m b/d and significant quantities of liquefied gas. *India*, already a major employer in Nigeria's economy, became the leading customer for its crude oil. Despite the cooling of relations, the US was still a major destination for Nigerian students, with more than 7,300 studying there.

Nigeria's *ailing power sector* remained a lucrative magnet for huge US investments. In May, the US Secretary of Commerce Penny Pritzker led a high-level delegation of investors, including General Electric, who, in December, signed an MoU for the implementation of a $ 1 bn investment plan. In addition, Nigeria's rapidly growing fast food sector and its shopping malls attracted companies such as Proctor & Gamble, which had established a factory in Ogun State. Against this background, Nigeria's president joined African leaders at the US-Africa Leaders' Summit in Washington on 4–6 August. The following day, after a court ruling, the US government revealed that it had taken control of more than $ 480 m looted by the late dictator Sani Abacha and would return the money to the Nigerian government in due course.

Legal issues also shaped relationships with *Britain*. At the start of the year, the two governments finalised an agreement to allow the transfer of prisoners between their countries. In September, Jeffry Okafor was arrested in Asaba and extradited to the UK, charged with a murder committed in 2009. He had fled to Nigeria using a passport belonging to his brother, who had already been prosecuted and jailed for four years. The case went to trial in London on 7 November. On 26 February, two young British nationals of Nigerian ancestry, Michael Adebolajo and Michael Adebowale, were found guilty of the murder in 2013 of Lee Rigby, a British soldier out of uniform; they were eventually sentenced to life imprisonment and life with a minimum of 45 years, respectively.

In April, there was another twist in the James Ibori saga. In 2012, the former governor of Delta State had been sentenced to 13 years in prison for fraud and money laundering. The case was somehow closely related to a pending complicated *confiscation of assets hearing*. £ 80 m had been temporarily confiscated from Ibori and his associates and frozen. The British crown prosecutor, however, called for a re-trial of the entire case and Southwark Crown Court adjourned the hearing, this time to April 2015. On 4 November, the Metropolitan Police disclosed that the British government was set to return another £ 6.8 m to the Nigerian government, having already transferred £ 1.2 m. It was not known whether the money had been handed back to the true owner and beneficiary, the Delta state government.

In April, the Nigerian Access Bank commenced the implementation of the judgment of a British court against its former manager, Erastus Akingbola, with the sale of two of his properties, which fetched more than £ 13 m. In 2012, he had been ordered by a British court to the pay Access Bank £ 654 m for *fraudulent practices* while in charge of the now defunct Intercontinental Bank, which Access Bank had later acquired. On 8 April, following the UK court judgement, the Lagos Federal High Court ordered him to pay the bank NGN 212 bn. In addition, Akingbola was facing trial for allegedly stealing depositors' money to the tune of NGN 47 bn.

Between September and November, British branches of two of *Nigeria's charismatic mega churches* were under investigation by the UK Charity Commission. After an altercation between the founder, Chris Oyakhilome, and his wife Anita, the Commission opened a statutory inquiry into a controversial payment of more than £ 3 m to the Christ Embassy. At the same time, the famous Winners' Chapel International was investigated following its request to establish an independent school, which would teach 'biblical truths' in each subject, and because of its methods of exorcising children believed to be witches or possessed by evil spirits.

In mid-May, Mark Simmons, the UK's Foreign Office minister for Africa, was in Abuja exploring long-term solutions to the Boko Haram issue. On the occasion of the global *summit to end sexual violence in conflict* held in London on 12 June, the foreign ministers of Nigeria and its neighbouring countries, the US, the UK, Canada and a representative of the AU re-affirmed their strong commitment to defeating Boko Haram and securing the safe return of the Chibok students. In addition, the UK promised to increase its military and educational aid, thereby setting aside possible cuts in aid due to Nigeria's anti-gay law. During a meeting of the Nigeria-UK Honorary International Investment Council in London on 21 November, the country's anti-terrorism campaign took centre stage, with President Jonathan attending in person.

Jonathan's attendance at the World Economic Forum in Davos (Switzerland) on 22 January was a prelude to the World Economic Forum on Africa, which took place in Abuja on 7–9 May. At this summit, economic *cooperation with China* was furthered by the presence of Chinese Prime Minister Li Keqiang, who was on a four-nation tour of the continent. Subsequently, on 20 November, the China Railway Construction Corporation signed a deal worth some $ 12 bn to build a railway along the coast connecting Lagos in the west with Calabar in the east.

Jonathan's two-day pilgrimage to *Israel* on 25–26 October, the first by a sitting Nigerian president, underlined Nigeria's close relationship with Israel. It was alleged that the relationship was instrumental in Nigeria's abstention in the crucial vote on the status of Palestine at the UNSC on New Year's Eve. On 6 January, both sides had already signed a bilateral air services agreement.

All of Nigeria's *diplomatic activities on the African continent* were shaped by Boko Haram. Even the centenary of the country's founding – the then colony of Nigeria came into existence on 1 January 1914 – celebrated in February, was turned into a conference on security and even saw French President François Hollande attending. On 17 May, Jonathan joined a security summit in Paris, hosted by his French counterpart. Nigeria's president attended the AU's Peace and Security Council meeting in Nairobi (Kenya) on 2 September, held talks with his Chadian counterpart Idriss Deby on 8 September, took part in an extraordinary meeting in Niamey (Niger) on 8 October and was a member of a three-man ECOWAS delegation on 5 November, which helped to resolve the crisis in Burkina Faso. Earlier in the year, in January, the president participated in the AU summit in Addis Ababa but had to cut short his attendance at the summit in Malabo (Equatorial Guinea) in June. At the beginning of the year, Nigeria took its seat as a non-permanent member at the UNSC for a two-year period. On 24 September, Jonathan addressed the UN General Assembly and on 27 November, Minister for Petroleum Ms Diezani Alison-Madueke was elected as the first female president of OPEC; soon afterwards, on 16 December, she emerged as president of the gas exporting countries forum.

Socioeconomic Developments

Oil prices, well above the $ 100 per barrel mark, remained high only until mid-year, while production levels in the Niger Delta were kept fairly stable at about 2.3 m b/d. The last four months of the year saw a *dramatic decline in oil prices*, which at the end of the year reached the $ 60 per barrel mark. Against this background, foreign reserves were under pressure, standing at $ 35 bn in December, while the Excess Crude Account, a rather controversial financial instrument used to share some of the windfall profit from oil and gas at federal and state level, stood at $ 3.5 bn. The national currency was under pressure as well and, in November, the Central Bank slightly deval-ued the naira to an exchange rate of NGN 168:$ 1. On 19 December, the rate fell to NGN 187:$ 1, partly due to the approaching Christmas and New Year celebrations and to currency speculation, with the lat-ter probably having the greater impact. The depreciation however, heralded a further decline of the naira in the coming year.

As of 30 September, the *total debt* of the federal government, the 36 federal states and the Federal Capital territory Abuja stood at $ 69.6 bn, being $ 9.5 bn of external debt and $ 60 bn of domes-tic debt. The states' share, however, was some $ 10 bn domestic and $ 3 bn external debts.

Nevertheless, in April, after it had rebased its nominal GDP, *Nigeria emerged as the biggest economy on the continent*, with an es-timated $ 509 bn for the year 2013, up from $ 285 bn, thereby over-taking South Africa by a clear margin. The sectoral distribution put services on top with 52%, of which retail and wholesale emerged with 20% and the booming telecommunication market with 8%. Industry, still dominated by the production and export of oil and gas – the main source of foreign exchange proceeds – and agricul-ture followed at 25% and 22% respectively.

As in previous years, the signing of the *federal budget* into law was delayed. The 2014 budget, totalling NGN 4.695 trillion ($ 29.3 bn) based on a benchmark of $ 77.5 per barrel of crude oil, a produc-tion of some 2.4 m b/d and an exchange rate of NGN 160:$ 1, was not signed by the president until 21 May. Unsurprisingly, the lion's share of the budget, NGN 968 bn, went to the security sector, to include the military, police, the office of the state security advisor and para-military services. On 17 December, the government presented its 2015 budget proposal of NGN 4.358 trillion, based on a benchmark of $ 65 per barrel of crude in the expectation that prices would average about $ 65 to $ 70 in 2015. The exchange rate was pegged at NGN 165:$ 1, although the rate was already falling towards the NGN 190:$ 1 mark.

There was little or no real improvement with regard to the sup-ply of electricity, despite the fact that the government had allegedly accelerated deregulation. Gas shortages and inadequate distribution infrastructure continued to depress both power generation and supply output from the national grid with an average of less than 4,000 MW. According to local estimates, private generators produced around 6,000 MW. Interestingly, some private companies such as the Dangote Group and other cement, food and beverage manufacturing plants across the country had built their own power plants and were generating more than 15,000 MW for the exclusive use of their own companies. Against this background, it was no wonder that, in April, the US firm General Electric, one of the world's leading power companies, considered Nigeria a significant power market. This was in line with the commitment of the World Bank, which, in May, supported Nigeria's power sector reform programme with $ 700 m over the next few years. In addition, on 18 November, the Central Bank signed a NGN 213 bn ($ 1.3 bn) memorandum of understanding with the Ministry of Petroleum Resources, the Ministry of Power and the Nigerian Electricity Regulatory Commission on the CBN-Nigeria Electricity Market Stabilisation Facility. Its aim was to resolve the power sectors' liquidity challenges. Local observers, however, regarded this agreement as yet another source of enrichment to some dubious players in the field.

On 20 July, the Liberian-US citizen Patrick Oliver Sawyer, working for ECOWAS, arrived at Lagos airport knowing that he carried the *Ebola virus*. On arrival, he collapsed and was admitted to a private hospital, where he died on 24 July. Although Sawyer denied being infected, consultant physician Ms Ameyo Stella Adadevoh was able to establish that Sawyer was Nigeria's first Ebola patient. On 28 July, all flights to and from Monrovia (Liberia) and Freetown (Sierra Leone) were suspended and, on 9 August, Nigeria's president declared the outbreak of Ebola "a national emergency" and all schools were closed until October. Unfortunately, the physician, the protocol officer who had received Sawyer, and five other individuals also succumbed to the disease. A dozen confirmed cases survived the outbreak. WHO officially declared Nigeria free of Ebola on

20 October and Nigeria won praise for its swift containment of the disease at a very early stage. In early December, the president signed the National Health Bill into law.

On 18 June, the *Aare Musulmi of Yorubaland*, Alhaji Abdul-Azeez Arisekola-Alao, passed away in London at the age of 69. The Ibadan-based religious leader, wealthy businessman and military contractor had played a dubious and controversial role in the aftermath of the botched democratisation process in the 1990s under the then military dictators Ibrahim Babangida and Sani Abacha.

Nigeria in 2015

The March and April elections at the federal and state level dominated the political scene. For the first time in Nigeria's history, a sitting president was voted out of office. Muhammadu Buhari won decisively and was given a strong political mandate. An improved election commission conducted the most credible elections yet in Nigeria's history, although it had initially appeared that the postponement of the elections would derail the whole election process with unforeseeable repercussions. However, at the end of the day, the political class and the vast majority of the elites demonstrated their willingness and ability to stabilise the Fourth Republic. The new government intensified the fight against the Islamist insurgency in the North-East, which improved the security situation as a whole. However, Buhari faced economic challenges amplified by plummeting oil and gas prices.

Domestic Politics

The most prominent issues were the *general elections*, scheduled for 14 February (presidential and National Assembly), 28 February (gubernatorial and state assemblies), and the ongoing threat of Boko Haram. At the beginning of the year, all eyes were on the elections, in which the incumbent President Goodluck Jonathan, a Christian from the Niger Delta, and the former military dictator and three-time presidential candidate Muhammadu Buhari battled for the presidency, a repeat of the previous election in 2011. While Jonathan, of the ruling People's Democratic Party (PDP), kept his vice president, Namadi Sambo, a Muslim from the North as running mate, Buhari, of the All Progressives Congress (APC), named former Lagos state attorney general, Yemi Osinbajo, a Christian from the South-West. The other 12 aspirants and their respective running mates played little to no role in the outcome

© KONINKLIJKE BRILL NV, LEIDEN, 2017 | DOI 10.1163/9789004347410_013

At the start of the year, logistical and technical problems within the *Independent National Electoral Commission* (INEC), along with the ongoing Islamic insurgency in the North, meant that only two-thirds of the 67.4 m registered voters had collected their 'Permanent Voters' Cards' (PVCs). Accordingly, the INEC extended the collection deadline until 8 February. At this point, doubts were raised as to whether the elections would take place at all, given the undercurrent of political change in favour of Buhari. However, the ability of the APC to seal a strong alliance between the North-West and South-West, which Nigeria had last seen on the eve of the civil war, presented Jonathan with an insuperable challenge, despite the fact that the presidency and the PDP had a level of resources no other candidate could hope to match. In fact, the credibility of Jonathan and the PDP had already reached a nadir from which they never really recovered. Moreover, the APC was able to demonstrate unity and stayed away from any provocative language during the election campaign.

On 22 January, at Chatham House in London, Sambo Dasuki, the national security adviser, insinuated that elections would not take place as scheduled. This was the prelude to similar indications by the security agencies, who were about to commence a six-week special campaign against the Islamist insurgents in the North-East and would not be available to support the planned elections. Thus, on 7 February, the well respected INEC chairman, Attahiru Jega, announced that *the polls* would be shifted to 28 March (presidential and National Assembly), and 11 April (gubernatorial and state assemblies). Although the elections were delayed, they still met the constitutional deadline.

Soon afterwards, the two main presidential contenders accepted the postponement and the incumbent pledged that the new president would be sworn in on 29 May, the day that marks the beginning of a new presidential term. In addition, the INEC extended the deadline for collecting the PVCs to 8 March and almost 80% of the registered voters eventually collected their cards. The uneven distribution pattern, however, indicated a comfortable lead of the North over the South, which was to a large extent related to the fact that many former pro-Jonathan voters, particularly from the Igbo heartland in the South-East, abstained from the election process. In the final analysis, this paved the way for Buhari to win by a clear margin. These issues notwithstanding, there was much uncertainty in the days and weeks that followed, as to whether the INEC could withstand the mounting pressure from influential inner government and security circles. The card reader issue in particular became a serious bone of contention since the *biometric machines* had been put in place in order to prevent and reducing electoral malpractice. Furthermore, the INEC had selected top personnel from tertiary institutions as returning officers. Against this background and the general political climate for change, it emerged that forces close to the government had advocated either a postponement or an indefinite delay of the elections.

Finally, the INEC's determination prevailed, with the support of the business community and well known tycoons such as Aliko Dangote, the international community and a broad alliance of civil society groups such as the Nigerian Civil Society Situation Room. The latter mobilised people to cast their vote and closely monitored events.

The presidential and National Assembly elections on 28 March, in which 31.7 m accredited voters eventually took part, was well covered by the media and it soon became clear that the expected change was in the offing. On 31 March, hours before the official announcement of the results, *Jonathan conceded defeat*, thereby confirming that the electorate, for the first time in Nigeria's history, had voted out a sitting head of state. Buhari polled closed to 54% (28.6 m votes) and won by a large margin of almost 2.6 m. Consequently, on 1 April, the INEC declared Buhari the winner. Buhari immediately accepted the mandate.

The results for the bicameral National Assembly resembled the results from the presidential elections. The APC won a landslide victory, securing an absolute majority in both the 109-member Senate and the 360-member House of Representatives.

A fortnight later, on 11 April, the PDP suffered another humiliating defeat in the gubernatorial and state assembly elections. While state assembly elections were held in all 36 states, only 29 gubernatorial mandates were contested because the tenure of seven sitting governors had not yet expired. Nineteen APC front runners triumphed, while the PDP won nine states, all but two (Gombe and Taraba) in the South. In some rare cases such as in Imo, Taraba and Abia states, results were inconclusive and supplementary elections were to be held two weeks later. The outcome of the elections was a *sharpened North-South divide*, which shaped the political landscape.

Most observers saw the poll as the most credible in Nigerian history, despite some shortcomings and lapses with regard to card readers and logistics. There were also some *violence*, in the form of election-related killings and isolated bomb blasts, various forms of aggression, arson and hijacking of election materials in a number of states. Such incidents occurred mainly during state elections. Moreover, the PDP did not challenge Buhari's victory in court, which, together with Jonathan's attitude towards the defeat, might indicate a constructive change in the political culture, at least in the medium term.

Nevertheless, 680 results, most of them for parliamentary seats, were challenged at *election tribunals* and in the courts, although these cases were for the most part dismissed. In Rivers state, the tribunal annulled the outcome of the gubernatorial election that saw Nyesom Wike of the PDP victorious, a ruling that was upheld by the Court of Appeal on 16 December. In Taraba, however, the election tribunal's verdict of 7–8 November in favour of the defeated APC candidate, Ms Aisha Alhassan, led to a violent clash between supporters of the two parties, leaving at least 12 people dead. On 31 December, the November verdict was repealed in favour of the PDP candidate Darius Ishaku. Ms Alhassan vowed to appeal. On 3 November, the Abia state tribunal had dismissed the petition by the All Progressives Grand Alliance (APGA) candidate, Alex Otti, challenging the INEC's decision to declare the PDP candidate Okezie

Ikpeazu the winner. On 31 December, however, the Court of Appeal rejected the supposed winner and directed the INEC to make arrangements for Otti's swearing in. Shortly before, on 18 December, a court nullified the election of PDP Governor Udom Emmanuel of Akwa Ibom state and ordered a re-run within 90 days. At the end of the year, the controversial verdicts on these four gubernatorial election results, together with other less disputed cases, were still pending at the Supreme Court.

The gubernatorial election in Kogi state, not due until 21 November, became a focal point of *legal wrangling* after the ballot was declared inconclusive and the APC candidate, Abubakar Audu, who was on the verge of winning against the sitting PDP governor, Idris Wada, died before the final result could be announced. In a disputed process, Yahaya Bello, the runner-up in the APC primaries, eventually replaced the deceased and, following supplementary elections on 5 December, was declared governor elect.

In Bayelsa state, the ballot on 5 December was marred by *malpractices and violence* and was eventually cancelled in southern Ijaw. Accordingly, the INEC fixed supplementary elections in the affected areas to take place on 9 January 2016. The incumbent, Seriake Dickson, had a clear lead and was widely expected to win.

With only hours to go before the end of his tenure, the outgoing president signed six bills into law, among them the Tobacco Control Bill, and issued 72 radio licences to dubious clients. However, he refused to sign the adopted constitutional amendments titled 'Fourth Alteration Act 2015'. A *silent power struggle* between the outgoing executive and the legislature over sensitive clauses relating to a reduction in the power of the executive had been going on since 2010, and was eventually brought before the Supreme Court. Legal experts, backed by a Federal High Court, had originally insisted that amendments passed by the National Assembly and backed by the necessary majority of at least two-thirds of all the 36 state assemblies must be signed by the president. The then president abided by the contentious verdict and in early 2011 put the first constitutional amendments into force. The National Assembly rejected this argument and the issue was left pending for years.

Against the backdrop of an imminent change of government, the court suggested defusing some clauses, particularly that concerning the presidential power to put constitutional amendments into force. However, given the fact that the Constitution offers no clear guidance, the court was reluctant to take a final decision on such a fundamental issue. Eventually, on 26 May, both sides agreed on minor constitutional amendments such as a pension for life for the National Assembly's leadership, the admission of independent candidates, reformed citizenship, the president's annual state of the nation address and a simplified process to deregister political parties, which Jonathan vowed to sign into law. He ignored the agreement, however, and the whole alteration process collapsed.

Buhari was sworn in on 29 May. After the inauguration of the 8th legislative period on 9 June, the overwhelming APC majority in the House of Representatives elected the APC members Yakubu Dogara from Bauchi State and Yusuf Lasun from Osun state as speaker, and deputy speaker, respectively. One month later, and after a lot of political wrangling, on 9 July, APC-senator Olubukola Saraki from Niger state emerged as senate president, while PDP-senator Ike Ekweremadu from Enugu state was somewhat surprisingly returned as his deputy. Interestingly, the *distribution of power* among the top three positions in the Nigerian political system was not balanced between the six geo-political zones, since it excluded the South-South from where Jonathan originates.

In successive steps between his inauguration and the forming of a cabinet in November, Buhari dissolved almost all federal parastatals and agencies and appointed new personnel. In addition, he immediately made appointments to *key positions within the presidency*, including the then president of the Nigerian guild of editors, Femi Adesina, as chief spokesman (30 May), Alhaji Ahmed Idris as the new accountant general of the federation (25 June) and Ms Amina Bala Zakari as acting chair of the INEC following the departure of Attahiru Jega, whose five-year term expired on 30 June. Later in the year, however, on 21 October, Ms Zakari was replaced by Mahmood Yakubu and appointed as INEC commissioner, representing the North-West. Lawal Musa Daura was named as the new director general of the Department of State Security (DSS; also known as the State Security Service: SSS) on 2 July, retired Major General Babagana Monguno was appointed national security adviser and retired Brigadier P.T. Boroh became the coordinator of the amnesty programme for former militants in the Niger Delta. In August, further important appointments were made, such as that of Emmanuel Ibe Kachikwu as head of the Nigerian National Petroleum Corporation (NNPC), Babachir David Lawal as secretary to the government of the federation and Alhaji Abba Kyari as the president's chief of staff.

More than five months after his inauguration, on 11 November, the president presented his *cabinet*. The number of ministries had been reduced from 29 to 24 and, in a deft move, security and law related portfolios were given to the crisis-shaken North, while key positions concerning finance and the economy were handed over to appointees from the economically better off South, in particular from the South-West. Two retired high-ranking military officers, Mansur Maman Dan Ali and Abdulrahman Bello Dambazau, emerged as defence minister and minister of the interior, respectively, the latter including authority over the police force, while Abubakar Malami took over at the Ministry of Justice. Ms Kemi Adeosun was appointed minister of finance, former Lagos governor Babatunde Raji Fashola was given the Ministry of Power and Infrastructure, another former governor, Rotimi Amaechi from Rivers state, was named minister of transportation, and Udoma Udo Udoma minister for budget and national planning. As expected, the president kept the decisive Petroleum Ministry – a repeat of Olusegun Obasanjo's approach during his incumbency – but called on the head of the NNPC, Kachikwu, to oversee the ministry's day-to-day business. In addition, Buhari approved the appointment of 18 new permanent secretaries in the federal civil service, some of whom were recruited from private sector fields such as banking and engineering.

Against the backdrop of the still *precarious security situation*, Buhari enforced wide-ranging changes within the military. Immediately after his inauguration, he directed the army to move its 'central command and control centre' to the Borno state capital Maiduguri, a move in which he hoped to consolidate 'Operation Zaman Lafiya' previously known as 'Operation Lafiya Dole'. This operation – the fight against Boko Haram was placed under a unified command structure coordinating GOC 3 and 7 Divisions.

In a sweeping shake-up on 13 July, all service chiefs were retired and replaced. Major General Abayomi Gabriel Olonishakin became chief of defence staff, Lieutenant General Tukur Yusuf Buratai emerged as army chief of staff, Rear Admiral Ibok-Ete Ekwe Ibas was promoted to navy chief of staff, and Air Vice-Marshal Sadique Abubakar became air force chief of staff. Air Vice-Marshal Monday Riku Morgan took over the position of defence intelligence chief. On 4 August, the senate confirmed these appointments. Prior to that, on 31 July, the new army chief of staff had handed over command of the Multinational Joint Task Force (MNJTF) to Major General Iliyasu Isah Abbah.

At the end of July, more than 300 army officers of the upper echelons, including some *General Officers Commanding* (GOC), were redeployed. Major General Adeniyi Oyebade became commander of the GOC 1 Division. Major General L.C. Ilo took over the GOC 2 Mechanized Division, and Major General Hassan Umaru emerged as commander of the GOC 3 Armoured Division. Less than six months later, on 18 December, Umaru replaced Major General Yusha'u Mahmood Abubakar, appointed in August, as commander of 'Operation Zaman Lafiya'; Brigadier M.S.A. Aliyu took over GOC 3. However, Major General I.H. Edet was appointed commander of the GOC 81 Amphibious Division, while Major General Ibrahim Attahiru became the new head of the GOC 82 Airborne Division. Only Major General Lamidi Adeosun, appointed in January by the previous

government, was kept on as commander of the GOC 7 Infantry
Division, garrisoned in Maiduguri. A few weeks later, in early
September, the air force and the navy also undertook a major shake-
up, redeploying most of their senior officers.

In addition to the shake-up and redeployment, president Buhari
and his government inherited a number of *serious military problems*.
For instance, on 16 January, more than 200 soldiers of the GOC 3
Armoured Division had protested against their dismissal a few days
earlier. Shortly thereafter, on 22 January, 22 officers were court-martialled in Lagos, among them Brigadier J.O. Komolafe and 14 colonels,
for alleged cowardice and desertion. In Abuja, on 11 March, another
batch of 30 officers, including another brigadier, Enitan Ransome-
Kuti, a member of the famous Kuti-family in Yorubaland, suffered
the same fate, being held responsible for failing to repel terrorists
who had attacked the headquarters of the MNJTF in Baga at Lake
Chad in January. Later in the year, on 15 October, it emerged that the
first count of 'cowardly behaviour' against Ransome-Kuti was struck
out and he was given a six-month prison term and dishonourably
discharged from the army for neglecting his military duties.

On 20 May, the Nigerian army disclosed that about 579 officers
and soldiers were facing *general court martial* in Lagos and Abuja for
various offences such as insubordination, cowardice, refusal to carry
out orders and indiscipline. In addition, it was reported that hundreds of rank and file soldiers had been dismissed. On 22 May, the
soldiers, sentenced to death in December 2014 for alleged mutiny,
filed a suit before a civil court in Abuja to prevent the army from
executing them. In July, another group of sacked soldiers hauled
the army before the National Industrial Court to seek redress. On
2 August, the new chief of army staff ordered a legal review of all
court martial verdicts and, on 3 September, the army confirmed the
pardon and reinstatement of more than 3,000 of some 5,000 convicted soldiers. In addition, on 19 December, all death sentences were
commuted to ten year' imprisonment, a decision that could still be
challenged in a civil court. Earlier, on 21 September, 5,000 soldiers

fighting Boko Haram were promoted in a measure aimed at boost-
ing their morale. Previously, around mid-year, it was reported that
the challenges of the Islamist insurgency and conflict within the
army had led to the re-engagement of retired officers to serve as
consultants and instructors at the artillery school in Kachia, Kaduna
state. At year's end, it transpired that within 12 months the army was
intending to raise another division in the North-East.

The *police forces* also underwent major changes. Much to the surprise of the public, the then president Jonathan, on 21 April, sacked
the inspector general of police, Suleiman Abba, whom he had appointed only in August 2014. Hailing from the North, Abba had allegedly acted in bad faith in the run-up to the state elections in Rivers
state by ignoring an order from the presidency to recall the deployed
assistant inspector general, Tunde Ogunshakin. It was surmised that
the presidency considered Ogunshakin sympathetic to the outgoing
Governor Amaechi and his party (APC), and that he would not allow
the PDP to win.

Solomon Arase, a deputy inspector general of police from the
South, emerged as inspector general and retained his appointment
under the new president. At the end of August, Ms Olabisi Kolawole
was named as the police force's spokesperson, the first woman to
hold this position. A redeployment of all commissioners of police
in the 36 states and the capital Abuja and of most of the assistant
inspector generals followed suit. At the same time, the new leadership enforced a presidential order calling for immediate *withdrawal
of police security for VIPs* who were not entitled to the service. Until
then it had been common practice for the political class and self-proclaimed eminent business people to make improper use of policemen for their personal security. Last but not least, 260 senior police
officers were promoted and, at the end of September, the police service commission reinstated more than a dozen officers and recalled
and/or retired several others, thereby reversing their unfair dismissal. In addition, between late August and early September a purge
hit the top echelon of the State Security Service (SSS), including

Gordon Obua, Abdulrahman Mani and Ms Marilyn Ogar abut called on the head of thend dozens of other senior staff. On 27 November, Buhari appointed 30 new judges to the Federal High Court in line with the recommendations of the National Judicial Council.

Over the course of the year, the once precarious security situation in the crisis-ridden North-East improved, thanks to *a new and massive military campaign* that began in mid-February. The improvement allowed for elections to take place in most parts of the affected area. As in previous years, however, Adamawa, Borno and Yobe states were the main targets of the *Islamist insurgency*. The deadly attack on the MNJTF base in Baga only a few days after New Year's Eve, which cost hundreds of lives, as well as suicide bomb attacks in Damaturu (Yobe state) and Maiduguri (Borno state) on 9 and 10 January, heralded yet another year of the insurgency. Eventually, some 2,000 persons were killed during the attacks and counter-attacks, bringing the total number of victims, at a rough estimate, to 20,000. However, the number of injured persons is not known, and is certainly several times higher. In addition, the number of IDPs rose close to 2 m.

Early in the year, the army and the air force began a large-scale operation that included the use of drones. On 21 February, Baga was recaptured and, in late April, military forces, backed by air strikes, started to invade Sambisa Forest, the insurgents' last known stronghold. It was reported that Boko Haram fighters stoned to death some of the women they had abducted as security forces approached. Towards the end of the year, all areas but Sambisa Forest were retaken and some 2,000 abductees, mostly women and children, were rescued. Two months earlier, on 28 October, the army had published photographs of 100 top suspected Boko Haram terrorists. By year's end, the effects were at best mixed, since only very few suspects had been arrested. In one case, on 18 December, the army had to set free one Abubakar Sadiq who had been wrongly detained a month earlier.

This notwithstanding, *suicide bombings* went on unabated, mostly undertaken by young girls, most of whom were probably unaware of their deadly mission. Yola, the capital of Adamawa state, more or less considered out of reach of terrorist attacks, was eventually hit on 17 November, just days after Buhari's visit. The bomb blast killed more than 30 people. Shortly after Christmas, on 28 December, two bombers struck a market in Madagali, the headquarters of the local government of the same name, claiming more than 25 lives. At the same time, only days after Buhari had claimed that the war against Boko Haram had been 'technically won', Maiduguri was hit for the umpteenth time, causing more than 30 casualties.

Kano state and the capital of the same name along with the Federal Capital Territory Abuja, as well as Gombe, Kaduna and Plateau states, suffered similar attacks, though not on the same scale as before. For example, on 24 February, a suicide bomb attack killed more than two dozen persons in a bus at a motor park in the Kano state capital along Zaria Road. Another blast occurred on 6 July outside the Umar Ibn al-Khattab mosque, located along the same road, when a teenage girl detonated explosives after she had been prevented from entering. Fortunately no one else was killed. On 18 November, a market in Turani local government in Kano State was hit by a twin blast, claiming at least 15 lives. On 27 November, some 20 members of the Muslim Brethren, also known as the Islamic Movement in Nigeria, who consider themselves 'Shiites', were killed by a bomb blast near Kura Town, on their way from Kano to the sect's main base in Zaria in neighbouring Kaduna state, where they were to participate in the Ashura festivities.

A day after Buhari's *address to the nation* on the occasion of the 55th Independence Day on 1 October, a twin blast occurred in the urban districts of Kuje and Nyanya within greater Abuja, claiming the lives of 15 and three persons, respectively; dozens were seriously wounded. Much earlier, on 2 April, a young woman had dropped a bag at a shop within a motor park in Gombe town. The improvised explosive device went off, killing more than a dozen people, including six soldiers. In Plateau and Kaduna states, almost 50 people lost their lives in two bomb attacks in the state capital Jos (5 July) and at least two dozen were killed by a bomb in Sabon Gari, a local government within greater Zaria.

In North-Central Nigeria, including the Middle Belt states, cattle rustling, disputes over grazing rights and rights over fertile land led to deadly skirmishes in which hundreds of peasants, herdsmen, soldiers, policemen and uninvolved citizens lost their lives. In early July, for example, even as far as Zamfara state in the far north, gunmen raided some villages in Birnin-Magaji local government, killing dozens of people and taking their livestock. Despite the alarming number of deadly clashes in Benue and Taraba states, Barkin Ladi and Riyom local governments in Plateau state remained the focal point of *sectarian and ethnic clashes*, in which mainly ethnic Birom and Fulani were involved. One of the cruellest incidents occurred in Foron Town on 2 May, when a church building of the Church of Christ in Nations was set on fire, allegedly by Fulani herdsmen; 27 worshippers were killed, including the pastor Luka Gwom. In the days and weeks that followed, the situation spiralled out of control in both local government areas. Eventually, on 13 August, the new Plateau state governor, Simon Lalong, imposed a dusk-to-dawn curfew.

Over the course of the year, the crisis in the North and the general elections kept public attention away from the unabated spread of bank robbery and organised crime throughout the country, particularly in the South, and from a number of disturbing incidents in the *Niger Delta and the Bight of Biafra*. According to the International Maritime Bureau, 14 incidents were reported during the period under review, with nine vessels boarded, though many attacks were believed to have gone unrecorded. For example, on 3 February, a tanker sailing under a Maltese flag was attacked while waiting to load at Qua Iboe in Akwa Ibom state. One crew member was killed and three others were taken hostage. A French oil industry supply vessel came under attack on 8 April, when pirates kidnapped three Nigerians. In another incident in the eastern Cross River state, pirates on speed boats attacked the marine police armoury in the state capital Calabar, making away with two gun boats and caches of weapons. The authorities denied claims that officers were killed.

On Good Friday, 3 April, ethnic Urhobo militants blew up a gas pipeline in Delta state, allegedly drawing attention to their exclusion from lucrative protection contracts with the NNPC. Barely a month later, on 29 April, militants from the same ethnic minority in the state claimed responsibility for two explosions that rocked two major trunk lines in Ughelli north and south local governments. Following the navy's destruction of 50 illegal camps in Burutu local government area in Delta state on 11 October, the Federal High Court in Lagos, on 30 October, convicted seven men to jail terms of 12 years each for *unlawful dealings in petrol*, ordering the forfeiture of their vessel and the assets of the convicts' company.

Kidnapping for ransom, mostly targeting Nigerians, remained quite rampant, particularly in the southern and south-western parts of the country. On 1 April, five local members of staff of a subsidiary of ExxonMobil were kidnapped in Akwa Ibom state by unknown gunmen. In neighbouring Rivers state, the vice chancellor of the Ignatius Ajuru State University, Ms Rosemond Green-Osagholu, was taken hostage on 20 June as she was leaving the campus. At least temporarily, Ekiti state somehow became a hub for this profitable business. For example, on 7 May, a former chief medical director, Patrick Adegun, was taken hostage, along with his wife Kikelomo. The following day, a university lecturer, Femi Omisore, suffered the same fate, with his driver killed during the incident. On 15 May, three women along with their husbands and children were abducted on their way from Oyo to Ekiti state. Eventually, the captors dropped the men and the children while the women were driven away. Emmanuel Akingbade, a Catholic priest of the diocese in the state, who was taken hostage on 9 June, was held captive for several days.

In neighbouring Kogi state, a US citizen and missionary of the Free Methodist Church, Ms Phyllis Sortor, spent more than three months in captivity after being kidnapped on 23 February. Prior to her release, on 25 May, a state high court judge, Samuel Obayomi, was attacked and abducted and his orderly shot dead on the spot. He eventually had to spend more than a month in his captor's custody. The well-known former politician, septuagenarian Olu Falae, was kidnapped on his farm in Ondo state on 21 September. He survived his kidnapping unscathed, as did the vast majority of abductees. However, the killing of Samuel Okpara, a medical doctor who was taken hostage on 20 February in Port Harcourt, and the discovery of the decomposing body of a university lecturer, Paul Erie, in Edo state on 1 October, underlined the fact that the *citizens' everyday life was still vulnerable*. Erie had allegedly died at the hands of his captors soon after being kidnapped on 16 June. The former vice chancellor of the Federal University of Technology in Akure, Ekiti state, 79-year old Albert Ilemobade, was killed on 22 June by two of his servants, who were intending to steal his car. Soon afterwards, both were apprehended. One Catholic priest and lecturer, Dennis Osuagwu, was murdered by a kidnap gang in Imo state on 15 August; and an Israeli citizen lost his life, when he resisted a kidnap attempt in Abuja on 9 September.

Against this backdrop, the newly elected Rivers state governor, Nyesom Wike, assented on 7 August to an amended *kidnap prohibition law*, stipulating that persons convicted of this crime would forfeit their assets to the state.

Despite a *great deal of crime*, the police forces, in conjunction with the DSS broke up several notorious gangs, particularly during the second half of the year. One of the cruellest crimes however, occurred on 16 September in Ogun state, where ten DSS operatives were killed in Arepo area by pipeline vandals who were siphoning off fuel. Earlier, towards the end of July, the DSS in Imo state had arrested a notorious gang leader, simply named Chibueze but popularly known as 'Vampire', alleged to have kidnapped and killed individuals in their dozens. Prior to that, on 6 July, Lagos state police command had smashed a gang that had carried out various robberies on waterways and highways in the state, including a bank in Lekki peninsula, where, on 12 March, three policemen and two civilians had been killed. In early October, while half a dozen ethnic Fulani herdsmen, suspected to be the kidnappers of Olu Falae, were detained in Ondo and Niger states, Lagos state police command claimed to have arrested some 100 suspects in September alone for offences ranging from armed robbery to kidnapping, murder and sophisticated fraud. On 28 October, the police in Imo state smashed the gang of one Musa Isah, alias Yahaya Ibrahim, that had killed Reverend Father Osuagwu.

The precarious security situation in most parts of the country had serious effects on *human rights*. On 4 June, AI maintained that the Nigerian military was responsible for the deaths of more than 8,000 prisoners detained during the campaign against Boko Haram; more than 7,000 had starved to death or died of disease, while some 1,200 were executed without trial. The military vehemently denied these allegations. Despite this accusation, AI was permitted to open an office in Abuja on 13 October. Earlier, on 10 June, the Federal High Court in Enugu acceded to the prosecutor's application to proceed in secret with the trial of members of the 'Biafra Zionist Federation'. The leader, Benjamin Onwuka, and some of his followers were charged with treason for crimes allegedly committed in 2014. No verdict had been reported by year's end. On 12 December, a motor-cade of the Army Chief of Staff Buratai made headlines when it was attacked on its way to a ceremony in Zaria, allegedly by members of the so-called Shiites; the soldiers opened fire without warning, causing dozens of fatalities. In a climate of reciprocal accusations, the official investigation into the grisly incident commenced rather reluctantly. The above is nowhere near a complete list of the terror-attacks, counter-attacks, kidnappings and murders that took place during the year.

On 27 November in Abuja, the Federal High Court turned down an application by the DSS aimed at quashing the decision of the National Human Rights Commission (NHRC) to pay compensation in the so-called 'Apo killings case'. The NHRC had held the government responsible for the *extra-judicial killings* of eight squatters in

September 2013 and awarded monetary compensation to the victims' relatives. In 2010, an amended act had made the Commission's decisions and recommendations legally binding and enforceable by the courts.

On 25 June, after a secret trial in an upper *sharia court* in Rijiyar Lemo in Kano state, nine people, including a cleric, were sentenced to death for blasphemous statements. Four others, arrested with those convicted, were found not guilty and were discharged. The sentences had not been carried out by year's end. The charge of murder brought against a 15-year-old girl was eventually dropped by a Kano state High Court on 20 May. At the age of 14, she had allegedly poisoned her 35-year old husband and four others. However, the constitutional legality of the death sentence was upheld on 24 April by the Supreme Court, when it rejected the appeal of a convicted armed robber.

As the unprecedented scale of corruption under the previous government gradually became clear, Buhari vowed to take drastic measures in his *anti-corruption campaign*. Despite the appointment of Ibrahim Mustafa Magu as the new chairman of the Economic and Financial Crimes Commission on 9 November, it had not gained any significant momentum by the end of the year. The serious charges against the former national security adviser, Sambo Dasuki, were considered as the litmus test for the government's ability to convict high ranking officials of the previous government on charges of looting public funds. In addition, controversial multi-million dollar contracts between the ousted government and former Niger Delta militia leaders such as Mujahid Dokubo-Asari and Government Ekpemupolo, alias Tompolo, came under severe scrutiny.

Foreign Affairs

Over the course of the year, the new leadership reshaped Nigeria's foreign policy. The fact that US Secretary of State John Kerry was present at Muhammadu Buhari's inauguration on 29 May was a strong indication of the *gradual improvement of relations with the* USA. The visit was a clear sign of the Obama administration's willingness to strengthen diplomatic relations, which had become severely strained under former president Goodluck Jonathan. The attendance at the ceremony of the head of the US Africa Command, General David Rodriguez, confirmed America's renewed commitment to cooperation with Nigeria.

From 19–22 July, Buhari paid a state visit to the USA and held bilateral discussions with President Barak Obama on 20 July, in which the US administration offered its assistance in *tracking down millions of dollars of stolen assets*. In addition, it committed $ 5 m in support for the MNJTF's fight against Islamist insurgencies. However, the trip produced a disappointing result with regard to military assistance as Buhari failed to secure an arms deal. On the positive side, USAID agreed on 11 June to expand its humanitarian assistance to northeastern Nigeria to the tune of some $ 44 m.

On 2 November, Musa Jack Ngonadi, believed to be the son of former military leader Yakubu Gowon, was released from prison and deported. He had served more than half of a 40-year sentence for his involvement in a drugs cartel.

As in previous years, *legal issues shaped the relationship with Britain*. Days before his inauguration, president-elect Buhari undertook a six-day trip to the UK (22–27 May) where, on 23 May, he held discussions with Prime Minister David Cameron. As expected, the meeting focused on the Islamist insurgency and the UK's continuing commitment to provide military training and intelligence support. The timing of this visit had the effect of avoiding publicity in the run-up to the inauguration, which was attended by British Foreign Secretary Philip Hammond.

At the end of March, 36 year-old Ms Franca Asemota was arrested in Edo state by the National Agency for the Prohibition of Trafficking in Persons and extradited to the UK, where she was wanted for *trafficking young women and underage girls* to Europe using

Heathrow Airport as a transit hub. On 1 April, Woolwich Crown Court sentenced Jeffrey Okafor to a minimum 17-year jail term. The verdict ended a murder case and manhunt after Okafor had stabbed another Nigerian, Carl Beatson-Asiedu, to death in 2009. The victim was a well-known DJ on the club scene. Using his brother's passport, the culprit had fled to Nigeria where he was eventually apprehended and extradited to the UK in 2014. His brother, Junior Okafor, had already been given a four-year jail term in 2010 for assisting an offender. In a similar case, 39-year old Abdul Adewale Kekere-Ekun was sentenced on 7 September to life imprisonment for a murder committed in 2001. He had fled to Nigeria in a bid to escape prosecution but was arrested in February 2015 for identity theft offences, which revealed that he was on a UK wanted list.

On 2 October, former minister for petroleum resources, Ms Diezani Alison-Madueke, was temporarily arrested in London by the UK National Crime Agency over allegations of corruption perpetrated during her tenure as minister. Shortly thereafter, the UK government formally asked Nigeria to assist in investigating her activities as minister. In another corruption case, former bank manager Erastus Akingbola had been tried for serious fraud at the Federal High Court in Lagos, but on 20 February, the Court of Appeal ordered his retrial, basing its decision on the verdict of a UK court in 2014. In 2012 the Federal High Court had cleared Akingbola of all charges for lack of diligent prosecution. Once again, these incidents highlighted the fact that *numerous wealthy Nigerians owned expensive, luxury real estate in the* UK. The NGO African-British Returnees International claimed in February that Nigerians spent at least £ 300 m a year on British education.

Probably the most spectacular international corruption case involved a former minister for petroleum, Dan Etete. On 15 December, Southwark Crown Court in London prevented the release of $ 85 m to Etete's allegedly fraudulent Malabu Oil & Gas Company in Lagos. The money was seized at the request of Italian prosecutors who were investigating a disputed oil deal worth more than $ 1 bn, involving Etete's company, the multinationals Shell and ENI, and the Nigerian government under then president Jonathan.

Due to the Islamist insurgency in the Lake Chad region, Nigeria's relationships with African countries focused on the West African region. Towards the end of February, military chiefs from Nigeria and the four neighbouring countries began finalising their ambitious strategy for the creation of an 8,750-strong force aimed at taking on Boko Haram. N'Djamena, the Chadian capital, would serve as the overall command centre. By May, however, during a state visit by Chad's President Idriss Déby, it emerged that the strategy was too ambitious, although the military chiefs met again in N'Djamena on 20–21 August. Nigeria's *structural web of arrogance, corruption, incompetence and shame* and the deep-seated and long-existing mutual mistrust between Nigeria and the neighbouring francophone states undermined and delayed potentially promising cooperation. Moreover, the weakness of Cameroon's and Niger's security forces offered Boko Haram an opportunity to regroup after they had been largely driven out of Nigerian territory.

On 11 June, an extraordinary meeting of heads of state and government of the Lake Chad Basin Commission and Benin met in Abuja and approved *Nigeria's retaining the leadership of the* MNJTF. Cameroon's President Paul Biya did not attend the meeting, being represented by senior staff member from the Ministry of Defence, but he did receive Buhari in Yaoundé on 30 July. Apart from endorsing the commitment made at the extraordinary meeting, Biya and his guest agreed to complete the demarcation of the common land border before the end of the year. Earlier, on 13 June, Buhari had attended the 25th AU summit in Johannesburg (South Africa). On 7 September, he paid a one-day state visit to Ghana, where he held talks with President John Mahama; he welcomed Togolese President Faure Gnassingbé on 10 September and, on 22 September, hosted an extraordinary meeting of ECOWAS, which aimed at resolving the impasse in Burkina Faso.

Buhari's busy travel schedule provoked sceptical reactions both within elite circles and amongst the public. He attended the G-8 summit in Germany (7–8 June), and travelled twice to Paris, for a three-day state visit on 14–16 September, and later, to address the summit on climate change, which began on 30 November, flying in the meantime to New Delhi to participate in the India-Africa Forum (26–29 October). On 23 November, he attended the summit of the Gas Exporting Countries Forum in Tehran (Iran) and was in Malta on 27 November to participate in a meeting of the Commonwealth Heads of Government.

Nigeria's relations with the UN remained friendly. On 9 January, the UN Secretary-General Ban Ki-moon announced the appointment of Major General Salihu Uba as the new commander of the UN Mission in Liberia (UNMIL). On 8 July, Nigeria abstained from voting on a UNSC resolution that would have dubbed the 1995 massacre at Srebrenica a 'crime of genocide'. Despite Nigeria's abstention, the resolution still had the necessary majority, but Russia eventually vetoed it. On 23 August, Ban Ki-moon arrived in Nigeria on a two-day official visit, and Buhari addressed the UN General Assembly on 28 September.

On 24 September, *a stampede in Mecca* (Saudi Arabia), caused by a collapsed crane, killed several hundred pilgrims on the Hajj. The number of injured was much higher. The first northern female newspaper editor, Bilikisu Yusuf, and the Chief Imam of the Sultan Abubakar iii Jumaa'a Mosque in Sokoto were among the more than 200 Nigerian victims.

On 28 May, Akinwumi Adesina, was elected as the 8th president of the *AfDB Group* and took over on 1 September. He was the first Nigerian to occupy this position after Nigeria's previous bids had failed three times. On 24 July, Ms Arunma Oteh was appointed vice president and treasurer of the World Bank with effect from 28 September.

Socioeconomic Developments

Plummeting oil and gas prices fell below the $ 40 per barrel mark by the end of the year. The decline had a serious impact on the economy and highlighted Nigeria's overdependence on its main export commodities and developments on the international energy market. The national currency immediately came under pressure. By New Year's Eve, the exchange rate of the naira had fallen to NGN 300 to the dollar in the parallel market as against the official rate of NGN 197, stubbornly maintained by the Central Bank of Nigeria (CBN) and the government.

Earlier in the year, on 20 May, the spokesman of the then president confirmed that Jonathan, without the usual fanfare, had signed into law the *federal budget 2015*, totalling NGN 4.5 trn ($ 22.6 bn). The budget was based on a benchmark of $ 53 per barrel of crude oil and a production level of some 2.2 m b/d. It was slightly smaller than the previous budget and took the price fluctuations for oil into consideration. On 18 November, the new government sent a supplementary budget of NGN 465 bn to the National Assembly in order to cover fuel subsidies and gasoline imports. On 1 December, both chambers eventually approved an even higher budget of NGN 574 bn, but this increase was to fund a special military operation in the crisis-ridden North-East.

Despite the *volatile global oil and gas market*, shrinking foreign reserves of some $ 32 bn and a depleted excess crude account of just $ 1.7 bn at mid-year, President Buhari approved a rescue plan of NGN 1.2 trn on 6 July in order to help ailing states' budgets and and local governments. In addition, the CBN disbursed a special intervention fund to the states in the form of soft loans, repayable over a 20-year period at an interest rate of 9%. The fund was set up with the sole purpose of paying outstanding salaries. In September, in line with the government's anti-corruption campaign, the bank set up a nationwide monitoring mechanism to ensure that the fund was not diverted for other purposes.

On 22 December, the president presented his *2016 budget proposal* before a joint session of the National Assembly. The budget, totalling NGN 6.08 trn was based on a crude oil price of $ 38 per barrel and a production estimate of 2.2 m b/d and was aimed at reviving the economy by massively increasing capital expenditure. The government accepted a deficit of some NGN 2.22 trn, equivalent to 2.1% of Nigeria's GDP, which, unsurprisingly, gave rise to concern both inside and outside of Nigeria about the government's ability to handle financial and economic affairs.

Much earlier, at the end of January, the CBN had already commenced the Federal Government's Independent Revenue e-Collection Scheme, a platform to support the collection and remittance of all government revenue to a consolidated account domiciled with the CBN. This marked the beginning of the full implementation of a *Treasury Single Account (TSA) system* in Nigeria aimed at ensuring the accountability of government revenue, enhancing transparency and avoiding the misapplication of public funds. This controversial move forced the commercial banks to act as collection agents and, on 17 September, led to the governor of the CBN, Godwin Emefiele, trying to refute their claim that the policy had provoked a liquidity crisis. As early as 24 June, Emefiele had to defend the bank's decision to tighten foreign exchange control by excluding 41 items from the interbank forex market, an action some economic analysts criticised. Interestingly, the National Assembly rejected the TSA initiative, maintaining its role as an independent body of the constitutional order and triggering a silent power struggle with the presidency. By year's end, the issue had not been resolved.

Despite increasing economic hardship, the 2015 Global Wealth Report indicated a *rising number of Nigerian millionaires*, some 15,400, three times the number recorded in the previous study, published in 2000. Against this background, unsurprisingly, four Nigerian banks, including FirstBank of Nigeria and Zenith Bank, were among the top 500 banks worldwide.

As in previous years, Nigeria kept its position as Africa's largest and most lucrative telecommunications market with more than 140 m subscribers spending about NGN 200 bn on calls every month. In addition, there were almost 90 m users of the Internet, although the vast majority were still dependent on the outdated mobile technology GSM. In October, however, this booming sector suffered from an act of negligence on the part of the South African MTN Group, Africa's leading provider, which controls more than 40% of the Nigerian mobile phone market. MTN was fined $ 5.2 bn by the Nigerian Communications Commission (NCC) for refusing to deactivate almost 40 m improperly registered SIM cards. All competing companies had abided by the order, which was designed to undercut Boko Haram's communication capacity. For its part, MTN tried to have the heavy fine reduced. The NCC offered a 25% deduction of the original fine, payable by 31 December. The MTN in turn rejected that offer and challenged the fine in the Lagos Federal Court.

Last but not least, on 8 November in Chile, the Golden Eaglets retained the U-17 World Cup after defeating Mali 2–0.

Nigeria in 2016

Nigeria faced substantial economic and security challenges through-out the year. Plummeting oil and gas prices coupled with the emer-gence of new and violent militia groups in the Niger Delta caused the worst recession for 30 years. Increasing violence, and organized crime on an unprecedented scale in central Nigeria and the east-ern Middle Belt, compounded the already precarious situation and raised serious questions about the ability of President Muhammadu Buhari's government to handle the multifaceted crises in the finan-cial and economic sectors, as well as the security situation in at least three of the six geo-political zones, namely the North-Central, North-East and South-South. Despite the military's progress in the fight against Boko Haram in the North-East, it was obvious that the security forces were overstretched and thus would have been unable to deal with other security challengers elsewhere.

Domestic Politics

President Buhari and his government got off to a bad start, par-ticularly in the South-South, home of the oil and gas producing Niger Delta and the Ijaw, Itsekiri, Ibibio, Isoko, Urhobo and Yoruba. Early in the year, it became clear that the *2009 amnesty programme* had come to a standstill. Several new ethnic-based militia groups such as the Niger Delta Avengers (NDA), Red Scorpions, Niger Delta Greenland Justice Mandate (NDGJM), Egbesu Red Water Lions and Joint Niger Delta Liberation Force, appeared out of no-where. Following an interlude of relative peace, the region expe-rienced weeks of constant attacks and bombings of oil and gas installations. The affected companies included Chevron, Agip, Shell, Nigerian National Petroleum Corporation (NNPC) and the Nigerian Petroleum Development Company (NPDC). Gun battles involving the police and military forces once again turned the Niger Delta into a veritable battleground. The NDA militia, made up of ethnic Ijaw, was at the forefront of violence, challenging the state and the oil companies with piracy and guerrilla warfare. The public was reminded of the long-lasting civil strife associated with the Movement of the Emancipation of the Niger Delta (MEND), and with the thousands of victims in the early years of the Fourth Republic from 1999. Most attacks, however, took place in Delta and Bayelsa states, causing heavy losses and the deaths of dozens of soldiers, policemen, militia men and innocent civilians. Companies were frequently forced to suspend crude output and withhold gas supply to thermal power stations inside and outside the country. This significantly reduced Nigeria's export capacity and led to export receipt losses of around $ 7 bn.

To the consternation of the federal and the affected state governments, some *militia groups* invaded the creeks along the eastern state borders of Lagos, Ondo and Ogun states. On 5 February, for example, they ambushed and killed half a dozen naval personnel in the Wawa area of Arepo in Ogun state. This was seen as a reprisal against security agents who had previously raided the area as part of 'Operation Awatse' and had arrested a number of pipeline vandals. Nine operatives of the Department of State Service (DSS), also known as SSS, were killed in the same area on 13 September. This incident was probably connected with the killing of four DSS staff in nearby Ishawo area in Ikorodu local government in Lagos state. On 26 July, other militants engaged security forces in Igando in Lagos state. Soon afterwards, on 28 July, a joint task force, comprising navy, army, air force, police, state security service and the civil defence corps, launched an aerial bombardment on enclaves, camps and hideouts of pipeline oil thieves in Lagos and Ogun creeks that lasted for several days. Earlier, in June, the air force had redeployed additional combat and surveillance aircraft and helicopter gunships to the South-South, intending to carry out similar campaigns in the central Niger Delta region.

On 6 June, Vice President Yemi Osinbajo held an emergency meeting in Abuja with all the service chiefs, governors of the region and ministers of defence and petroleum in attendance. As a result, the federal government initiated a somewhat reluctant dialogue with militia groups and stakeholders, including some of the old political Ijaw elites such as octogenarian Edwin Clarke and septuagenarian Alfred Diete-Spiff, the first military governor of Rivers state (as the present Bayelsa and Rivers states had been known), who together represented the Pan-Niger Delta Forum (PANDEF). On 1 November, in a move aimed at helping to restore peace, leaders of the forum presented a 16-point plan to President Buhari, but the ethnic Urhobodominated NDGJM-militias carried out a damaging attack on the important Trans-Forcados pipeline in Delta state on 5 November, signalling that any peace deal was unlikely. In the following weeks, military operations, such as 'Pulo Shield', later renamed 'Delta Safe', 'Tsare Teku', Crocodile Smile', 'Crocodile Tears' and 'Python Dance', led to the killing and arrest of dozens of alleged militia commanders, but the campaigns did not prevent further attacks. Worse still, as part of the 2009 amnesty programme, the government was forced to resume cash payments to repentant militiamen, which had been stopped in February. Unabated killings, kidnappings and bomb attacks forced the government to admit that it would be unable to restore security for the foreseeable future, as it soon became apparent that even the *local elites had lost any respect and authority in their own spheres of influence.*

In the neighbouring ethnic Igbo-heartland, *advocacy groups in favour of an independent Biafra*, such as Indigenous People of Biafra (IPOB), Movement of the Actualization of the Sovereign State of Biafra (MASSOB), the Biafra Independence Movement (BIM) and the Biafra Zionist Movement, regained momentum. Tension grew throughout the year and led to numerous fatalities. On 19 January, in Aba, the hub of Abia state, soldiers opened fire on members of IPOB protesting against the continued detention of their leader, Nnamdi Kanu. Some half a dozen of his followers were killed. In May, further incidents in Anambra, Enugu, Imo and Ebonyi states provoked a chain of violence which culminated on 29–31 May in a bloodbath in Onitsha, in Anambra state. According to MASSOB and IPOB, some 60 members and sympathizers were shot by military forces. AI confirmed these numbers on 23 November, but the army rejected AI's preliminary report, and reported a lower number of deaths. Notwithstanding these events, Osita Okechukwu, the ethnic Igbo director general of the 'Voice of Nigeria', argued at a meeting of the Igbo socio-cultural organization Ohaneze Ndigbo on 28 September, that the actualization of Biafra was not feasible.

In several states of North-Central and North-East, particularly Zamfara, Adamawa, Niger, Benue and Taraba, the security situation went from bad to worse. A swathe of destruction affected the northern parts of the southern and eastern states of Cross River, Delta and Enugu. Against the backdrop of an *accelerated militarization of the region*, cattle rustling – traditionally part of Fulani herdsmen's culture of bravery and prowess – transformed into well organized banditry. In addition, disputes over grazing rights and fertile land led to deadly skirmishes in which hundreds of peasants, herdsmen, soldiers, policemen and uninvolved citizens lost their lives. Zamfara experienced at least two major attacks. On 6 February, gunmen raided Kwanar Dutse community in Maru local government area, gunning down some 50 villagers, razing most of their houses and taking away their livestock. On 7 November, Bindin village in the same local government suffered another tragedy, when gunmen on motorcycles killed about 50 miners and several gold merchants at a nearby gold mine. In a state-wide broadcast on 21 November, Governor Abdulaziz Yari, trying to address the security challenges by setting up a crisis management committee, disclosed that 155 people had been killed and more than 50 persons kidnapped in the past month.

On 24 January, at least 30 people, including members of a police team were killed by suspected Fulani herdsmen. The group had tried to stop the ongoing raids in the Girei local government (Adamawa state). The attackers were on a revenge mission following earlier clashes with local farmers. In another incident, Kodomun village in Demsa local government of Adamawa state was attacked twice within three days (on 30 July–1 August); dozens of people were killed and many more injured.

Agatu local government in Benue state, *for years a focal point of hostilities* between herdsmen and farmers, was again counting the cost when, at the end of February, incessant attacks on local people by Fulani herdsmen led to the deaths of more than 100 people. Other sources put the number at around 300, with some 7,000 people said to have been displaced and to be surviving in squatter camps. The dispute was not made any simpler by the fact that the hostilities were closely connected with the killing of scores of cattle.

Only after a raid on a community in Enugu state on 25 April, when heavily armed herdsmen killed scores of people, did President Buhari eventually break his silence and order the police and the military to take all necessary action to stop the carnage. The issue of *nationwide grazing reserve centres* re-emerged and, by August and September, the federal government had concluded arrangements to rehabilitate the more than 400 centres and stock routes, mandating 10 state governments to monitor the project. The military launched 'Operation Accord' to tackle the clashes between herdsmen in their own way. On 8 November, the government inaugurated a 16-member technical committee, chaired by Professor Oshita O. Oshita, director general of the Institute for Peace and Conflict Resolution (IPCR), to look into the recurring clashes. Despite these initiatives, deadly incidents in politically volatile southern Kaduna state occurred throughout the year. Endorsed by the president, the state government banned all processions and unlawful assemblies throughout the state on 21 December, imposing a 24-hour curfew in Jema'a, Kaura and Zango Kataf local governments which, except in Kaura, was reduced to a dusk-to-dawn curfew a few days later. Nevertheless, on 26 December, herdsmen were thought to have made an assault on locals, killing at least half a dozen people.

Meanwhile, the precarious security situation in the crisis-ridden North-East gradually improved thanks to an ongoing and better co-ordinated military campaign by the *Multinational Joint Task Force*

(MNJTF). Operations such as 'Lafiya Dole' and 'Gama Aiki' led to the arrest of dozens of Boko Haram commanders, including Mohammed Usman, better known as Khalid al-Barnawi, the rescue of well over a thousand hostages, among them the wife and daughter of the Shehu of Bama, and the death or surrender of several hundred insurgents.

Al-Barnawi was apprehended on 1 April in Kogi state. As a founder of the Islamist splinter group Ansarul (Ansarul Muslimina Fi Biladis Sudan – 'protectors of Muslims in Black Africa'), he had allegedly overseen the bombing of the UN office in Abuja in August 2011. Accordingly, *Boko Haram insurgents lost control of almost all the territory* in Adamawa, Borno and Yobe states, although they retained parts of the notorious Sambisa Forest in Borno state, just 60 km southeast of the state capital Maiduguri. The number of military rank-and-file who fell victim to the terrorists was still markedly high, and did not spare middle-ranking and commanding officers such as Lieutenant Colonels Abu Ali (4 November) and B.U. Umar (15 November). On 16–17 October, the military suffered a humiliating defeat when troops on the northernmost edge of Borno state were forced by the insurgents' superior firepower to abandon their base. They were eventually cornered, and, trying to escape over the Yobe River, most of the soldiers drowned, along with their commanding officer Lieutenant Colonel K. Yusuf. As a result, the military was reluctant to start a major offensive in the forest there, which was full of booby traps, and limited themselves to frequent bombings of Boko Haram camps by jet fighters and drones.

Against this backdrop, *suicide bombings* went on unabated, mostly carried out by young girls. The security forces were unable to prevent all such assaults but managed to foil quite a number. As in previous years, Borno state was the main target of suicide bombings and deadly assaults. On 30 January, more than 60 inhabitants of Dalori village on the outskirts of Maiduguri lost their lives and at least 130 were seriously wounded after a raid by Islamist insurgents. On 28 July, Boko Haram ambushed a UNICEF team returning to the state capital from an IDP camp in Bama. As a result, UNICEF suspended its mission in the area. On 12 October, a bomb blast near

Muna Garage, a car park, killed four female passengers and their driver. On 29 October, two suicide bombings, at the entrance to Bakassi IDP camp and the NNPC Mega Filling station in Maiduguri, left several people dead. On 18 November, in a rather rare case, a foiled suicide attack in the city centre led to the arrest of an unhurt female survivor.

On 13 October, 21 of the more than *200 missing Chibok school* girls were released, following a deal brokered by the Swiss government and the International Committee of the Red Cross. Credible sources stated that more than 110 captives were either dead, married off or radicalized and unwilling to leave their kidnappers. Earlier in the year, on 27 January, two female suicide bombers had targeted Chibok market in the local government of the same name and killed more than a dozen citizens.

On 9 December, a twin blast in Madagali in Adamawa state left more than 50 people dead and over 100 injured, reminding the public that the Islamist insurgency was far from over and contradicting the constant claims by the government and military leadership that the crisis in the North-East was ending. On 21 December, Major General Lucky Irabor, commander of operation 'Lafiya Dole', disclosed that the army had rescued 1,880 women and children in Sambisa Forest and arrested about 500 Boko Haram members, while more than a dozen had surrendered. On 24 December, President Buhari claimed in his Christmas message that the last Boko Haram stronghold, 'Camp Zero', had been seized in a sneak attack two days previously, and that the Islamist insurgency had finally been crushed. At the end of the year more than 1,000 civilians, among them some high-ranking Boko Haram suspects, were arrested in operation 'Rescue Final'.

Throughout the year, *crime was widespread*. Kidnappings, bank raids and murders remained frequent, in spite of the fact that dozens of notorious gangs were apprehended. Clement Abanara and his gang, for example, who were accused of four bank robberies in Lagos state, were arrested in mid-January. On 24 March, Toweki Joseph and his gang were engaged by special police forces while attempting to rob banks and some bureau de change operators at Seme, a border town between Nigeria and Benin Republic. The leaders and most of the gang, mainly ethnic Ijaws, were shot. They had terrorised states in the South-West and South-South for some time and were said to have robbed banks in Lagos and Ondo states, killing several people during their operations. In mid-December, the Lagos state police commissioner disclosed that over the past 12 months, 246 cases of murder and 486 of armed robbery had been recorded in the state.

On 26 March, army colonel Ismaila Inusa was robbed and killed in Kaduna by a four-man gang and his car sold for some NGN (naira) 800,000. Later in June, the same gang and its leader, Emeka Okeke, were apprehended. On 29 May, Thomas Adekoye, a 60-year old surgeon working with the Lagos University Teaching Hospital, was abducted and killed in Ijebu-Itele in Ogun state by suspected sympathizers of a 'native doctor'. On 8 June, the registrar of the Medical Laboratory Science Council, Mrs Olufunke Omotuyi, suffered the same fate in Abuja. She was due for retirement the following month. Shortly before, on 20 May, Denen Igbana, a senior assistant on security to Benue state Governor Samuel Ortom, was gunned down at his residence in Tionsha, close to the state capital Makurdi. The then governor of Ondo state, Olusegun Mimiko, experienced a similar incident when his chief security officer Idowu Oyewole was killed by armed robbers on 20 October, and four days later, in the run-up to the *gubernatorial election* in the state, Afolabi Olaposi, a leadership figure of the All Progressives Congress (APC) in Ondo state, was shot dead after a party meeting in Owo. This was the second APC chieftain to be assassinated, after Franklin Obi, who, together with his wife and son, had been killed by gunmen on 6 March in Omoku in Ogba-Egbema-Ndoni local government in Rivers state. Benue state suffered another blow on 2 October, when armed men attacked a police station in Igumale in Ado local government, killing all four officers on duty. In Sokoto, a Lebanese citizen, Moin Amsuri, a mathematics teacher at the well-known Nagarta College, was the victim of a holdup murder on 28 July.

More *captives were killed* than in previous years. On 5 January, the king of Ubulu-Uku kingdom in Aniocha south local government, Akaeze Edward Ofulue III, was abducted and allegedly killed by Fulani herdsmen. Samuel Okies and Inegite Inibia – the former a nephew and the latter the foster-father of former president Goodluck Jonathan – were taken hostage on 17 February. The nephew was found dead a few days later, but Inegite regained his freedom after more than a month in captivity.

In contrast, hostages such as a traditional Yoruba ruler Oba Gariola Oseni, who was kidnapped on 16 July in Lagos state, and Mrs Margaret Emefiele, wife of the governor of the Central Bank, taken on 20 September in Edo state, were released unharmed on 7 August and 30 September, respectively. In the Lagos case, four men were arrested and put on trial. On 11 November, the king gave evidence and acknowledged that his family had eventually paid a ransom of NGN 15.1 m, although the criminals had initially demanded NGN 500 m. No verdict had been reported by year's end.

On 11 April, *pirates* abducted a Turkish cargo ship. The six crew members were set free after two weeks. Last but not least, the Sierra Leonean deputy high commissioner and high ranking military officer, Nelson Williams, was kidnapped at gunpoint along the Abuja-Kaduna Expressway on his way to Kano on 1 July. The kidnappers demanded a ransom of $ 40 m for his safe return. He was rescued on 5 July. Whether a ransom was paid remained unclear.

This itemization of criminal incidents in no way completes the list of terror attacks, organized crime, kidnappings, killings and arrests.

Against this backdrop, *jail breaks* occurred in several states: on 24 June in Abuja, on 30 July in Kogi state and on 9 August in Enugu state. On 18 August, a jail break in Ebonyi state failed; several inmates and members of staff were killed. These incidents revealed the dismal prison conditions and the huge challenge of handling thousands of inmates in overcrowded prison cells. They further revealed that prison staff were frequently complicit in many cases. In the aftermath of these events, Comptroller General Ahmed Ja'afaru, appointed to this position on 24 May, dismissed several senior and junior staff.

President Buhari used his executive powers to appoint more chairmen and board members of the numerous *state agencies and federal parastatals*; these short-term lucrative positions served first and foremost to redistribute huge financial resources to the political elite. The appointment of Muhammad Abdallah to the National Drug Enforcement Agency (NDLEA) on 18 January, and that of Ms Adejoke Orelope-Adefulire as senior special assistant in charge of the office for Sustainable Development Goals (SDGs) on 7 March, are examples of such posts. On 18 April, Sule Kazaure became director general of the National Youth Service Corps (NYSC) and, on 24 May, Mohammed Babandele became the comptroller general of the immigration service. New chief executives were appointed to six state media agencies, among them the News Agency of Nigeria (NAN). A change of leadership at the federal budget office took place in June, when Ben Akabueze replaced Tijani Mohammed Abdullahi.

On 21 June, Ibrahim Kpotum Idris was promoted to acting *inspector general of police* after the retirement of Solomon Arase. In early July, against the backdrop of the crisis in the Niger Delta, the president removed Ibe Kachikwu as NNPC's group managing director, appointed Maikanti Kacalla Baru in his place, and dissolved and reconstituted the board. Kachikwu retained his posts as minister of state for petroleum and as the board's chairman. Victor Ndoma-Egba became chairman of the Niger Delta Development Commission (NDDC). The extension of Yemi Kale's tenure as statistician general of the Federation and as chief executive officer of the National Bureau of Statistics (NBC) for another five-year term, which took place in late October, was considered a rare case and an exception to the rule.

Soon afterwards, on 7 November, Sidi Dauda Bage and Paul Adamu Galinje were elevated to the *Supreme Court*, which brought the number of Supreme Court justices to 17 currently on the bench. On 10 November, against common practice, President Buhari swore in the most senior judge, Walter Onnoghen, as acting chief justice after the tenure of his predecessor Mahmud Mohammed had ended the previous day.

In November and December, President Buhari signed 17 bills into law including the 'Prevention of Crime Amendment Act 2016'.

The military redeployed their upper echelons at quite frequent intervals, an indication that *all was not well in the military*, particularly with respect to the ongoing insurgency in the Northeast. On 5 January, Major General Yusha'u Mahmood Abubakar handed over the command of operation 'Lafiya Dole' to Major General Hassan Umaru. Major General Lamidi Adeosun, general officer commanding (GOC) 7 Division, garrisoned in Maiduguri, was deployed to the MNJTF in N'Djamena (Chad) and replaced by Brigadier Victor Okwudili Ezeugwu. On 17 March, Hassan Umaru had to hand over his command to his deputy, Major General Lucky Irabor, and was assigned to the post of chief of training and operations, following the death of his predecessor Abubakar in a road accident not long before. On 14 July, Brigadier General Ali Nani emerged as the new GOC 8 Task Force Division.

Major General Kasimu Abdulkarim was appointed the new GOC 2 Division in Ibadan but later redeployed to take over as GOC of the newly created 6 Division in Port Harcourt. Brigadier C.M. Abraham became acting GOC 2 Division. On 19 November, Brigadier Ebenezer Oyefolu assumed office as GOC 81 Division in Lagos. Operation 'Delta Safe' in the *volatile Niger Delta* also saw a change of leadership when, on 17 November, Rear Admiral Apochi Suleiman replaced Joseph Okojie, making Suleiman the first naval officer in charge of military operations in the region. On 9 December, the army council approved the promotion of 21 brigadiers, 93 colonels and 113 lieutenant colonels to the next higher rank.

Earlier in the year, on 27 February, chief of army staff Lieutenant General Tukur Yusuf Buratai inaugurated a motorbike battalion in Damboa in Borno state to strengthen its counter-insurgency capability, and the army released a further list of 100 suspected members of Boko Haram wanted by the Nigerian state.

The compulsory retirement of dozens of high-raking military officers and several *courts martial* confirmed the incidence of widespread corruption and misconduct, which triggered a major shake-up of the top brass and investigations by the Economic and Financial Crimes Commission (EFCC) against former top military personnel such as retired Air Chief Marshal Alex S. Badeh. Between April and August, dozens of high-ranking officers were sacked for professional misconduct during the general elections in 2015 and the Ekiti gubernatorial election in 2014. In addition, others were sacked and investigated for gun running or for the illegal sale of military equipment. The most striking issue, however, was the alleged involvement of officers in the $ 2.1 bn arms procurement scandal, in which Sambo Dasuki, former security adviser to then president Jonathan, took centre stage.

In early May, two major generals, Ibrahim Sani and Patrick Falola, faced court martial behind closed doors for misconduct and dereliction of assigned duties. While Falola, former commandant of the Military Hospital in Lagos, was demoted to brigadier in September, the fate of Sani, the former chief of the Army Transformation and Innovation Centre, remained unclear. On 10 August, four officers and 16 soldiers were arraigned for having committed various offences within operation 'Lafiya Dole'. In early September, a brigadier was court martialled in a *secret trial* in Maiduguri on charges of selling arms to Boko Haram.

In contrast, on 1 March, the army council commuted the sentence of Brigadier Enitan Ransome-Kuti, who had been disciplined in 2015 for neglecting his military duties. He was demoted to the rank of colonel and the council also quashed his six-month prison term. However, the case highlighted that *procedures within the military* – the retiring or sacking of personnel regardless of their rank – were driven by dubious motives. Other senior officers, such as Major General Ijioma Ijioma and Lieutenant Colonel Mohammed Abdulfatai sought redress at the Industrial Court. The army council was notably absent and cases were still pending at year's end.

In the aftermath of the appointment of Ibrahim Kpotum Idris as the new inspector general, the *police forces underwent major changes*. No sooner had he taken office than he replaced the spokesperson Ms Olabisi Kolawole with Don Awunah. On 1 July, 21 assistant inspectors were compulsorily retired. In addition, within a period of less than four months, seven new deputy inspectors general and two dozen assistant inspectors general were appointed. Promotions and retirements notwithstanding, the police force also had to face adversity: on 23 November, a spokesman revealed that within the past three months 128 policemen had lost their lives in the line of duty, a figure which indicated a significant number of fatalities over the course of the year.

In Edo and Ondo states, statutory *gubernatorial elections* took place on 28 September and 26 November, respectively. The APC candidates, Godwin Obaseki and Rotimi Akeredolu, won the elections. Obaseki was finally installed as duly elected, while Akeredolu was to be inaugurated in February 2017. Earlier in the year, on 9 January, the *Independent National Electoral Commission* (INEC) concluded the ballot in Bayelsa state, which had been partially cancelled in some parts of the state in December 2015. The People's Democratic Party (PDP) incumbent, Seriake Dickson, already had a clear lead and eventually won decisively.

The *INEC* faced 680 legal challenges following the 2015 elections, although only 80 cases were dealt with by the courts. The outcomes of these trials affected federal and state constituencies, meaning that all the disputed governors-elect were eventually confirmed by the Supreme Court. Nevertheless, in Rivers state elections had to be postponed twice due to widespread violence, orchestrated unrest and killings across the state. On 10 December, the elections took place but they were marred by violence, despite the presence of thousands of policemen. The PDP defended its stronghold, but the APC took one senatorial district.

The *precarious security situation* in most parts of the country, often with an *ethnic and sectarian undercurrent*, had grave effects on human rights. On 31 May, Methodus Emmanuel, a trader, was killed in Rafi local government in Niger state by a mob accusing him of blasphemy. Three individuals, including Security and Civil Defence Corps personnel also fell victim to the mob. The issue of blasphemy triggered similar incidents in Kano's Kofar Wambai market on 2 June, where one Bridget Agbahime, an ethnic Igbo trader and wife of a pastor, was decapitated; in Talata Mafara local government in Zamfara state, on 22 August, a student and seven other people were burnt to death. Interestingly, the five suspected perpetrators of the Kano incident were discharged by a magistrate's court on 3 November.

In the aftermath of the killing by armed forces in Zaria in December 2015 of more than 300 members of the Muslim Brethren – also known as the Islamic Movement in Nigeria (IMN), who admire the Iranian revolution and consider themselves as 'Shiites' – the seriously injured leader of the sect, Ibrahim Zakzaky, was still in police custody at the end of the year. Zakzaky's residence was demolished by bulldozers. The official investigation into the killings was deliberately delayed and the Kaduna judicial commission of inquiry, which was boycotted by the IMN, eventually released its report on 31 July. On 6 October, the Kaduna state government declared the IMN to be an unlawful organization and, in the days that followed, several members of the sect were attacked and killed in the states of Kaduna, Katsina and Sokoto and their properties and vehicles burnt or vandalized. These orchestrated acts were carried out by youth groups. Nevertheless, on 2 December, a federal court ordered the release of Zakzaky within 45 days.

In May, AI accused the military of being responsible for the deaths of babies, children and adults in detention centres, including the notorious Giwa barracks in Maiduguri. In another report, published in September, AI accused the police force, particularly the Special Anti-Robbery Squad (SARS) of *torture and accepting bribes in exchange for freedom*. The inspector general rejected the report as biased and inappropriate and maintained that the police had not been given a fair hearing.

In the so-called 'Apo killings case', the National Human Rights Commission (NHRC) had held the government responsible for the *extra-judicial killings* of eight squatters in September 2013. In June, the ECOWAS court imposed a heavy fine of $ 3.3 m on Nigeria. The Incorporated Trustees of Fiscal and Civil Right Enlightenment Foundation had taken the Nigerian government, the army and the state security service to the ECOWAS court on behalf of the deceased. Earlier, on 19 April, a federal high court in Abuja had rebuffed the federal government's intention of conducting the trial of former national security adviser Sambo Dasuki in secret.

Nevertheless, on 26 February, the Supreme Court once again upheld the legality of the *death sentence* when it confirmed the verdict on Chukwuemeka Ezeugo, popularly known as Reverend King, who had first been arraigned in 2006. Furthermore, Lagos state was in the process of amending the criminal code to allow the death penalty for kidnappers. If the amendment was passed, it would bring Lagos into line with Edo and Ondo states.

On 20 August, Ms Abiola Akiyode Afolabi was elected as chairperson of the *Transition Monitoring Group*, a coalition of around 400 civil society organizations.

Although the president and his government had vowed to take drastic measures against *corruption*, first results were at best mixed and the campaign was making no progress. The arrest of seven high ranking judges on 7 and 8 October on allegations of corruption was seen as a serious blow to the judiciary's reputation. It was reported that a silent power struggle between Justice Minister Abubakar Malami and some courts over the cautious handling of corruption cases might have triggered the arrests. In the end, the judges were released after a few days and were later suspended until further notice. One of the accused judges, Adeniyi Ademola, who was handling two delicate litigation cases concerning Sambo Dasuki and Nnamdi Kanu, was awaiting prosecution. On 21 December, 11 federal high court judges were redeployed, including Okon Abang and Mohammed Liman, who were among those suspended.

On 3 November, the Corrupt Practices and Other Related Offences Commission (ICPC) filed a nine-count charge against Gambo Saleh, the outgoing chief registrar of the Supreme Court, and two other members of staff for diverting NGN 2.2 bn. Shortly before, Saleh had been confirmed by the National Judicial Council to take over as the Council's secretary in mid-2017.

Much earlier, on 2 May, Vice President Yemi Osinbajo acknowledged that about $15 bn, provided to support the counter insurgency in the Northeast, had been diverted through *fraudulent arms contracts and theft*. Furthermore, the publication in 'Premium Times' on 5 May of a list of more than 100 prominent Nigerians named in the database known as the 'Panama Papers' had no apparent impact on the investigations.

Apart from taking legal action, the EFCC tried to recover funds by targeting high-ranking former politicians and administrative officers such as Senator Iyiola Omisore, Musiliu Obanikoro and the former comptroller general of the customs service, Abdullahi Dikko, and was successful in recovering more than NGN 1 bn from the former customs boss.

Foreign Affairs

The *relationship with the USA continued to improve*. On 9 February, at a meeting in Washington DC on the regional impact of Boko Haram, Assistant Secretary of State for Africa Linda Thomas-Greenfield announced the resumption of training programmes for Nigerian soldiers, experts on cybercrime and the police, which had been aborted under Buhari's predecessor, former president Jonathan. Soon afterwards, the president returned to Washington to take part in the Fourth Nuclear Security Summit on 31 March. On 20 September, he addressed the 71st session of the UN General Assembly in New York, and held talks with President Obama.

On 30 March, US Secretary of State John Kerry hosted a meeting of the *bi-national commission* and, on 22–23 August, Kerry was in

Nigeria on a two-day official visit, where he was received by Nigeria's president in Abuja. One important item on the agenda was talks with the Sultan of Sokoto, the spiritual head of Nigeria's Sunni Muslim community, and with governors from the crisis-ridden North in the Sultan's hometown Sokoto. However, the meeting did not go down well with the Christian Association of Nigeria (CAN), which was denied a meeting with Kerry and accused the US of bias. Later in the year, on 18–20 October, those governors from the North attended a three-day symposium organized by the US Institute of Peace in Washington. In addition, Shaarik Zafar, the State Department special representative to Muslim communities, visited Nigeria on 17–19 October as part of his maiden visit to SSA.

Earlier, Samantha Power, the US representative to the UN, had led a delegation of US military, intelligence officers, business people and the diplomatic corps to Adamawa state capital Yola, the seat of the American University of Nigeria (AUN), underlining their joint determination to defeat the Islamist insurgents and rebuild a *devastated Northeast*.

In June, it was reported that, despite improved relations, the issue of *repatriating looted funds* stashed in US banks by the former military dictator Sani Abacha had been delayed. The matter remained unresolved. According to the US embassy, this was due to the cumbersome legal process and the complexity of the investigation.

On 30 August and 2 September, Facebook founder Mark Zuckerberg, on his first trip to SSA, paid a visit to the Yaba, the technological hub of Nigeria in Lagos, and to Abuja where he was received by President Buhari.

As in previous years, *Nigeria's relationship with Britain was shaped by various legal issues*. The extradition of Ms Franca Asemota, arrested in Nigeria in 2015, was delayed until 27 January. On 4 August, she was finally sentenced to 22 years' imprisonment by the Isleworth Crown Court in London for trafficking Nigerian girls to work as prostitutes across Europe.

Over the course of the year, there *was a further twist in the saga of James Ibori*, who was serving a 13-year prison sentence for money laundering and fraud. When the former Delta state governor was about to be released after serving more than half of his sentence, a British police officer was removed from the UK anti-corruption unit in May, after it emerged that he might have been paid for providing information in the case. More was to come when, in late November, the UK's Independent Police Complaints Commission (IPCC) launched a fresh investigation into alleged corrupt practices of further London Metropolitan Police officers in connection with the Ibori case. On 21 December, Ibori was eventually released, despite attempts by the British home secretary to keep him in prison, pending the ruling on a prolonged asset forfeiture case brought against him by the British government. The request was dismissed outright by a high court judge.

On 4 February, President Buhari attended an international conference on Syria in London. The previous day, he had addressed a special session of the European Parliament and held talks with the chairmen of the European Parliament and the European Commission. This was followed by another trip to London, where he participated in an anti-corruption summit on 12 May, and where, in early June, he underwent medical treatment. The result of the summit was a memorandum of understanding, signed on 30 August in Abuja, which was supposed to provide a mechanism by which *looted funds could be repatriated to Nigeria*, including an amount of £ 300 m kept in the Channel Islands, in Jersey. A similar agreement was reached concerning the return of illegal immigrants and visitors who had overstayed their visas. Earlier, on 13 April, the UK's Minister for International Development Nick Hurd arrived on his first trip to Nigeria.

Although advanced in years, Buhari kept a busy travel schedule, which took him in January to the UAE, where he attended the summit on future energy and signed agreements on returning stolen funds and on the extradition of convicted Nigerians. At the end of the month, he was on a three-day state visit to Kenya, from where he proceeded to the 26th AU summit in Addis Ababa (Ethiopia). In February, he participated in a business forum in Egypt, made the lesser Hajj in Mecca, and attended an OPEC meeting in Qatar. On 14–15 March, the president held talks in Malabo with the president of Equatorial Guinea on maritime security and returned on 23 November for the 4th Africa-Arab summit in the same city. In mid-October, he spent three days on a state visit to Germany, where he met Chancellor Angela Merkel and the then president, Joachim Gauck, whom he had received in Nigeria in February. Gauck had announced that the EU had pledged $ 50 m to support the fight against Islamist insurgents and the resettlement of IDPs. Against this backdrop, the sixth Nigeria-EU ministerial dialogue took place in Brussels (Belgium) on 16 March, focusing on strategic cooperation and migration issues.

On 14 November, Buhari went to the Moroccan city of Marrakesh for the summit on climate change (COP 22), and on 5–6 December, he travelled to Dakar (Senegal) for the International Forum on Peace and Security in Africa. A week later, on 13 December, the efforts of Buhari and his counterparts from Liberia, Ghana and Sierra Leone to persuade their host Yahya Jammeh to concede defeat in the recently concluded Gambian presidential election came to nothing. At the 50th ECOWAS Assembly in Abuja on 17 December, the Nigerian president was mandated to lead an *ECOWAS mediation team to The Gambia.*

The 27th AU summit in Rwanda in July was one of the few occasions in which Buhari was represented by Vice President Yemi Osinbajo.

When IMF Managing Director Christine Lagarde paid an official visit to Nigeria and neighbouring Cameroon on 4–9 January, Abuja was her first port of call. On 8–9 March, Buhari welcomed South Africa's President Jacob Zuma for a two-day state visit. He hosted the 2nd regional security summit on 14 May, which was attended, inter alia, by France's President François Hollande and the presidents of Benin, Cameroon, Chad and Niger. On 2 December,

King Mohammed VI of Morocco arrived in Nigeria for a three-day official visit.

Political and economic relations with China were strengthened. Buhari visited Beijing on 10–12 April, with a large delegation of businessmen and ministers, aiming to attract several billion dollars in investment for infrastructure projects such as the coastal railway line, energy, gas and oil pipelines and the downstream sector. As a follow-up, Minister of State for Petroleum Ibe Kachikwu organized the first Nigeria-focused road show in Bejing at the end of June.

On 18 November, a Nigerian, Chijioke Obioha, was hanged in Singapore for *drug trafficking*. Earlier, at the end of July, three Nigerians, along with other foreigners and locals, were executed in Indonesia for similar offences, and more were awaiting execution. In Cambodia, on 6 December, a court dismissed an appeal by another Nigerian, Chineme Nwoko, by upholding a 27-year prison sentence for drug trafficking.

India retained its position as the major importer of Nigerian crude oil, receiving a total of 63 m barrels. In addition, towards the end of the year, Kachikwu negotiated a $15 bn oil-for-cash deal aimed at easing Nigeria's depleted reserves of foreign currency and India announced an increased demand for crude.

The *relationship with the UN remained friendly*. Soon after the election of the new Secretary General António Guterres in December, Ms Amina Mohammed, formerly Nigeria's minister for environment, was appointed as his deputy. Earlier, on 26 April, Abiodun Bashua emerged to lead the special investigation into an attack on the UN Mission in Malakal in South Sudan (UNMISS). Against the backdrop of increasing criticism of the ICC and the intention of some African countries to withdraw from the Rome Statute, the Nigerian government pledged its support on 3 November to improve the ICC's mandate.

Last but not least, on 2 June, Mohammed Sanusi Barkindo was appointed secretary general of *OPEC*. He assumed office on 1 August, becoming the second Nigerian to hold that post.

Socioeconomic Developments

Oil and gas prices remained low but gradually rose to above the
$ 50 per barrel mark by the end of the year. Despite the modest
recovery, renewed civil strife and frequent bomb attacks on pipelines by militia groups seriously affected production levels, which
fell to 1.4 m b/d in May, far below the usual target of 2.3 m b/d.
However, during the last quarter of the year, production rose, at
least temporarily, almost to its normal level.

Foreign reserves decreased to $ 26 bn in December, although the
excess crude account gradually recovered and reached $ 2.5 bn by
the end of the year. The national currency was also under pressure
at a time when the exchange rate had sharply depreciated to close
to 500 NGN:$ 1 on the parallel market. The Central Bank eventually
applied a currency rate of NGN 305:$ 1 after it had, in May, rather
reluctantly, and only after Buhari's apparent change of heart, allowed the naira to fall to that mark from the previous rate of some
NGN 200:$ 1. Despite the efforts of the Central Bank, the naira's mas-
sive fall, coupled with declining revenues from oil and gas exports,
gave cause for serious concern both in business circles and among
the wider public over the government's ability to handle financial
and economic affairs. The government blamed the problem on numerous bureau de change operators who had broken the rules and
had traded foreign currency far beyond their mandate. Accordingly,
in November, state security staff clamped down on them, arresting
about a dozen. Several offices were closed, and markets were raided
in various parts of the country in search of illegal foreign currency
hawkers.

As in previous years, the signing of the *2016 federal budget*, totalling NGN 6.1 trn ($ 30.8 bn) based on a benchmark of $ 38 per barrel
of crude oil, a production of some 2.2 m b/d and an exchange rate
of NGN 197:$ 1 was delayed and only signed into law by the presi-
dent on 6 May. The budget had already been passed by the National
Assembly on 23 March but the president withheld his assent due to
controversial projects either added or removed by the lawmakers.

Somewhat surprisingly, the government accepted a *budget deficit* of around 30%, to be financed by internal and external borrowing, the removal of kerosene and fuel subsidies and the imposition of new stamp duties. On 1 November, the government's proposal to borrow $ 30 bn over a three-year period was rejected by the Senate. Against this backdrop, the AfDB approved a $ 600 m loan the following day, as the first tranche of a $ 1 bn budget support package.

Earlier, on 7 June, the World Bank approved an IDA credit of $ 500 m in support of a 'national social safety nets project', which laid the foundation for the establishment of the country's first system of this kind. Nigeria would contribute $ 1.3 bn.

The *high unemployment rate* particularly among young people, which the Central Bank and the National Bureau of Statistics estimated at almost 60%, prompted several social intervention projects worth billions of naira, among which were the Youths Entrepreneurship Support (YES), the N-Power and the Conditional Cash Transfer (CCT) programme. Inflation soared and soon reached the 18% mark, while the growth rate fell to almost zero, and, on 17 October, the finance minister announced the launch of a development bank early in 2017 aimed at providing small and medium-sized enterprises with easier access to capital.

On 14 December, the government presented its *2017 budget proposal* of NGN 7.3 trn ($ 24 bn), based on a benchmark of $ 42.5 per barrel of crude oil and an assumed production of 2.2 m b/d, while the exchange rate was pegged at NGN 305:$ 1.

The *enduring power problems* took their toll. Despite billions of dollars having been spent during the previous decade and several restructuring and deregulation reforms, the total power generated by Nigeria's power stations for transmission and distribution was nowhere near the envisaged 6,000 MW. In April, for example, production was 3,700 MW, due to the crisis in the Niger Delta and the disarray within the power sector as a whole. The situation was no better by year's end. Interestingly, according to the Sahara Group, a leading privately owned power, gas and energy conglomerate, businesses and households spent an estimated $ 22 bn on fuel for their generators. Big companies such as the Dangote Group and other plants across the country, however, had built their own power plants and were generating more than 15,000 MW, for the exclusive use of their own companies.

Nigeria kept its position as Africa's largest and most *lucrative tele-communications market*. Almost half of the population had regular access to the Internet. The South African MTN Group saga, which had begun the previous year, was concluded on 10 June. Initially, the Nigerian Communication Commission (NCC) had imposed a fine of $ 5.2 bn – at that time equivalent to NGN 1.04 trn – on Africa's leading provider for failing to deactivate more than 5 m unregistered SIM cards. The fine was eventually reduced to NGN 330 bn, which included a 'goodwill' payment of NGN 50 bn made in February. Accordingly, on 26 December, MTN paid the balance of NGN 30 bn for the current year, leaving the unpaid balance to be paid in tranches until May 2019.

Despite these problems, on 29 June, MTN, the sole bidder, won a 10-year licence to get access to a frequency spectrum, which made *4G LTE* services possible at a fee of about NGN 19 bn.

In addition, on 8 November, Nigeria reached a deal worth $ 5 bn with five international oil companies to cover outstanding financial obligations for joint oil and gas exploration and production. Over the years, Nigeria's state-owned company NNPC had refused to pay its dues and had amassed debts that it was now obliged to pay. Inter alia, this issue highlighted the fact that Nigeria's oil and gas exploration and production costs were comparatively high.

On 29 June, Captain Elechi Amadi (rtd), author of works such as 'Sunset in Biafra' and 'The Concubine', passed away at the age of 82. Later in the year, on 14 September, 93-year-old Ibrahim Dasuki, the 18th Sultan of Sokoto. He had been deposed by the then military dictator Sani Abacha in 1996.

Index of Select Names